Mastering
CD–ROM
Technology

Mastering CD–ROM Technology

Larry Boden

JOHN WILEY & SONS, INC.
New York • Chichester • Brisbane • Toronto • Singapore

Publisher: Katherine Schowalter
Editor: Tim Ryan
Managing Editor: Frank Grazioli
Text Design & Composition: Pronto Design & Production Inc., New York

Designations used by companies to distinguish their products are often claimed as trademarks. In all instances where John Wiley & Sons, Inc. is aware of a claim, the product names appear in initial capital or all capital letters. Readers, however, should contact the appropriate companies for more complete information regarding trademarks and registration.

This text is printed on acid-free paper.

This publication is designed to provide accurate and authoritative information in regard to the subject matter covered. It is sold with the understanding that the publisher is not engaged in rendering legal, accounting, or other professional service. If legal advice or other expert assistance is required, the services of a competent professional person should be sought.

Library of Congress Cataloging-in-Publication Data:
Boden, Larry.
    Mastering CD ROM technology / Larry Boden
             p. cm.
    Includes index.
    ISBN 0-471-12174-6 (PAPER/CD–ROM : alk. paper)
      1. CD–ROMs.   I. Title.
TK7895.CC 39B63   1995   95-34725
004.5'6—dc20   CIP

Printed in the United States of America
10 9 8 7 6 5 4 3 2 1

· · · · Dedication

*To Ms. Harriet Matthey, a source of knowledge, a fountain
of inspiration, and the ultimate provider of sustenance —
worldly, intellectually, and in spirit.*

• • • • • Acknowledgments

No book—especially this one—is the work of one person. The author would be remiss if he didn't acknowledge the following people who contributed so much to this effort:

Mike Green, who not only hatched the idea for this book, but put an "above and beyond" effort in getting it off the ground and into publication.

Tim Ryan and the staff at Wiley; they showed patience beyond belief. Thanks, Tim.

Philip Merrill, who contributed not only a mountain of research, but also rewrote, corrected, and provided original material.

Other contributions were made by: Pam Ballou, Mitch Brown, Rob Burr, Mark Englehardt, Irving Green, David Guenette, the staff at the Learning Annex, Dick Meixner, Mike Neff, John O'Connor, Pat Onderdonk, Mary Renfrow, John Sands, Eric Saslow, Gene Shiveley, Caternia Solomon, Perry Solomon, Patrick Theaker, Sam Theaker, Dick Wilkinson, and Mike Wintz.

• • • • • Preface

It was a wonderful spring day in 1986. I was pushing some paperwork across my desk at the audio recording studio I ran in Hollywood. My closest friend, Rob Burr, came into my office, and while looking me dead in the eye, said "Larry, you can forget this audio CD stuff— you and I are gonna put computer data on compact discs and make a lot of money!" Rob, as usual, was right, sort of.

The implications were staggering. For the first time in history, humankind would be able to send the archives to the scholar instead of the scholars having to journey to the archives. Medical and census data, learning tools, service manuals—all sorts of "can't miss" applications. Ahead of us was arguably the biggest revolution in information dissemination since the invention of the printing press. We knew it. We waited. And then we waited some more.

In some ways, we're still waiting. For all the success that CD–ROM has held up to now, the biggest growth curve, I believe, still lies ahead of us. We're just now learning how to use the platform to its best advantage and have only recently attracted the creative types who can exploit it

What a wondrous media! Seven hundred megabytes on a disc consisting of just eight cents worth of exquisitely durable raw materials that fit in your pocket, *and* can be manufactured at the rate of one every four seconds! The audio implementation of the media just paved the way for a multitude of applications.

More similar to the evolution of the printing press than the LP record album (remember those?), those early software tools were crude; the base of installed drives was microscopic and many decision makers who were charged with implementing CD technology lacked the vision to attract the resources that could exploit the medium to its fullest.

There were some exceptions: U.S. government scientists like Jerry McFaul of the U.S. Geological Survey saw the potential of CD-ROM technology, but even his earliest initiatives seem dull and strictly utilitarian compared the advent of game technology and the arrival of *MYST* and *THE SEVENTH GUEST.*

This book is about empowerment, about giving you, the reader, the ability to realize the full potential of CD-ROM. Once you understand how the *science* of CD-ROM works, you can begin to practice the *art* of CD-ROM . And it *is* an art, limited only by source material, digitizing methods, and your imagination.

Understanding is power. So read this book, understand, then join the revolution and make a contribution to the art. It's barely begun. Today it's encyclopedias, games, how-to applications, and all types of educational discs.

Tommorrow. . . You complete the thought!

Larry Boden

Pasadena, California
October 1995

···· Contents

Compact Disc Overview

Unless you happen to live in a very isolated environment you know about the rapid ascent of CD–ROM both as a computer peripheral and as a platform for games, movies, and such. Some visionaries have called CD–ROM the long-playing album of the computer world. Many people apparently agree, since research shows that the installed base of CD–ROM drives worldwide is approaching the 30 million mark, with almost one third of that number being delivered in 1994.

The research firm Inteco predicts that CD–ROM will supplant floppy discs as the main medium for software delivery by 1996. Almost 12,000 titles are now available, and that number will surpass 20,000 by the end of 1995. The research firm of Spade & Archer predicts that compact discs manufactured for other than audio delivery will surpass the audio market by 1998.

CD–ROM is a futuristic medium. CD read-only memory constitutes a giant step forward in information technology. For the first time, truly vast amounts of data, whether text, graphics, or sound, can be easily disseminated in a convenient and inexpensive format. The chief advantages of CD–ROM are high information density, durability, accessibility, and ease of both distribution and replication (see Table 1.1). The potential of the medium for information users is enormous.

While the first use of the compact disc format was as a replacement for the vinyl phonograph record, history points us to a different historical model when comparing the CD to other media of information distribution. Let's compare the CD with both the LP *and* the printing press (Table 1.2): It becomes apparent that having a medium that can adapt to virtually any resident source is not only appealing but functional as well.

TABLE 1.1 Characteristics of Common Distribution Media

MEDIA	CAPACITY	PROS AND CONS	COST	BEST USE
Paper	About 2 KB per page.	Random or sequential access. Nonvolatile. Difficult to cross-index for multiple retrieval strategies. Physically heavy. Data is not easily manipulated. Requires no equipment to use. Individual copies or mass production.	$5.00 per MB or more, depending on information and printing quality.	Information that will not be manipulated; single copies, and small amounts of information archiving.
Tape	Up to 60 MB	Sequential access. Volatile. Easy to transport, slow direct access. Requires tape equipment. Mass production is very difficult.	Less than $1 per MB.	Archiving and backup of data and program files.
Floppy diskette	512 KB–1.44 MB	Random access. Volatile, easily damaged. Easy to transport. Difficult to copy-protect. Data may be manipulated; reading equipment is widely available. Mass-production speeds are adequate with low data volumes.	Less than $2 per MB.	Program distribution, user data storage, small archives, and backups.
Hard disc	40 MB to 1 GB+	Random access, high-speed access. Volatile. Difficult to transport.	Around $0.55 per MB.	User data and program storage.
CD–ROM	700 MB	Random access, adequate access speed. Very durable, easily transportable. Suitable for mass production.	Less than $0.01 per MB in volume.	Distribution of reference and program data in large volumes.
On-line	Unlimited	Random access, very slow delivery compared with other methods. Central updating, high currency.	Very expensive delivery, can be over $200 per MB.	Distribution of current data from large central databases.

KB=kilobytes (1000 bytes); MB=megabytes (1,000,000 bytes); GB=gigabytes (1,000,000,000 bytes)

3

TABLE 1.2 Comparison of LP, CD, and Printing Press

	VINYL LP	CD	PRINTING PRESS
Can it deliver audio?	Yes	Yes	No
Can it deliver text?	No	Yes	Yes
Can it deliver graphics	No	Yes	Yes
Is it interactive?	No	Yes	Yes
All of the above at once?	No	Yes	No
Video?	No	Yes	No

Advantages of Distributing Information on CD-ROM

There are many advantages, from both a technological and financial standpoint, to distributing information via CD–ROM.

1. *Random access*: Both audio and video tape are sequential access media, meaning that their information is given out in a predetermined order

2. *Optically read*: A small, low-powered laser is used to read data from a CD–ROM; therefore, no wear takes place on the medium itself. The actual read surface is buried beneath a 1.2-mm layer of optical-grade plastic. This plastic is also used to make such items as football helmets and bulletproof glass. A motor failure or similar event in the playback unit will occur before a disc fails.

3. *Digitally stored*: The binary code used for storing data on a CD is finite and permanent. A one will always be a one, and a zero will always be a zero. Paper can yellow, color film can fade, and audio

records can lose high frequencies with multiple plays. A ten-year-old-disc has the same integrity as a day-old one.

4. *Affordable*: Compact discs can be replicated for well under a dollar. For larger quantities, 60 cents or less is the rule. The disc itself contains only 6 cents worth of raw materials, and the manufacturing time per disc hovers in the 4-second range. They are easy to store and ship, and lend themselves to elaborate decoration if desired. CD–ROM products are also affordable for the consumer. The average price for a CD–ROM title has continued to fall. The arrival of a $19.95 average price point has made the purchase of a disc more of an impulse decision than in the past.

5. *Common*: The price of playback drives has reflected the economy of scale of mass manufacturing. Additionally, "juke-box" units capable of holding up to 1000 unique discs are available.

6. *Permanent*: Several disc replication houses will warrant their product against manufacturing defects for over 50 years. Advances in plastic and lacquer technology have been substantial in recent years. Accelerated aging tests at separate facilities have given the industry great insight on both materials and manufacturing techniques.

7. *Read only*: The data on a manufactured disc cannot be altered or deleted. The typical consumer is unlikely to purchase a book with corrections written in the margins. CD–ROMs are also impervious to viruses. Data stored on a CD–ROM has integrity equal to the original source.

8. *Standardized*: The physical specifications are defined in detail in The Yellow Book (more on this later). Indeed, the only variable is the demand put

on the host computer system for the vagaries of the retrieval program.

9. *Lasting format*: From time to time stories surface about some medium or other that is being heralded as a successor to CD–ROM's throne. The truth is this: Such a medium would have to have the ability to exceed CD–ROM's storage capacity of 700 megabytes, be manufactured for a lesser cost (remember, a CD uses only 6 cents worth of raw materials), and have a faster rate of manufacture. Since CD–ROM has ridden the coattails of the success of the audio disc in terms of scale of production, this is unlikely.

10. *More CD–ROM drives*: More and more new computers are coming out of the factory with a CD–ROM drive built in. The Software Publishing Association of Washington, D.C., estimates that 47 percent of PCs sold for home use in 1995 will be so equipped. Their figure for 1996 sales is 68 percent.

11. *Maturing distribution channel*: The distribution channel continues to expand. Not too long ago most commercial CD–ROM titles were sold by mail order houses or direct to the end user at computer shows and the like. The distribution channel has widened and matured parallel to the acceptance of CD–ROM. The rise of computer superstores such as Babbages, Comp USA, and Businessland has created valuable shelf space to display popular titles. Book and software wholesalers have also entered the fray: Merisel, Ingram, and Baker & Taylor now offer CD–ROM applications from stock. It should also be noted that Waldenbooks, B. Dalton, and Crown have all announced that they will dedicate floor space to CD–ROM product.

12. *Increased acceptance in education*: Educational institutions have embraced the medium. As the cost

for hardware and software has declined, the enthusiasm of teachers, institutes of higher learning, and school boards has escalated. Not only can the use of audio, images, video, and animation bring academic matters to life, studies done at the University of Pittsburgh show that student retention of facts from a multimedia presentation rose by anywhere from 12 to 40 percent. Moreover, the real power of multimedia educational software lies in its potential to unleash the curiosity of the user as well as accommodating his or her individual needs. For instance, a student need not stumble over unfamiliar concepts or vocabulary within an application, since related materials, glossaries, and the like can be cross-referenced and accessed instantly via "links" to supplemental material and included vocabulary.

13. *Platform independence*: CD–ROMs are no longer platform dependent. It is now possible to make one disc that will perform just as well on Windows, DOS, and Macintosh machines. The advantage of such a universal product is clear—distributors and retailers are no longer faced with the prospect of stocking double inventory. Additionally, users can change platforms without making their CD–ROM inventory obsolete. That cannot be said for specific software applications such as word processors, database management programs, or utility programs.

What Will Fit on a CD?

Without question, the compact disc has redefined the meaning of efficient distribution. Distribution of what? Well, just about anything. Sony and Philips (the joint patent holders) did the world a big favor when they totally separated the physical specifications of the disc itself from the contents. If items can be converted to digital, they can be stored on a compact disc.

The contents of a compact disc must be in binary form. Binary is by nature digital, so anything that can be digitized can be put on a CD. This includes not only audio, but text, graphics, all manner of images, and moving pictures as well.

Efficient? Yes. A compact disc can be injection molded in about four seconds and can hold over 700 megabytes of any of the items just noted. It can be economically shipped, isn't very picky about how it is stored or handled, and is a worldwide standard. It is important to make a comment about the actual capacity of a compact disc. Often, confusing and conflicting numbers are bandied about.

- • For audio, the standard volume is 74 minutes; however, in actual practice a disc could be as long as 81 minutes.

- • For data applications (CD–ROM), 660 MB is usually the limit, although I have put as much as 722 megabytes on a disc. You may not want to do this, for reasons to be discussed later. 700 megabytes is over 716,000,000 characters or "bytes." That is almost 2000 floppy discs worth of data and is equivalent to 275,000 pages of single spaced text. Such a volume of text would completely fill 14 standard four-drawer filing cabinets. One expert figured out that a typist working at 65 words a minute would take 10 years at 24 hours a day to fill a CD–ROM. If the text were put in one long continuous line, it would stretch from New York City to somewhere just west of Chicago.

- • As for images, over 5000 can be put on a single disc in a high-resolution format. That number could easily quadruple if standard resolution were used.

The Evolution of CD-ROM Formats

The compact disc is an optical medium (unlike a floppy disk or a tape backup system, which are magnetic). It is read from beneath by a beam of light, so there is no physical wear on the disc itself. This is as good a time as any to make a short detour in order to understand the common conventions regarding the use of *disc* and *disk*. Magnetic media are the recipients of the *disk* moniker, while optical creatures, both great and small, have inherited the *disc* label.

The principle of optical discs was first demonstrated way back in 1927. Using a disc made of wax and a crude forerunner of today's optical scanner, John Logie Baird showed a system he called Phonevision. The system used standard phonograph discs and an off-the-shelf disc recording system. Mr. Baird recorded and played back 30 line pictures at the rate of 12.5 frames per second using flying spot scanners and crude mechanical scanning discs.

By the late 1950s, scientific advancement led to increased interest in optical recording and playback. The 3M Company showed a prototype system in 1962. Westinghouse announced their proprietary system, called Phonovid, in 1965.

In 1970 Teldec (a joint venture between Telefunken and Decca) showed their TED system. By using a diamond playback stylus on a non–rigid 8-inch disc, five minutes of video and audio could be recorded and played back.

Research efforts to marry the then newly developed laser to optical disc mastering and reproduction, specifically a video product, began to pick up speed in the early 1970s (although its conception dates back to

World War II, the first fully implemented laser was
born in 1961 (laser is an acronym for *l*ight *a*mplifica-
tion by *s*timulated *e*mission of *r*adiation).

By the mid-1970s and beyond, several corporations had
competed to establish market dominance in the field of
consumer video applications. The LaserVision format
developed by MCA and Philips won out, beating RCA's
SelectaVision platform as well as JVC's VHD standard.

The LaserVision format survives today. You've seen the
12-inch video discs in specialty stores or perhaps at the
house of a friend. Chances are that you don't own a
player yourself, since just 1 percent of American homes
had them as late as the end of 1994. VHS and Beta
proved to be far more popular with consumers than the
video disc, perhaps because they had read/write technologies rather than LaserVision's read-only capability.

All this background leads us to 1982, when Sony and
Philips bounced their new baby—the compact disc. It
was launched initially as a delivery medium for music.
By 1985 it was obvious that large chunks of data could
also be mastered to compact disc, hence the beginnings
of CD–ROM. Though CD–ROM was touted long and
hard as a useful computer peripheral, the early years
(1985 through 1989) were lean because of the lack of
an installed base of drives and the lack of sophisticated
software to retrieve the information from the disc in a
meaningful fashion.

Distributed multimedia took another step forward with
the introduction of the CD–I format, which stands for

---

*John Logie Baird was an amazing inventor who experimented with
long-distance television transmission, stereo sound, and even color TV.
A good account of his work in the optical disc field can be found in the
book Electronic Motion Pictures (University of California Press, 1955).*

compact disc–interactive. CD–I was not designed as a computer adjunct but rather as a system—a special player that connects directly to the user's TV and allows him or her (with a generous remote control) to control the flow of information at whim.

Progress is ever advancing, with new flavors of compact discs arriving with almost the certainty of new government tax forms. Next came CD–ROM XA, a variation of CD–ROM that allowed for the use of ADPCM (for adaptive pulse code modulation). ADPCM is a very economical form of compressed audio that was first used in the CD–I world. Its advantage is that it takes up far less space than audio in 16-bit PCM format. CD–ROM XA was little used until the advent of the next compact disc variant, Photo CD.

Kodak introduced the Photo CD primarily as a consumer product: Take a roll of film in to be developed and get your pictures back on a CD. Your photos can then be viewed (if you have the appropriate player) on a standard television set. Although this option is still available, Photo CD has found its real home in the *professional* community. Specifics of each of these "little sister" formats will be discussed later.

Kodak's desire to enable the consumer to append additional photos to an existing disc spurred the development of CD write-once technology. By doing this, the concept of sessions came into being. Understanding sessions is really quite easy, since only two variations, single session and multiple session, exist:

- • *Single session*: All data is transferred to a disc in a continuous fashion, in one operation called a session.

- • *Multisession*: In this case, data is placed on the disc in sections. When all the desired sections are fully set, the disc is frozen by writing a complete table of contents (known as the TOC) adjoining the boot-up tracks.

The XA variation was implemented for this use. If you can play a Photo CD, then your drive is also XA compliant. (Older XA drives can only read the first session on a multisession disc, but it is virtually impossible to purchase a single-session XA drive today.)

Different types of compact discs are often differentiated by using the name of a color. This practice came into being when the specifications of each disc were sent to licensees. The first format, audio, was delivered in a red binding and hence became known as the Red Book Standard. When you see or hear the term Red Book Audio used, it means that the program material conforms to this standard of 16-bit, 44.1-kHz sampling. It is possible (but sometimes not desirable) to put Red Book Audio tracks on a CD–ROM. But let's not get ahead of ourselves.

Here's a summary of the books by colors:

Red Book   CD Audio

Yellow Book   CD–ROM

Green Book   CD–I

Orange Book   Photo CD and Write–Once CD

White Book   Video CD

Blue Book   CD–Plus

Because it is important to understand the derivation and antecedents of CD–ROM, both technically and in terms of their growth, the following chapters continue with the chronological and format advances as they occurred.

A Technical Look at CD–Audio Disk

THE FATHER OF THE FAMILY

Since 1982, the world has been enjoying the sound quality that we now take for granted. In a sense, the technology for digital playback was long overdue (Figure 2.1). Immediately after the October 1982 announcement of the CD audio format, players, and discs were available at retail outlets in both Europe and Japan. Initial capacity for manufacture was limited, and this delayed the U.S. introduction until the following March.

The price of early audio players approached the $1000 mark but declined to under $300 by 1984. By early 1985 the fate of the vinyl record was sealed, as consumers upgraded to CDs at an astonishing rate. Less than three years after the beginning of the compact disc age, player sales were over a million units per year. This rates as one of the fastest uptakes of new technology ever.

Audio CDs have many advantages when compared with the previous standard—the 12-inch vinyl album (Table 2.1). The phenomenal acceptance of this new medium was a rational market response to its technological supe-

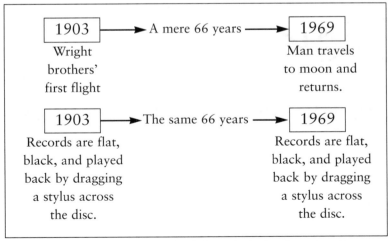

FIGURE 2.1 Development of digital playback technology versus aerospace technology.

TABLE 2.1 Audio CD and Vinyl LP Comparison

FEATURE	AUDIO CD	VINYL LP
Wow & Flutter	None, due to precision of timing circuit	Higher, sometimes 1% or more
Wear Characteristics	No surface wear due to laser playback	Pops, ticks, and noise increase with playing due to contact of stylus with record
Signal-to-noise ratio	>90 db	Approaching 60 db
Speed of manufacture	4 seconds	20 to 30 seconds
Portability	Excellent	Inconvenient

riority. The physical layout of the audio compact disc format is the foundation on which CD–ROM technology is built. You could say that the Yellow Book has to go on top of the Red Book. A review of some of the prominent features of CD–DA will, therefore, have an immediate bearing on our later discussion.

CD Size Specifications

The compact disc is one of the great marvels of twentieth-century engineering. Light, rugged, and small, the CD has a diameter of 120 mm, a height of 1.2 mm, and a weight of between 14 and 33 grams (the hole in the middle is 15 mm). The size of a data area may vary depending on how much programming has been recorded, but the data shown in (symmetrical) Table 2.2 is typical. If we include the lead-in and lead-out sections, the total recorded area may be considered to be 35.5 mm. Some quick math will show some impressive facts.

TABLE 2.2 Cross-Section of the Diameter of a Compact Disc

1.5 mm	0.5 mm	33 mm	2 mm	15.5 mm	15 mm	15.5 mm	2 mm	33 mm	0.5 mm	1.5 mm
empty	lead-out area	**data area**	lead-in area	empty	**hole**	empty	lead-in area	**data area**	lead-out area	empty

The track pitch specification calls for a value of 1.6 microns (the distance between adjacent tracks). Since the track pitch is essentially equal to one track, we can compute the total number of tracks as follows (the 1000 in the numerator is to convert microns, or micrometers, to millimeters):

$$\frac{35.5 \times 1000}{1.6} = \begin{array}{l} 22,188 \text{ tracks crossing a radius of} \\ \text{the disc} \end{array}$$

The track of a compact disc is actually a continuous spiral, recorded from the innermost beginning of the lead-in area to the outermost end of the lead-out area. When viewed from the reflective surface, the compact disc is rotated counterclockwise when it is read.

We can calculate the total length of this spiral of recorded material by taking the average circumference of a track and multiplying it by the total number of tracks. Please remember that when we speak of multiple tracks, it is for convenience, since in reality the compact disc traces a single groove from hub to rim. Taking our average track to be half of 35.5 mm (17.75 mm) and adding that to the hole and empty inner area [(15 mm/2) + 15.5 mm = 23 mm], we derive a radius for our average track of 40.75 mm. Plugging this into the formula 2r for circumference, we get an average circumference of 256.04 mm (or about 10¹/₄ inches). So we have the length of the spiral = 256.04 mm × 22,188 tracks = 5,681,015.5 mm/1000 = 5,681.0155 m, or about 5.7 kilometers, which is about *3.52 miles!*

So the recorded portion of a CD can be viewed in a linear fashion as a line 1.6 microns across that stretches for just over 70 New York City blocks (blocks run uptown-downtown). (By the way, if you're a stickler and have heard the length as being 3.54 miles, the different result is caused by determining the average track as being midway in the data area, instead of midway in the data plus lead-in plus lead-out areas.)

The size of our imaginary line has been seriously exaggerated but not the *length!* You've seen the calculations. The width is not really 1.6 microns, it is actually half a micron. You see, the recorded portion is only half a micron wide, but like the shoulder of a microscopic highway, there is just over another half micron on either side. How small is half a micron? Consider these comparisons:

1. The prick of a pin is 700 times larger.

2. Five hundred atoms of hydrogen, end to end, would fit inside.

3. The average fingernail grows half a micron in about seven minutes.

Now back to our imaginary street. It's full of potholes. Each pothole is called a pit and is only 0.1 micron deep. They vary in length from 1 to 3 microns (see Table 2.3 for exact measurements). How small is a pit? Its proportions (or aspect ratio) are similar to a grain of rice, but it's much smaller. If one pit on a compact disc were the size of a single grain of rice, the proportional size of the total CD would be over 400 yards in diameter (instead of 120 mm). That is the length of four football fields laid end to end. The proportionate length of the spiral (10,602 miles) would be longer than the diameter of the earth (7920 miles).

TABLE 2.3 Pit Specifications

The following pit-structure dimensions are required to achieve the necessary signal during playback.	
Minimum pit length:	0.833 micron (1.2 m/s) to 0.972 micron (1.4 m/s)
Maximum pit length:	3.05 micron (1.2 m/s) to 3.56 micron (1.4 m/s)
Pit depth:	Approximately 0.11 micron
Pit width:	Approximately 0.5 micron

The higher level of the surface that the pits are set into is called a land. So our spiral set of tracks is really just an alternating pattern of pits and lands (Figure 2.2). Traveling along the spiral would feel like "step up, step down, step up, step down." The storage of data in these pits and lands is achieved by assigning every step (be it up or down) to digital 1 and assigning the absence of a step to digital 0.

CD Speed Specifications

For this binary code of pits and lands to work, movement along the spiral must be at a predictable speed. Since zeros are coded by the absence of a step—the absence of change—that means time must be used to calculate how many zeros come between the ones. This is accomplished by moving the compact disc at a constant linear velocity (CLV). The linear dimensions of the track are the same at the start of play as they are at the end of the data, so the drive must rotate the disc faster when the head is reading data near the center and more slowly as the outer tracks are read.

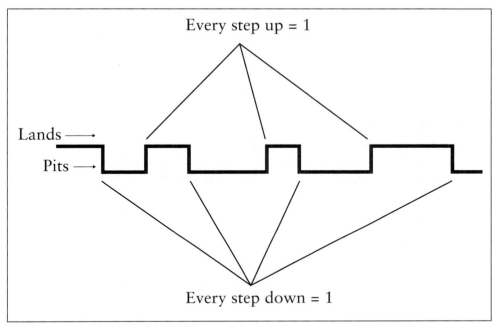

FIGURE 2.2 The surface of a CD–ROM.

The CLV is a natural determinant of the audio CD's length of play. If we pick a mathematically convenient speed midway within the CLV range of 1.2 to 1.4 m/s—namely, 1.28 m/s—we can relate this easily to our previous calculations. Looking at it in terms of miles per hour, 1.28 m/s is equivalent to slightly under 3 mph. At this speed, our imaginary street of 3.5 miles (the length of the spiral track) will take a little over an hour to travel. Seventy-four minutes is a standard length of play for CDs, and our conveniently chosen 1.28 m/s speed can calculate to this as follows:

Length of play (in minutes)

$$= \frac{\text{length}}{\text{speed}} = \frac{5681.0155 \text{ m}}{1.28 \text{ m/s} \times 60 \text{ s/minute}} = 73.97$$

Expressing CLV in rotations per minute shows us the other side. A vinyl album doesn't have CLV; it has constant angular velocity (CAV). A $33^1/_3$ rpm record album will always rotate at a steady $33^1/_3$ rpm, but the stylus will have a faster speed at the outermost grooves (because it is covering more distance) and a steadily diminishing speed as the record album progresses and the stylus moves closer to the center (where the circumference is smaller). A compact disc, on the other hand, begins play at the end of the spiral nearest the center, with an initial rate of rotation ranging between 486 and 568 rpm. As the compact disc continues to play at its CLV speed, it rotates more slowly, until its final rate may be between 196 and 228 rpm. The CLV for any single disc is fixed; it does not fluctuate. Given the CLV of a single disc, the beginning and ending revolutions per minute will also be fixed.

The main advantage of CLV over CAV is the consistently dense recording of information that this makes possible, regardless of distance from the center. One might say that a CAV record album has its information stretched out farther from the center, whereas a CLV CD stays densely packed throughout.

CD players regulate the rotational speed of the disc to maintain a constant clock rate of 4.3218 MHz, which also produces a constant bit rate. CD players don't need to directly concern themselves with the exact speed and rotation requirements of different discs (falling within allowable ranges). If they are concerned with the digital signal processing, the exact speed and rotations required can be treated as natural concomitants to the signal and adjusted accordingly.

Audio CDs are sampled at a rate of 44.1 kilohertz (kHz). A hertz is a measure of cycles per second, so 44.1-kHz sampling means that a finite value (a quantized sample) is assigned to the music once every 1/44,100 seconds. Audio compact discs use what is known as 16-bit sampling, which means that each sample is restricted to the informational size of a 16-bit word (16 bits = 2 bytes). Therefore, each word or sample can assume one of 65,536 different possible values (that's 216). Since the source music is stereo, both the left and right channels must be sampled separately, creating a 2-word, 32-bit (or 4-byte) slice of the time frame. This is what is known as analog-to-digital conversion.

A little more simple math will tell us the constant bit rate required for audio compact discs. Since each second at 44.1 kHz will contain $44,100 \times 2$ words (because of stereo) $\times 16$ bits each, the result is 1,411,200 bits per second. We can divide this by 8 to get the value 176,400 bytes per second. So that's how many bytes per second must be read to achieve playback of a CD–Audio disc.

CD Optical Specifications

Perhaps the most common visual association with compact discs is their reflective properties. Because the CD is an optical medium, this appearance is strongly connected to the underlying technology.

The rainbow effect you observe when inspecting a disc results from the pits (at a constant track pitch on the disc surface) acting like a diffraction grating. Refraction of light is frequently explained by the "experiment" of making a pencil appear broken—placing the pencil in a glass of water so that it is half-in and half-out. The pencil appears broken because the change from traveling through air to traveling through water has bent the light. The wavelength of light changes and bends when it passes from one medium to another, provided that these media have different refraction indices.

If you hold up a CD and look at its reflective surface, you are looking through polycarbonate plastic with a refractive index of 1.55. (The refractive index of air is 1.0 by definition.) The side of the disc's plastic that is nearest to you is smooth (unless it's been damaged). The far side of the polycarbonate has had a distinctive pattern of pits and lands imprinted on it (by any of several methods). The polycarbonate was then metallized (generally by aluminum), after which lacquer and some sort of labeling information were applied to the other side of the metal. Polycarbonate plastic is most commonly used for its clarity, strength, and moldability, but really any transparent material is possible provided that its refractive index is 1.55.

Looking at a disc "upside down," from the perspective of the read head, means that the pit surfaces are closer to you than the lands, like bumps in the surface of the disc's metallized layer.

Our discussion here is primarily concerned with the compact disc itself, not the machinery that accomplishes playback or "reads" the CD (covered in Chapter 8). A cursory review of playback fundamentals is necessary, however, to account for the specific properties of the CD per se. Once rotating, the compact disc is read by a movable head (or read head), which can slide along a straight line from a position close to the disc's center to a position immediately facing the disc's outermost tracks. This head directs a miniature laser beam (through a lens) onto the disc's reflective surface. The binary information on the CD's surface is then reflected back toward the lens by the beam. This reflected beam has been modified in different distinctive ways (only two of which are most important, since the information is binary) by the pattern of pits and lands on the disc surface (Figure 2.3).

When the playback light beam transitions from air into the CD's plastic substrate, it slows, becomes bent, and focusing occurs. The wavelength of the playback read head's laser is 780 nanometers in air, so once it enters the polycarbonate this changes to just over 500 nanometers (780 divided by the plastic's 1.55 refractive index = 503).

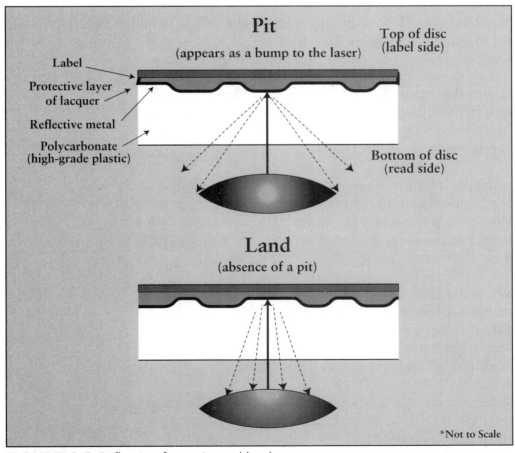

FIGURE 2.3 Reflection from pits and lands.

Since we are looking at the disc upside down, we can now refer to the pit depth as the *pit height*. The 0.11-micron specification for pit height bears an important relationship to the wavelength of the read head's laser beam. A micron (or micrometer) is 1000 times bigger than a nanometer (nm)—10^{-6} m versus 10^{-9}. This means that the pit height can be expressed as approximately 110 nm in comparison with the laser's wavelength in plastic of 500 nm.

Basically, the laser's wavelength is equal to four times the pit height. This is only approximate, but for the discussion that follows we will treat it as if it were true. You may ask: "Why didn't they just make the pit height 0.125 micron instead of 0.11 micron?" The answer is that, in practice, this deviation optimizes the tracking signal. Conventionally, this is where we should refer you to the many excellent reference books on the subject, but the point is that we won't elaborate on it here (nor the issues presented of pit depth variance when the depth goes to 0.13 micron).

Consider a lightwave as a ripple of high and low points. If you add a second lightwave that begins half a wavelength later, these two cancel out. The high point of one occurs at the same instant as the low point of another, and vice versa (Figure 2.4).

When the laser strikes a land on the CD, about 90% of its light is reflected back at the lens. This light can then pass through the playback head's assembly, where it meets a detector photodiode and an RF signal is created, indicating that there is light (Figure 2.5).

When the laser strikes a pit, the light reflected back at the lens has traveled a distance that is half a wavelength shorter. The light bouncing off a land had to travel an additional 0.11 micron to the land surface and an

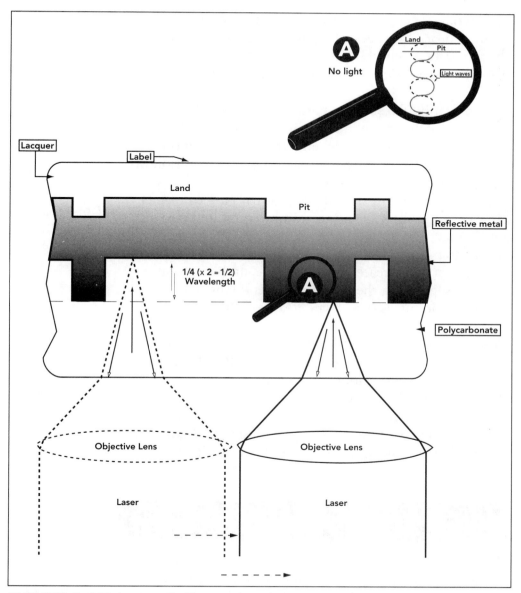

FIGURE 2.4 Lightwaves half a wavelength apart cancel out.

additional 0.11 micron on the trip back, approximately half a wavelength. As a result of this phase difference between the light emitted by the laser and the light returning to the lens after it has been reflected off a pit, the two cancel each other out and the light is effectively scattered or absorbed. The photodiode within the playback head's assembly will not register light, and an RF signal is created indicating the absence of light.

The pulsating RF signal records this series of light and no light conditions in a data stream that can then be analyzed in terms of (1) when a transition from one state to a different state occurs, and (2) the duration of time separating these transitions. In other words, the step up, step down, step up, step down pattern of pits and lands on the CD surface can be translated into step, no change, no change, step, no change, no change, step. Every step or change of condition (from light to no light or vice versa) is treated as a binary 1, and the duration of time separating these transitions is quantized to produce a series of 0s (yes, I said a *series* of them).

You see, the head's light beam is focused to a spot size of about 1.7 microns at the pit surface. Recalling our table of pit specifications, this means that the focused beam is more than three times larger than a pit's width and just over two times the minimum length of a pit. This seems like an inconsistency in design that could create problems. The solution is why I say "series of 0s."

Eight-to-Fourteen Modulation (EFM)

Compact disc technology can be seen as a marriage between two different technologies: miniature lasers and precision manufacturing. The wavelengths of light impose constraints on laser technology that are more difficult to work around than any problems posed by precision manufacturing processes. In particular, red laser technology effectively limited the focused spot size to 1.7 microns (reflecting off a pit depth one quarter of

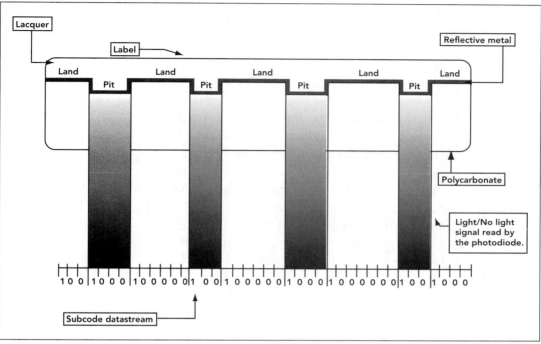

FIGURE 2.5 Pulsating RF signal.

that) at the time the Red Book standard was developed. Philips already had disc manufacturing experience with its LaserVision format, which involved pit specifications even smaller and more densely packed than the pits on an audio CD. So the question became one of optimization based on a history of "workbench" engineering experience. What pit specifications would achieve the optimum combination of performance and reliability?

A comparison can be made to producing large-print books for readers whose eyeglasses are already about as thick as anyone wants eyeglasses to be. At a certain point, you accept limited acuity of vision, and instead of tinkering around with the reader, you magnify the symbols in the book that is being read. The advantage of binary signal processing is that you can also translate the book into a totally different set of symbols, give the reader a translation key known as a *look-up table* (LUT), and choose symbols purely on the basis of what works out as being easy to read—in other words, maximizing performance and reliability.

In the world of compact discs, the answer is a surprising one: The symbols for every 8 bits of data are 14 bits long, and they are separated from each other by three connecting bits (Table 2.4). The 8-to-14 look-up table converts disc-surface symbols into standard data or vice versa. When standard data is being recorded, digital software translates it using the LUT in 8-to-14 mode. When the data of the pulsating RF signal streams off the recorded disc surface, the LUT is used in 14-to-8 mode to convert the easy-to-read symbols back into standard data. Implementation of this look-up table translation is accomplished electronically at nearly imperceptible speeds.

Another way to describe this is to say that the data stream is, in effect, "stretched" to a level that allows for more reliable playback and a more workable duty cycle for the playback mechanism. If the data stream weren't

TABLE 2.4 Standard Data versus Disc-Surface "Symbols"

8 BITS OF STANDARD DATA = 1 BYTE	14-BIT DISC-SURFACE SYMBOLS (+ 3 CONNECTING BITS)
$2^8 = 256$ possible combinations	$2^{14} = 16,364$ possible combinations, from which 256 were chosen as being "easiest to read"

Examples:

00000010 becomes 10010000100000
01111111 becomes 00100000000010
01101010 becomes 10010001000010
01011001 becomes 10000000000100

expanded by this process of 8-to-14 modulation (EFM), then it would be very possible for the playback laser to "see" a pair of neighboring transitions simultaneously (see Figure 2.6), irretrievably corrupting the integrity of the data stream.

Contrary to what you may have been told, pits and lands do not directly designate the 1s and 0s of standard binary code. The disc surface has its own native code. The 16,364 possible combinations of 14 binary bits may seem like a staggering number, but it can be reduced to a mere 267 combinations by applying three selection criteria to these many permutations:

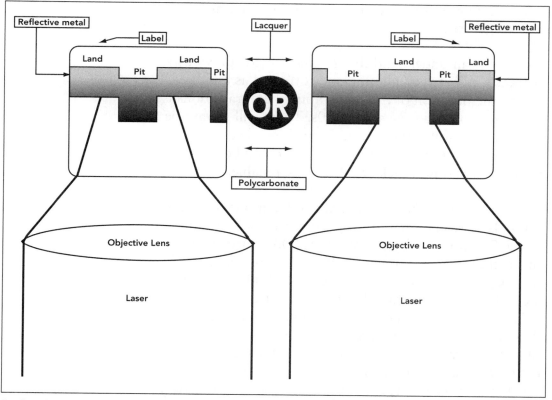

FIGURE 2.6 Narrow pit misread as land, and narrow land misread as pit.

TABLE 2.5 CD–Audio's Two Data Streams

The standard data stream (1 byte = 8 bits)	The direct-from-the-disc-surface data stream (1 byte generally equals a 14-bit symbol + 3 coupling bits, but it's *more* complicated than that)
1 frame of audio contains 6 four-byte stereo samples = 12 samples of 16 bits each = 192 bits of "code"	 588 bits of "subcode"

1. 11 is not allowed.

2. 1001 is as close as two 1s are allowed to get.

3. 100000000001 is as distant as two 1s are allowed to get (ten 0s).

Now you can understand the statement made previously: A transition between pit and land is treated as a binary 1, and the duration of time separating these transitions is quantized to produce a series of 0s. There will always be a series of 0s following pit–land transitions because if this were *not* true, adjacent transitions could be incorrectly read and playback would not be reliable.

So 256 out of the 267 permitted combinations of 14-bit symbols were chosen and assigned in the look-up table to the 256 possible byte formations. One consequence of this is that there are now only 9 possible pit lengths: 3T through 11T. The T is one of the 4,312,800 cycles per second, which is the mandatory clock rate, so 3 bits is 3T is 3 cycles, and so on. The definition of a land as the "absence of a pit" makes more sense when it is thought of as the negative image of these pit lengths. Don't forget that since the RF signal is analyzed in terms of step, no change, no change, a 3T pit will be logically identical to a land of the same length—namely, 100.

One additional problem presents itself: When these 14-bit symbols are placed in a series on the disc surface, how can one ensure that the three EFM criteria will be consistently met? Phrased another way: How can one prevent the end of one symbol and the beginning of the subsequent symbol from violating the pit length restrictions? Mathematically, the answer is achieved by adding 3 bits between every 14-bit symbol.

The 3 bits that are added between every symbol are called *merging bits, coupling bits, connecting bits,* or *packing bits.* Like grout separating enamel tiles, this makes what we're dealing with a little bigger, but it also glues it together. During recording, the digital processor assigns values to these 3 bits that maintain the EFM criteria. During playback, these coupling bits are logically discarded.

As we will see, EFM points us to the fact that discussion of the data on an audio CD is different depending on whether it is from the perspective of the disc surface's native language or from the perspective of standard data coded in samples that are words of 2 bytes each.

Does CD–Audio Have Sectors? Yes and No

Since this is a book about CD–ROM, we will take the liberty of telling you that an audio CD has 75 sectors per second. Although this is not strictly true, the engineering is such that one can treat it as if it *were* true, and CD–ROM people generally do so. They also generally discuss audio CD as containing nothing but raw audio data in 16-bit samples.

You should be prepared to encounter digital audio experts who will insist that audio CDs have no sectors and no logical blocks. They will claim to debunk CD–ROM people's claim that there is only raw data by referring to the *sync words, control words, and error correction* that are digitally encoded within an audio CD's data stream.

How can both groups be right? Get ready for a little math again. Now that you're used to thinking of 8-to-14 modulation, we can show you how the math is a little different depending on whether it is approached from the point of view of standard data or else in the disc surface's native language. First let us trot two CD facts back out for your inspection:

Audio samples per second	Clock rate (equivalent to bits per second)
44.1 kHz =	4.3218 MHz =
44,100 Hz	4,321,800 Hz

In an earlier discussion we argued (from the point of view of standard data) that the audio data stream was 176,400 bytes per second. We arrived at this as follows:

16-bit samples × 2 channels for stereo × 44,100 samples per second = 1,411,200 bits per second

Dividing 1,411,200 by 8 bits in a byte gave us 176,400 bytes per second, but

1,411,200 bits per second ≠ 4,321,800 bits per second

So how do we make sense of this? Retreating back into the CD–ROM way of looking at it, from the standard data perspective, we can argue as follows:

1. The data rate is 176,400 bytes per second.

2. There are 75 sectors per second.

3. There are $(176,400/75) = 2352$ bytes per logical block or sector.

4. Each sector is composed of 98 frames of 24 bytes each $(98 \times 24 = 2352)$.

5. Each 24-byte frame of audio consists of twelve 2-byte samples (words) or 6 stereo samples of 4 bytes each.

6. Stereo samples per second divided by 6 stereo samples per frame yields 7350 audio frames per second.

7. Audio frames per second $\times$ 6 four-byte stereo samples per frame = 7350 frames per second $\times$ 192 bits/frame = *1,411,200 bits per second.*

So we're back where we started, in a sense. But the number of audio frames per second (7350) is just what we needed to make sense of the 4.3218 MHz clock rate. If we take 4,321,800 bits per second (from the point of view of the disc surface's native language) and divide that by 7350 audio frames per second, we get an answer of 588 bits per audio frame. This is exactly right!

In other words: "Yes, Virginia, there are two data streams" (Table 2.5). There are various ways to refer to the distinction. Reference to the disc surface's native language has been our colorful metaphor thus far. Since standard binary data is commonly referred to as code, the information composing the 588-bit frame can be referred to generally as subcode. We will adopt this convention for the rest of the chapter.

The subcode that streams off the CD surface through the pulsating RF signal organizes every group of six stereo 4-byte samples into a 588-bit audio frame. The circuitry (or software) of the CD player reconstitutes this data stream of subcode into a secondary data stream of code, which only contains the audio samples' digital data.

This 588-bit frame is a part of the Red Book specification for audio CD that does not carry over into CD–ROM in an important way. It should be noted, however, that the error correction techniques developed for CD–Audio *are* also implemented in CD–ROM. The details of CD–Audio subcode are delightfully complicated, and we present only an encapsulated overview.

Minding Your P's and Q's

The reason that the 588 number of bits (in the audio frame subcode) is not readily divisible by 17 is because it always starts with the same 24-bit sync word:

Sync word = 100000000001000000000010

This permits system synchronization for the playback mechanism, which can rely on it as a flag, calling attention to the start of discrete data units, and use the frequency of sync words in its speed-control circuitry for calibration. The sync word is followed by three padding bits. Thereafter, the rest of the frame consists of subcode organized into EFM's predictable $14 + 3$ configuration of symbols ($588 = 27 + 561 = 27 + (33 \times 17)$). So we can lay out the 588-bit configuration as follows:

NUMBER OF BITS

27	27	Sync word (24 bits) + 3 padding bits
17×1	17	Control word of which the P- and Q-bits are most important
17×12	204	Audio samples (6 samples, 2 symbols each)

NUMBER OF BITS

17×4	68	Error correction Q (not related to the Q-bit of the control word)
17×12	204	Audio samples (6 samples, 2 symbols each)
17×4	68	Error correction P (not related to the Q-bit of the control word)
	$\overline{588}$	Total

Figure 2.7 provides a helpful illustration of this.

Let's dive in and tackle some of the parts of this that can be the most confusing:

- • The control word is properly called *subcode* (unlike our use of the term as a general reference to the disc surface native language). The control word is demodulated 14-to-8, and each of its 8 bits is assigned a letter: P, Q, R, S, T, U, V, and W (Figure 2.8). Each of these letters can be considered a *subcode channel,* which is how we will refer to them.

- • The term *control word* sometimes crops up in error correction terminology, although *codeword* is pre-

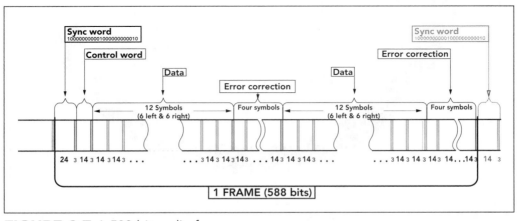

FIGURE 2.7 A 588-bit audio frame.

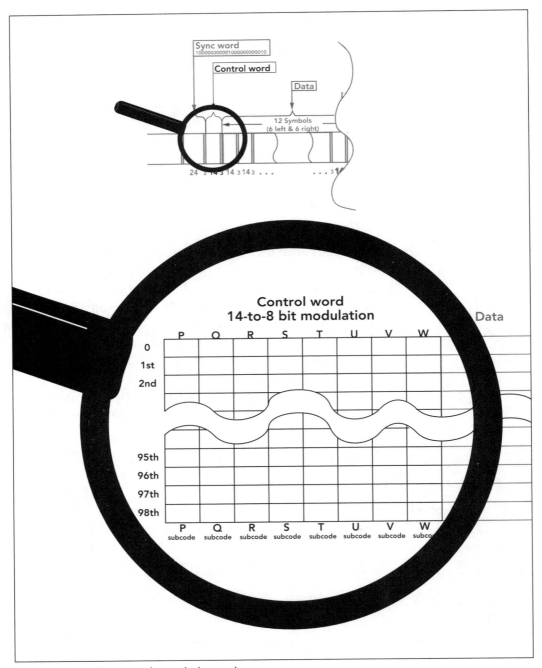

FIGURE 2.8 Control word channels.

ferred. Here it is used in the same general sense as the word header. The information in the control word is generally used to help control the information in the audio samples. The control word does, however, contain some self-referential error correction of its own.

• • Error corrections P and Q are so named because the inventors of this particular error correction technique use P and Q in their equations to describe redundant information that can be used to correct or locate errors. We refer to them as *expressions* because of their essentially mathematical nature. The P-expressions and Q-expressions are redundant to the sampled audio information. They do not relate to the eight subcode channels, which are confusingly similar (by pure coincidence).

Now that we've taken care of a few terminological pitfalls, we can get back to talking about what the subcode does and how it is organized.

The Control Word

Of the eight channels in the control word, R through W were originally unassigned by the Red Book (what is called "reserved for future use"). They have since been utilized to encode other information, such as pertains to video, but we can safely ignore them here. It's interesting to note, however, that the G-channel contains the words "read by Karaoke players."

The P-channel was a simple flag for use by primitive CD players, such that a 0 indicates a musical track in progress and a 1 indicates the lead-in pause before a track, which the read head seeks when a particular track has been requested. If a series of frames has alternating

1s and 0s, this indicates that the lead-out area for the CD is being read. The Q-channel is much more complex.

The Q-channel of the control word only makes sense if it is retrieved from 98 frames assembled together. The second bit of the control word, taken by itself, would only be able to contain two states of information, but 298 allows a structured data block to be mapped out that can convey a great deal of information. The common way to visualize the Q-channel is by stacking 98 frames on top of each other and reading the Q-channel going down from the top.

The reason digital audio people will sometimes assert that CD–Audio does not have sectors or logical blocks is because the code in and of itself is composed of only audio samples. Although the subcode is handled in blocks of 98 so that the Q-channel can be read, this is not what purists think of as a logical block for data processing purposes. In some ways, it is just an efficient way to store header-type control information. So even though the CD player handles blocks of 98 frames at a time, these are not clearly delineated sectors—unlike the situation in the CD–ROM standard, which we will cover subsequently.

When we do the math showing that a sector has 2352 bytes of code (6 samples $\times$ 2 bytes each $\times$ 2 for stereo $\times$ 98 frames), this does not include the Q-channel information. So the Q-channel is plucked from the subcode during playback and is considered as an auxiliary source of coded data. The 98 bits of Q-channel information contain their own sync data and their own error correction, plus an extensive assortment of contents, which can range from the common (notably time information such as that used for SMPTE) to the uncommon (notably a 12-character ISRC number, the conventions for which are only consistently observed by CDs released on Philips-owned labels such as Polygram).

The Audio Samples

Each frame has six stereo samples organized in the two separate data areas as follows:

Left 1

Left 3

Left 5

Right 1

Right 3

Right 5

Left 2

Left 4

Left 6

Right 2

Right 4

Right 6

These are shuffled in arrangement to protect sequential samples from disc damage. This final arrangement, however, is simple in comparison to the shuffling, which is a built-in part of arriving at the error correction data. Remember that since each sample is 16 bits of code, it will be recorded on the disc surface as 34 bits of subcode.

Error Correction

The type of error correction used for the audio samples is known as *cross-interleave Reed-Solomon Code* (CIRC). It is named after Irving Reed and Gustave

TABLE 2.6 CD–Audio Sales Compared with Total for Recording Industry

YEAR	UNITS	% OF INDUSTRY TOTAL	$ SALES	% OF INDUSTRY TOTAL
1984	5,800,000	1% of 679.8 M	$103,300,000	2% of $4.37 B
1990	286,500,000	33% of 865.7 M	$3,451,600,000	46% of $7.54 B
1991	333,300,000	42% of 801.0 M	$4,337,700,000	55% of $7.83 B
1992	407,500,000	45% of 895.5 M	$5,326,500,000	59% of $9.02 B
1993	495,400,000	52% of 955.6 M	$6,511,400,000	65% of $10.05 B
1994	662,100,000	59% of 1122.7 M	$8,464,500,000	70% of $12.07 B

Solomon, who invented it in 1960 (*J. Soc. Indust. Appl. Math*, 8:300–304). A simpler type of error correction, known as *cyclic redundancy code* (CRC), is used by the Q-channel.

One thing CIRC and CRC have in common is that they arrive at a polynomial expression (for example, $x^3 + x^2 + 1$) by which the data can be divided. If there is no remainder to the division—which is to say a remainder of zero—then the data is presumed to be correct. If the remainder is nonzero, then this remainder contains meaningful information regarding the size or location of the error in the data.

Remember that analog data is continuous, so random damage to the storage medium will generally produce meaningless noise or scratchiness. Since digital data is discrete, errors may not be so harmless. A digital glitch in the data is theoretically capable of producing any type of sound within the range of the playback equipment, so errors must be detected and prevented from reaching the playback circuitry. If an error in audio data cannot be corrected, then the sample that contains it can be

• • *Replaced with silence*: Because speakers vibrate, a theoretically silent sample is a practical impossibility. Use of this muting or erasure technique is ardently avoided.

- • *Replaced with the previous sample*: With 44,100 samples per second, "previous word hold" is the most expedient technique to use. The detail that this robs from the data is not subjectively noticeable if the technique is only resorted to occasionally.

- • *Replaced with an interpolated sample*: Taking an average between the previous and subsequent samples is superior to merely repeating the previous sample, but this technique cannot be implemented by low-end CD players.

The simplest errors to correct are those affecting a single bit. There is a theoretical measure of the distance between erroneous information and correct data known as the *Hamming distance*. For binary single-bit errors, the Hamming distance will always equal 1, because only one bit needs to be changed to correct the error. Imagine a field of coins with tails facing up, except for

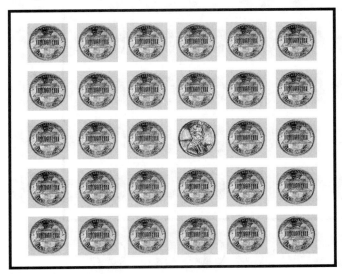

FIGURE 2.9 Single-bit error.

one rogue coin showing heads; all you have to do is flip over that one coin (Figure 2.9).

All error correction requires information redundant to the data itself, so the simplest case would be to repeat the data exactly. While this technique has been used, its storage disadvantages are glaring. Another simple technique is the use of checksums. For example, a two-dimensional matrix could have horizontal and vertical totals stored beside it. An erroneous element of the matrix would throw off one vertical checksum and one horizontal checksum, so you could calculate where the error occurred and what the size of the deviation was (for binary it would always be 1) (Figure 2.10).

Since binary data only has two values at each place-position, taking a checksum (of the different places in a number) yields an odd or even number such that any

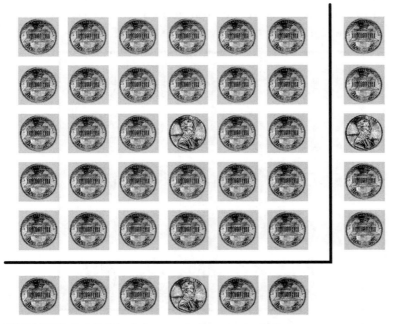

FIGURE 2.10 Modular totals locate deviation.

TABLE 2.7 Characteristics of Audio CD

CHARACTERISTIC	MEASUREMENT
Outer diameter of disc	120 mm ± 0.3 mm
Eccentricity	0.2 mm
Diameter of center hole	15 mm ± 0.1 mm – 0 mm
Thickness of disc (outside clamping area)	1.2 mm ± 0.1 mm
Maximum eccentricity of track radius	±70 microns
Track pitch	1.6 microns ± 0.1 micron
Clamping area	26 mm–33 mm
Maximum angular deviation of the reflected beam	±1.6°
Maximum outer diameter of lead-out area	Program area + 1 mm
Maximum starting diameter of lead-in area	46 mm
Starting diameter of program area	50 mm + 0 mm – 0.4 mm
Thickness of disc (overall)	1.2 mm + 0.3 mm – 0.1 mm
Label printed area	46–116 mm
Rotation	Counterclockwise when viewed from reflective surface
Material	Any transparent material with a 1.55 refraction index
Modulation system	EFM
Error correction code	CIRC
Number of channels	2 channels
Quantization	16-bit linear quantization
Audio sampling frequency	44.1 kHz
Disc weight	14 g–33 g
Disc warpage	±0.4 mm max
Skew angle	±0.6° max
Vertical acceleration	10 m/s^2 max
Radial acceleration	0.4 m/s^2 max

single-bit error will change the checksum from odd to even or vice versa. This means that instead of storing totals, one can more efficiently add a parity bit to each row and column so that every total should always come out even (or odd, as the case may be). To modify the example with the coins, this means that if the parity bits are all 0 for a matrix except for a 1 in one column and a 1 in one row, you can easily find the error and change it. This is an oversimplified example; such parity bits will generally present a series of 1s and 0s calculated to make the checksums uniformly even (or odd) (Figure 2.11).

Burst errors are far more difficult to detect and correct than single-bit errors. One must determine not only their location but also their size, and they may exceed the capacity of what the redundancy can deal with. With CIRC, for example, more than one small burst error can be detected and corrected, but if errors are

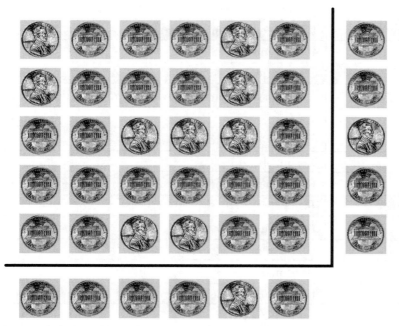

FIGURE 2.11 Checksum parity totals.

sufficiently large and/or numerous, correction will become impossible.

The reason error correction shuffles data all about is that the process tries to turn burst errors into single-bit errors. As illustrated in Figure 2.12, reading a matrix row by row will produce a burst error if there is one row that is all bad, but it may produce only single-bit errors if it is read column by column. As we said, the layout of audio samples on the compact disc becomes relatively simple after recording, but, between the beginning and end of recording, the data is shuffled every which way in order to calculate powerful error correction data.

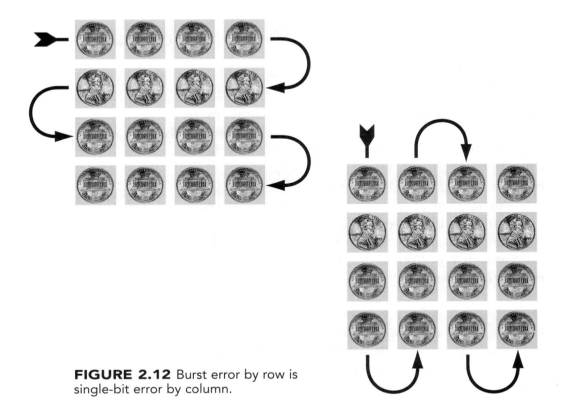

FIGURE 2.12 Burst error by row is single-bit error by column.

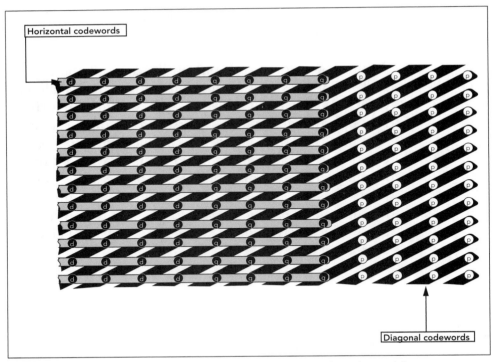

Horizontal codewords

Diagonal codewords

FIGURE 2.13 Horizontal versus diagonal codewords (adapted from *The Art of Digital Audio* by John Watkinson.)

Various terms describe the shuffling or scrambling of data. *Multiplexing* and *interleaving* are used together to separate the two bytes of each sample and shuffle the first bytes of different samples together, the second bytes of different samples together, and so on. *Cross-interleaving* shuffles the data even more and so requires more effort to implement with proportionately greater rewards. If this seems convoluted, that's a desirable property for the shuffled data—although *convolved* is the preferred term.

Once data has been fully convolved, CIRC calculates horizontal and diagonal divisors (Figure 2.13). Using polynomial division with binary data is a very powerful way to store information and locate erroneous data. The various powers that go into the P-expressions and

Q-expressions move data around into different place-positions, so the remainders contain meaningful descriptions of the error. Actually locating an error, however, is done by experimenting with different values in the calculation until the error is found, which is known as a Chien search. The mathematical name of a field containing polynomials to different powers is a Galois field, and this is fundamental to the principles used by CIRC.

Although CIRC has been proven to be the optimal form that redundant error-correcting information can take, all error correction is subject to certain limitations. Error correction must be designed with a strict sense of error probability in mind. Since the calculations or algorithms are used to change erroneous data, there is always the possibility that a big enough error will be made even worse by error correction. Implementation of error correction thus requires a time-out or off switch that causes it to stop when the scope of an error exceeds the parameters of the error-correction scheme.

CD Sales: Over 2 Billion Served

Up to now, almost everything we've described about CD–Audio is the foundation of CD–ROM technology. Besides revolutionizing audio reproduction, the Philips/Sony standard of 1982 has brought a new power of precision mass manufacturing into every household.

Although the CD is often compared to computer chips, chips are not mass-manufactured in the general sense of the term—their precision is a product of fabrication plants that are few and far between, and extremely difficult to set up. In contrast to this, replication factories for compact discs are starting to proliferate, to the point where digital piracy has become an international issue. Setting up a CD replication facility is relatively straightforward.

It's the *precision* of CD mass manufacturing that is bringing in a new era. The only mass-manufactured household item with such precise specifications is the gap in a VCR's read head. However, many of the basic techniques used to mass-replicate CDs (notably stamping in a press) have been around for centuries. When you consider that audio CDs are now bouncing along in cars and hanging from the shoulders of kids walking down the street, the playback reliability of the medium is a triumph!

Since 1993 more than half of the units of recorded music sold have been in CD format, accounting for sales of almost $15 billion (Table 2.6). In case the total of "over 2 billion served" fails to stagger your imagination, let's remind ourselves that a year only has a little over 31.5 million seconds in it, so 2 billion is equivalent to the number of seconds in over 63,000 years! That's a lot of CDs.

CD–ROM is in a tantalizing market position now. Everyone wonders if it's here to stay, while its growth continues beyond all (but the most exaggerated) expectations. Text, video, animation, and all sorts of hypertext, programming, and software engines have all been brought to 650-MB-plus reality on CD–ROM discs that can now be manufactured for under $1. Even as new state-of-the-art storage media gain in appeal that humble CD–ROMs, flaunting new and ever-escalating capacity, CD–ROM continues installing itself as the common heavy-storage medium of choice. But whatever CD–ROM's present and future achievements, it is almost completely in debt to CD–Audio: the father of the family (or mother, if you prefer). (See Table 2.7.)

Onward to the Big Sister, CD–ROM, and the Lesser Sisters

Breaking the Audio Barrier

For CD technology between 1982 and 1985, the term *software* meant the digital audio content recorded on the compact disc. Since 1985, this meaning has been expanded to include all data recorded using CD technology as a medium, for example CD–ROM, CD–I, and so on. Now this data can represent audio, video, graphics, and text. *Software* has also come to include the programs that are used to format and create the data to be stored on the disc, as well as the programs that are used to retrieve data from discs. In fact, in the CD–ROM industry, *software* generally refers to the latter meaning.

Philips and Sony produced the Yellow Book data format standard for preparation and accessing digital data in read-only fashion on a compact disc: CD–ROM. Instead of 2336 bytes of user data per frame in Mode 2 (CD–A) systems, 2048 bytes were available in each logical sector on Mode 1 (CD–ROM) systems. The remaining 288 bytes are used for a second layer of EDAC (error detection and correction) to further decrease the bit error rate from the 1×10^{-9} figure suitable for audio (where the occasional loss of a sector only affects 1/75 second of sound) to the 1×10^{-15} figure that is quite

TABLE 3.1 Comparison of Data Recorded on CD–ROM and CD-Audio

DATA RECORDING CHARACTERISTIC	CD–ROM (MODE 1) VALUE	CD–A (MODE 2) VALUE
Bytes of user data per sector	2048	2336
Sectors per second	75	75
Minutes per disc	Up to 60–74	Up to 60–74
Total bytes in 60 minutes	552,960,000	630,720,000
Total bytes in 74 minutes	681,984,000	777,988,000

TABLE 3.2 Storage Requirements for Digital Audio in CD–ROM

Bytes per Minute of Audio			
SAMPLING RATE (in kHz)	RESOLUTION	MONO	STEREO
44.1	16-bit	5,292,000	10,584,000
22.254	8-bit	1,335,273	2,670,545
22.05	16-bit	2,646,000	5,292,000
	8-bit	1,323,000	2,646,000
11.127	8-bit	667,636	1,335,273
(with 3:1 compression)		222,545	
(with 6:1 compression)		111,273	
11.025	16-bit	1,323,000	2,646,000
	8-bit	661,500	
7.418	8-bit	445,091	
5.563	8-bit	333,818	

acceptable for digital data processing. Table 3.1 shows the comparative figures in data capacity of the two modes.

So CD–ROMs can include CD–A-quality sound in addition to their capacity to store video, graphics, and text. Digital sound quality is a function of the kilohertz used for sampling and the bit resolution used for data storage. Especially for spoken material, inferior sound quality is often used on a CD–ROM in order to liberate the megabytes that would be required to store superior quality audio. Of course, data compression can accomplish the same purpose and is often used. Table 3.2 illustrates various audio storage needs. You may notice that the bytes required for stereo equal mono-times-two, and the same is true for 16-bit versus 8-bit sound; so for any given sampling rate, 16-bit mono will use the same number of bytes as 8-bit stereo.

Data Requires More Robust Error Correction

Fortunately, the architects behind the compact disc format were visionary enough to know that the key to the format's success would be a robust error correction scheme that was easily implemented and had redundancy approaching absurdity. Now that you're knowledgeable about sectors, let's glance at the error correction system in the audio CD. An entire data sector (2340 bytes) translates to less than 1/75 second of audio. If an error (or several) occurs during any given sector, the playback electronics can easily substitute the previous sector for the faulty one. Such a switch will be undetectable to the listener. Such an error on a CD–ROM disc, however, would be a major catastrophe.

In the world of computer data storage, the accepted level of reliability is no more than one byte error per 10^{12} bytes. In the language of CD–ROM, that figures out to one erroneous byte in every 2000 or so discs.

To accomplish this level of reliability, CD–ROM error correction would have to be over 1000 times greater than that of the audio disc. What could be simpler than just moving a continuous binary string over, around and through the various processes, right? Not so fast. Would that it were so easy. Slight playback glitches on an audio CD can be corrected quite easily. If a bit is lost or reversed, the performance is not compromised. Such a situation on a CD–ROM cannot be tolerated. A missing or reversed bit could not only provide erroneous or missing information, it could crash the system.

After experiencing low error rates during the first few years of commercial compact disc manufacture, the Sony/Philips consortium saw additional use of the CD format linked to the growing popularity of the personal computer. After yet another level of error correction, the CD–ROM format was officially announced in 1983. Since the physical standards were identical to audio discs, no changes in the manufacturing process were needed. Here's a visualization of a CD–ROM block structure in Mode 1:

Sync 12	Header 4	User data 2048	EDC 8	Blank 8	ECC 272

= 2352 bytes total.

Here's how Mode 2 looks:

Sync 12	Header 4	Data 2336

= 2352 bytes total.

The overwhelming majority of CD–ROMs are in Mode 1. Mode 2 discs are usually in XA Mode. Briefly, Mode 2 discs rely solely on CIRC for error correction. It is the basis for sound and image storing in both CD–I and CD–ROM XA formats.

The basic logical unit of data storage on a CD–ROM disc is the sector, which derives from the audio heritage of the discs. On both CD audio and CD–ROM discs, a sector is 1/75 second of playing time, which would be a section of the pit spiral about 1.5 cm in length. Because the formats are the same, a CD–ROM disc's sector addresses are in the same format as an audio disc's: minute:second:sector. These are minutes and seconds of playing time measured out from the hub, not minutes and seconds of arc.

A CD–ROM sector contains 2352 bytes, of which 2048 are user data and 304 are positioning, error detection/correction, and speed information. Since sectors are 1/75 second playing time and discs can be up to 72 minutes "long" (chosen to accommodate a slow-tempo rendition of Beethoven's *Ninth Symphony*), it follows that the data capacity of a CD–ROM disc is $72 \times 60 \times 75 \times 2$ Kbytes, or about 630 Mbytes. The 304 bytes of nonuser data in a sector are used for location, disc speed, and error correction. These are allocated as follows: The first 12 bytes at the beginning of each sector are synchronization (*Sync*) data, used to regulate the speed of the player's motor, which must constantly adjust rotational velocity to maintain a constant linear velocity and constant data intake. The next 4 bytes are the sector's *header*; 3 of these provide the sector's address, and the fourth is mode information (data or zero, with zero indicating that the error correction bytes are available for storage). At the end of the *user data* in each sector are 288 bytes. Of these, 4 are used for error detection. A further 276 bytes are used for error correction. The remaining 8 bytes are reserved for information about sound and video.

Data integrity for CD–ROM discs is made possible by scrambling and by multiple levels of error detection and error correction codes (EDC and ECC, also abbreviated as EDAC). Scrambling/unscrambling is done according to a bit-shift algorithm that acts to disperse related data through a sector, to reassemble them for error detection and correction (if necessary), and to deliver them to the user. Once data is unscrambled, the initial check of a block of data that is to be transferred to the user's computer is the cross-interleave Reed-Solomon code (CIRC). This is the first-level system; it functions invisibly to detect and correct errors.

When the CIRC cannot repair an error, the system moves to the cyclic redundancy code (CRC), calculated similarly to a parity check of the sync, header, and user data, to detect the location of the error. Then, to regenerate bad data, the drive utilizes the error correction code bytes created during data preparation. To insert the ECC bytes, the data bytes in a sector are arranged mathematically into a virtual block. The ECC algorithms then calculate two bytes for each column and row, which are appended as bytes at the "end" and "bottom" of the rows and columns. Since the block is virtual, not actual, the ECC bytes are actually interleaved among the data.

When the drive needs to correct a sector of data, it subjects the bytes in the sector to the same mathematical algorithms that were originally used to calculate the ECC bytes, in a process similar to a parity check. The test determines whether the bytes calculated by the drive match the ECC bytes it has just read from the sector. Because the location of a sector's data is known from the CRC bytes, the regeneration algorithms can be applied to it. When a block of data requires correction, the drive's electronics apply Reed-Solomon algorithms to the defective data, based on the ECC bytes. This allows a burst of up to 450 bytes of defective data to be regenerated correctly. When the defects in a sector exceed the ability of the ECC algorithms to regenerate data, the system times out and reports a data error.

Green, Orange, and White

CD–I Systems (Base-Case Level)

Base-case CD–I systems can be either a CD–I system or a (future) CD–DA player with a CD–I decoder. A pointing device is available for input. If the application software tries to accept input from the keyboard (tries to read the keyboard buffer) and no keyboard is connected, then a keyboard image will be displayed on the screen and the pointing device used to "key" the keyboard.

CD–DA discs can be played. Base case CD–I discs can
be played for fully functionality. A CD–I disc of greater
than base-case level must perform usefully on a base-
case-level system. This will probably be a constraint on
the disc content developer. A CD–ROM disc in Mode 1
that conforms to the ISO 9660 Level 2 format and contains text files and 68000 code and calls to the CD–
RTOS operating system is playable; otherwise, the data
can be transferred. This is one of several possible standard systems for the reference departments of libraries
and a possible standard system for the home.

CD–I Systems (Extended System)

CD–DA discs can be played. Devices such as a keyboard and/or floppy disc are included. These allow a
wider range of applications to be run on the system.
Additional memory and other features can be present.
A base-case-level CD–I disc will play because all CD–I
systems must perform base case. A CD–ROM disc in
Mode 1 that conforms to the ISO 9660 Level 2 format
and contains text files and 68000 code and calls to the
CD–RTOS operating system is playable; otherwise, the
data can be transferred.

CD–R

Perhaps most pressing at the moment are the various
issues surrounding CD–R (Table 3.3). These discs can be
written on once, although this may be accomplished
during multiple sessions as you burn the photoresist
from the hub of the disk toward the rim (also see Table
1.6). With the cost of CD–R drives now under $2000
(and the disc cost below $12), their appeal will now be

TABLE 3.3 Comparison of CD–ROM and CD–R

CRITERIA	CD–ROM	CD–R
Is mass production possible?	Yes	No
Durability	50+ years	Unknown, perhaps 50 years
Transfer Rate	300 KB/second	300 KB/second
Transportability	Light, easy to mail or ship	Special packaging
Capacity	700+ MB	600 MB
Ease of update	Requires new manufacture	Very easy
Error rate	$1 \times 10 \,(12)$ bits	
Best use	Distribution	Storage or small number of users
Mass replication	Fast, economical, low cost per disc	Blanks are expensive and are copied individually
Encryption	Encryption software/ firmware separated	Encryption software/ firmware separated

felt not only in the commercial sector but also in the "data-mongers for hire" service sector.

To draw a couple more comparisons between these media: CD–R is the medium of choice for product prototyping, proof copies, and as a short-term transfer medium. CD–ROM is the medium of choice for economical distribution of data in a durable, standardized form. Its ability to withstand adverse physical conditions is unexcelled.

Cross-Platform Compatibility

The innovation of CD–DA and CD–ROM technology has produced a diversity that is both wonderful and intimidating at the same time. It's certainly intimidating to keep track of. This instills nervousness among consumers because the suspicion arises that anything you buy will be obsolete by the time you get it home.

Don't expect brand-new, consistently adopted standards to solve *all* the problems caused by diversity. Have you ever heard a bunch of programmers gripe about MS-DOS? No matter how well something works or runs, once it's adopted we're all going to have to be limited by whatever unique restraints and inefficiencies it imposes on us. Also, bad standards are worse than no standards at all because they are a financial and intellectual burden on programmers and developers. An absence of standards *can* also foster creativity, as programmers try to ensure that their creations can run on different hardware.

Table 3.4 is a guide to *some* of the big competitors on the digital disc scene. It is not exhaustive by any means (for example, it does not include Photo CD, 3DO, etc.). This indicates some of the complexity involved in answering the question: "What is compatible with what?"

Because many perceive disc/system compatibility, specifications, and standards issues to be significant problems, most of these issues are being controlled by standards organizations or key vendors. The others are controllable by system integrators.

An example of a standards organization that has worked to resolve many of the basic CD–ROM issues is the AAP with its electronic manuscript standard. It is

TABLE 3.4 CD Disc Player Compatibility

DRIVES	CD–DA discs	CD–I base case discs	CD–I extended discs	CD–ROM Mode 1 discs	CD–ROM Mode 2 discs	CD–R DISCS (readability ONLY)	CD–V (video) discs
CD–DA players	✔	CD–DA formatted tracks only	CD–DA formatted tracks only	CD–DA formatted tracks only	CD–DA formatted tracks only	CD–DA formatted tracks only	✘
CD–I systems (base case level)	✔	✔	mandated to be compatible	✘	possibly, depends on logical formatting	possibly, depends on logical formatting	✔
CD–I systems (extended systems)	✔	✔	✔	✘	possibly, depends on logical formatting	possibly, depends on logical formatting	with an adapter
CD–ROM Mode 1 drives	✘	✘	✘	✔	✔	✔	✘
CD–ROM Mode 1 or 2 option A drives	✔	only with CD–1 controller	only with CD–1 controller	✔	✔	✔	✔
CD–R drives (write-once/ WORM)	for some option classes	✔	✔	✔	✔	✔	✔
CD–V (video) drives	✔	CD–DA formatted tracks only	CD–DA formatted tracks only	CD–DA formatted tracks only	CD–DA formatted tracks only	CD–DA formatted tracks only	✔

hoped that this will provide low-level common access to textual (nonbibliographic) databases, which are frequently found in the reference departments of libraries. Further standardization of text index structures is not feasible in light of the need to optimize performance and access techniques at the application-specific level. The designers of sophisticated CD–ROM based systems will optimize performance for their end users. As a result they will effectively choose to be less than fully compatible. This approach is similar to that used by other microcomputer systems developers.

The desired compatibility solution might be best achieved by action of the National Information Standards Organization (NISO), by reasoned local area network solutions, or by voluntary action on the part of the major software houses. Current local area network implementations are beginning to address these issues in a primitive way. However, most have implemented CD–ROM drives as network disc servers instead of as network database servers. In addition, they tend to use private protocols instead of (the international standard) Internet protocols. The result is lower throughput capabilities and the inability to operate outside of the single local area network. Presumably, pressure from larger users will hasten conversion to standardized network protocols and database server functionality.

Some organizations have demonstrated commendable initiative in approaching the integration of CD–ROM into end-user networks. However, there needs to be a whole new standards focus for portable media (not just CD–ROM) that addresses how CD–ROM fits into the architecture of a system. This could be a reasonable extension of the work at the International Standards Organization, which applies to distributed systems, or that of IBM, which pertains to system applications architecture (SAA).

The following trends underscore the immediacy of these issues:

Usage of local area networks in offices and homes.

Fiber-optic LANs are moving into offices.

LANs are well underway for homes in Europe and Japan.

Development of chipsets for both MPEG and JPEG encoding/decoding and set-top interactive TV boxes.

Integration of CD–ROM with video games (i.e., NEC, Nintendo, Sega).

Integration of video game components such as Nintendo with educational or other information services.

Computerization of consumer electronics including televisions and VCRs.

Migration from analog to digital video.

Today most end users are primarily concerned with very basic compatibility and usability issues such as "Does it work on my system?" and "Do I have to reboot when I change CD–ROM discs?" Someday these questions, or their underlying causes, will have found some permanent resolution and will be governed by relatively fixed sets of standards, but you can count on the fact that there will be new questions and new standards issues that come up in our electronic world on a more or less steady basis. Welcome to the future—you're here.

Photo CD—An Orange Book Sister

The Orange Book specification covers recordable CDs and was first issued in 1991. Photo CD, being a writeable format, falls under this category. Since its announcement in 1990 and introduction in 1992, Kodak's Photo CD system has been filling voids in the professional market. Originally touted as a consumer item, the lack of success in that market has been more than compensated for in other areas.

There are two distinct parts to the Orange Book. Part I covers CD–MO (magneto-optical discs). This subsection is specific to discs that can be overwritten. Part II is concerned with CD–WO (write-once discs). In this section, discs can be recorded once, but additional information can be added sequentially until the existing space available for recording is used up. There are two modes to Part II of the Orange Book.

> Disc at once: Here, all data is written in one pass. None can be added later.

> Track at once: Under this section, recording to disc can take place at many different times, but the data is not available for reading until a final TOC (table of contents) is added.

Don't confuse either of these with multisession mode. Multisession allows for separate record sessions until the disc is full. Data is still able to be read back before the last session is completed.

An individual Photo CD image is stored on the disc in a file known as Image Pac. Each Image Pac consists of five files that contain both compressed and uncompressed image data. Mercifully, Kodak has built in their own compression method. The highest resolution image (2048 lines by 3072 pixels) would be 18 MB in size. The compression program stores the same file in only 4.5 MB. The decompression software resides in firmware as well as other access programs and in some plug-ins. There are five Image Pac formats, which are shown in Table 3.5.

When written to Photo CD in Kodak's master format, a full-range Pac may be written between 3 MB and 4.5

TABLE 3.5 Five Image Pac Formats

| NAME | HEIGHT | WIDTH | GENERAL DESCRIPTION | APPROXIMATE FILE SIZE (True color, uncompressed) | |
				PICT	TIFF
Base/16	128	192	Thumbnail	48 KB	78 KB
Base/4	256	384	Low-resolution TV	171 KB	294 KB
Base	512	768	High-resolution or zoomed TV image or VGA monitor	732 KB	1158 KB
Base *4	1024	1536	HDTV	3078 KB	4614 KB
Base *16	2048	3072	High-Resolution HDTV or 35-mm quality	13,533 KB	18,438 KB

MB in size, depending upon the composition of the image and the density of compression. When an image is written to Photo CD in Kodak's Portfolio format (in base resolution), each file is always 768 KB in size. All images are stored on Track 1 of the Photo CD as digital data, and audio annotations and stereo sounds are stored as a single, continuous audio data recording on a second track. Track 2 is industry-standard (Red Book) stereo audio playable on a consumer compact disc player. Precise start and stop points on this track are identified during the design and mastering process for Portfolio format discs to specify which sound bites are to be played when associated images are displayed. For a minute of play, digital audio files require approximately 9.2 MB of data storage space on the disc.

Because Photo CD technology is based upon the aspect ratio of a 35-mm film exposure (not television or computer displays), photo CD images are slightly larger than will fit on a television screen. Although not much of the image extends beyond the edges, Kodak players provide a four-direction panning feature so that viewers can see to the very limits of their photographs.

Photo CD Software Support

One of the main reasons for the increasing acceptance rate of the Photo CD format is the wide variety of hand-in-glove supporting software packages. Among them are

Kodak's CMS Photo CD plug-in for Adobe Photoshop: This add on uses Kodak CMS (color management system) to convert the photo YCC color encoding metric used on Photo CD to Photoshop's LAB or RBG format.

Kodak's Arrange-It CD Portfolio: This software aid allows developers to import images from presentation applications such as Persuasion and to develop high-level multimedia applications such as talking slide shows.

Kodak's Create-It: Here, users can implement image editing and design functions. Finished products can be turned into interactive presentations or output in more conventional forms such as slides or prints.

Kodak's Picture Exchange: This package allows for downloading of images by modem.

Kodak's Shoebox: This nifty package is an image management tool that simplifies the cataloging and retrieval of not just Photo CD images, but also files in PICT, WPG, TGA, BMP, GIF, PCX, and TIFF formats. Additionally, UVAV audio files and Quick-Time movies can also be included. Developers define keywords, captions, and the like. They can later search on these fields to find a specific file.

Photo CD

The manufacturing process for raw photo CDs differs significantly from standard CDs. A continuous groove with a *wobble* is cut into a master disc. This wobble has a base frequency of 22.05 kHz and is annotated with ATIP (absolute time in pregroove). This prerecorded "time" signal is used to control the spindle speed of the playback drive. Remember, CDs don't rotate at the same speed across the disc as a 33⅓ r.p.m. record album. The components of a blank photo CD (and all other write once CDs) are a clear substrate, a layer of dye, a gold reflective layer, and a layer of protective sealant.

The photo CD system continues to evolve. Today write-once photo CD mechanisms can transfer data at the rate of 900 KB per second, thereby allowing a full disc to be completely cut in just ten minutes. At a suggested retail cost of only $25 (about 4 cents a megabyte), photo CD has blazed a trail to compact, easy storage of virtually any image source.

CD-PLUS

CD-plus is defined in the Blue Book. CD-plus is a way to add ancillary data such as song lyrics, technical credits, graphics, and animations to an audio CD. You won't be able to access that information on your audio CD; however, your CD–ROM unit will handle the data, regardless of whether you're running Windows or a Macintosh. Audio CDs are 100 percent Red Book–compliant. The specifications for a mixed-mode CD–ROM call for data to be located on track one so all audio files are appended to the data. Raw data sounds awful on audio speakers. How do you negate this "track one problem?" The answer is to generate a multisession master disc, and "hide" data in the disc's "pre-gap," thereby leading us to a track zero disc instead of a track one disc. In essence, the computer data is "buried" in the disc's lead-in area and is only accessible by rewinding to a point before the audio program begins. This solves the problem for CD audio players. New versions of driver software solve the problem for CD–ROMs.

VIDEO CD

This is in the White Book. Don't confuse this rendition with its high-density cousin, DVD. The pits, lands, and other physical characteristics of this format coincide 100 percent with standard CDs. Using standard MPEG 1 compression, the total available playing time is 74 minutes. Video CD is considered to be a "bridge" format, mainly because it will play on both CD–I players as well as either Windows or Macintosh computer setups. It is fully capable of carrying a signal in all the worldwide video standards (PAL, SECAM, and NTSC), and has full motion capability along with freeze frame, fast scan playback, and slow motion.

CD-ERASABLE

CD–E can be recorded too, much like today's one-off discs, but will allow for erasure and rewrite. The format's proposed discs have been submitted by Philips Electronics NV, but will not be compatible with current CD–ROM drives, unless the drives are modified to create variable laser power. The technology behind this format is a variation of the phase-change technology that is the basis for magneto-optical recording and will be included in new CD–ROM drives. In its raw state, a CD–E disc is amorphous. When struck by the beam of a record laser, however, the exposed areas change to a crystalline state. During playback, the read laser is either reflected by the crystalline areas or scattered by the amorphous surface, thereby emulating standard CD playback. In order to record over existing data, a record laser of a higher power has to be used. This is true for each re-recording. All phase-change media suffers from the fact that the number of times re-recording can be accomplished is limited.

Premastering CD–ROMs

Virtually every urban area on earth has some sort of zoning laws. These statutes dictate where structures of specific size and height can be built and define commercial versus residential areas. These ordered laws prevent factories from being built in residential areas and so on. Civilization has long recognized the need for such order, since facilities and structures have specific needs for public utilities (power, water, etc.) and place corresponding demands on utilities (waste disposal, etc.) at the same time.

In effect, premastering is nothing more than the zoning restrictions governing the placement of data onto a compact disc. Having a set order of premastered data assures all of us of having a compatible disc, playable on not only drives of various manufacturers but on different computer platforms and operating systems as well.

The main premastering formats are

- • ISO 9660
- • High Sierra
- • Apple HFS
- • UNIX UFS
- • Apple ISO 9660 Extensions
- • Rock Ridge
- • Updatable and Frankfurt

There also exist various combinations of these formats, a topic with too many variations to be adequately covered here. Suffice it to say that discs exist that combine, for example, ISO 9660 and HFS. Discs of this type are known as *hybrid* discs (or *Janus discs*, named after the Roman god with two faces). In this chapter we review ISO 9660 thoroughly, provide a general description of the other formats, and then describe some premastering software and hardware options for the small digital publisher.

ISO 9660

CD–ROM technology was appealing in its infancy because of its incredible efficiency as a means of information storage and distribution—more than 650 MB replicated by a stamping die-mold process with costs falling to below $2 per CD. The emerging CD–ROM industry, however, required cross-platform standardization so that it could grow to its fullest potential, as it is now only beginning to do. ISO 9660 is amazing both technologically and socially because it accomplished this.

Bluntly put, ISO 9660 is a file system designed specifically for CD–ROM. Since by nature CD–ROMs were not designed to be changed or altered, ISO 9660 does not provide a way to change or add data.

Since its purpose is to allow a CD–ROM to be read over several operating platforms, it includes information that can be recognized and used by these platforms. It is the lowest common denominator of file system structure.

Before the first development of a uniform standard (the draft of ISO 9660 known as High Sierra), CD–ROM was a nightmare for developers: Every application had to install its own drivers in order to address its own unique file system.

Naming Conventions

Although ISO 9660 has three levels of interchange, only level 1 is fully compatible with DOS. This is primarily because of the 8 + 3 limit that DOS sets on the length of a file name and its extension (e.g., FILENAME.EXT). Directory and subdirectory names are also limited to a length of 8 characters. Our discussion does not specifically cover the less-restrictive ISO 9660 levels 2 and 3 because they will not become cross-platform unless the 8 + 3 DOS limit becomes outmoded.

In fact, ISO 9660 is even more restrictive than DOS when it comes to naming files and directories. Naming possibilities are severely restricted to the uppercase characters A–Z, 0–9, and the _ symbol. The lack of the space (ASCII 32 = 0X20) character as well as several others permitted by DOS can be extremely frustrating and provides fertile ground for human error during the premastering process. Additionally, only eight directory levels are supported, so there can be only eight levels of folders within folders. Although that should be suffi-cient for most applications, programmers with unusual-ly strong nesting instincts will find this limitation confining.

Looking at this from the equipment and systems side, however, presents a very different perspective. Instead of being aghast at draconian naming restrictions, we can appreciate the fact that strong zoning laws make CD–ROMs more readable. File names are far from the most important issue in computer programming, and the ideal of cross-platform functionality is well worth certain trade-offs. (See "Why Do We Have a Standard Such as ISO 9660?" on page 82.)

The Primary Volume Descriptor

The word *volume* is used here to describe an individual CD–ROM title. As with books, this means that a *vol-ume set* will be a collection of volumes such as a two-volume encyclopedia or a set of three CD–ROM discs that are designed to function as a collective unit. The word *descriptor* refers to the function of providing extensive descriptive information about the disc and how to read its contents. Also note that the word *identifier* bears the same general meaning as name (although a *file identifier* includes extensions and version number).

Using our zoning metaphor, ISO 9660's primary volume descriptor can be compared to a plan for a uniform orientation area that many different communities would have in common. No matter which community you went to, you could look in the same place for signs telling you where you were, how big the place was, and where to find maps to get around. It would also give you more general facts and information.

To break out of the metaphor, since a compact disc is a binary digital environment, this orientation area must be built out of bits and bytes. Specifically, the primary volume descriptor can always be found at Logical Sector 16 (or Block 16) of an ISO 9660–compliant disc, and the subsequent 2048 bytes of information are strictly laid out by byte position (BP). Review the summary in Table 4.1 of how these bytes are assigned to get a sense of what is actually involved in such standard formatting.

The challenge being addressed by ISO 9660 and the various restrictions it contains is the logical layout of the whole compact disc (see Table 4.2).

It is not enough to know that the wealth of information laid out by the primary volume descriptor will be ready and waiting at the data bytes contained in Logical Sector 16. What is needed is a systematic organization of all the contents on the disc so that the computer's operating system can access any of the application's files (by having the CD drive perform accurate seeks). Or, to go back to our zoning metaphor, the visitor to the orientation area needs to be provided with maps that will let her go out into the community and travel where she wants.

TABLE 4.1 Primary Volume Descriptor Layout by Byte Position (BP)

BP	INFORMATION PROVIDED
1–8	Uniform to all ISO 9660 discs 1 *Volume Descriptor Type:* "1" indicates that this is the *primary* volume descriptor. 2–6 *Standard Identifier:* "CD001" indicates ISO 9660, versus "CD-ROM" for High Sierra, or "CD–I." 7 *Volume Descriptor Version:* "1" indicates ISO 9660 version of the Volume Descriptor Set Terminator. 8 (Unused field padded with zeros)
9–40	*System Identifier:* what kind of system can process Logical Sectors 0–15?
41–72	*Volume Identifier:* indicates the title of the compact disc.
73–80	(unused field)
81–88	*Volume Space Size:* the number of recorded logical blocks on the disc.
89–120	(unused field)
121–124	*Volume Set Size:* "1" for a standalone or more for a multi-CD set.
125–128	*Volume Sequence Number:* "1" for set of 1, "1" or "2" for a set of 2, etc.
129–132	*Logical Block Size:* as measured in bytes.
133–140	*Path Table Size:* the length, in bytes, of the path table(s).
141–144	*Location of Occurrence of Type L Path Table:* Type L is least-significant-byte-first method, typical of Motorola/Macintosh chips.
145–148	*Location of Optional Occurrence of Type L Path Table*
149–152	*Location of Occurrence of Type M Path Table:* Type M is most-significant-byte-first method, typical of Intel/DOS-PC chips.
153–156	*Location of Optional Occurrence of Type M Path Table*
157–190	*Directory Record for Root Directory:* points to location of the root directory set of multiple directory records by providing a single, minimal directory record for it.

The Path Table and Hierarchical Directories

ISO 9660 provides two different kinds of map to every single file:

• • The *path table* map gives the location of every individual file. It is like the citywide map, if you will, and includes a list of all the bewildering

BP	INFORMATION PROVIDED
191–318	*Volume Set Identifier:* the title of multi-CD set containing this volume (if applicable).
319–446	*Publisher Identifier:* contains information on publisher, or identifier for file* containing information.
447–574	*Data Preparer Identifier:* contains information on preparer, or identifier for file containing information.
575–702	*Application Identifier:* information on how data is recorded, or identifier for file with information.
703–739	*Copyright File Identifier:* identifier for file with copyright statement (re ownership).
740–776	*Abstract File Identifier:* identifies file with summary statement describing this volume.
777–813	*Bibliographic File Identifier:* contents are not standardized.
814–830	*Volume Creation Date and Time:*† for the original creation of the data.
831–847	*Volume Modification Date and Time:* for the last modification.
848–864	*Volume Expiration Date and Time:* left blank if data-obsolescence is not anticipated.
865–881	*Volume Effective Date and Time:* left blank if data may be used immediately.
882	*File Structure Version:* "1" indicates ISO 9660 formats of the path table and Directories
883	(reserved for future use)
884–1395	*Application Use:* contents are not standardized (see discussion of Rock Ridge below).
1396–2048	(reserved for future use)

*This and the files referred to in subsequent fields are restricted to the root directory.
†The last byte of this and subsequent time fields is offset from Greenwich Mean Time.

byways in one handy place. Although one path table is all you need, versions in different languages—least- versus most-significant-byte-first—are provided for our disc-community's polyglot visitors. (This is comparable to the hard disk path table known as the *file allocation table* or FAT.)

TABLE 4.2 Overview of CD–ROM Organization

PHYSICAL LAYOUT		LOGICAL LAYOUT	
LEVEL 1	LEVEL 2	LEVEL 3	LEVEL 4
Converts pits and lands into a 24-byte frame; provides EFM encoding; inserts CIRC and PQ codes.	Converts ninety-eight 24-byte frames into blocks of 2352 bytes, including 12 sync bytes, 4 header bytes, 2048 data bytes, 280 bytes of EDC and ECC Mode 1 (8 bytes reserved).	Blocks are converted into files.	Files are converted into directories and volumes.
[Red Book]	[Yellow Book]	[ISO 9660]	

- • The *directory* maps break the city down into parts, indicating what these big divisions are but only providing detailed information on files that fall within that directory's immediate neighborhood.

For clarity's sake, we'll make a brief digression on what a directory is. Macintosh users are familiar with these as the folder windows on the desktop containing document or application icons, or else icons for additional nested folders. DOS users often have a clearer sense of directories because the operating system is less intuitive and frequently demands that a file name include its entire path. For example, every time they save a document, WordPerfect users will receive a prompt reading something like this:

Document to be saved:
C:\JOURNAL\DAYNOTES\JAN0995.WPD

This path just means that the JAN0995.WPD document is contained in a subdirectory named DAYNOTES, which in turn is contained in a subdirectory named JOURNAL, which is stored on the hard drive. This painstaking accuracy can leave DOS users feeling like the butler to some powerful potentate—every time you want to address them you have to give the long version: "Your Right Honorable Overseer to the Lands Immediately Posterior to Your Exalted Person." But this accuracy is just what any computer's operating system needs in order to instruct the drive's moveable head to seek the exact address on the storage medium. Like the Post Office, the computer needs more to go on than just John Smith, New York, NY 10028.

We can visualize the system of maps as leading from the orientation area to the all-in-one compilation of directories—the *path table*—and also to the top of the hierarchically organized system of smaller directories—the *root directory* (see Figure 4.1). Any file (or directory) can be accessed by either one of these two methods, but different seek times will be involved depending on the starting position of the CD drive's read head.

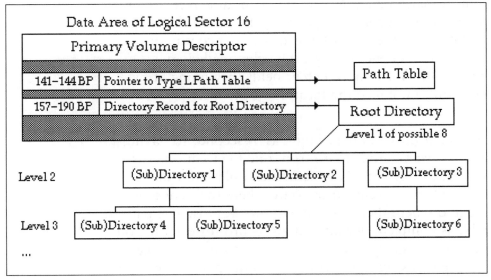

FIGURE 4.1 Simplified disc layout.

TABLE 4.3 Path Table Record Layout by Byte Position (BP)

BP	INFORMATION PROVIDED
1	*Length of Directory Identifier:* describes the total byte-size of this record.
2	*Extended Attribute Record Length:* total byte-size of extended attribute record, if any.
3–6	*Location of extent:* points to the first logical block where (sub)directory is located.
7–8	*Parent Directory Number:* path table record number for the (sub)directory's parent.
9–	*Directory Identifier:* first path table record is "00" self-reference; others are characters.
—	*Padding Field:* absent if length of directory identifier is even; "00" if it is odd.

Tables 4.3 and 4.4 illustrate the various byte positions of information contained in the path table records and the directory records, respectively. Be aware that since all ISO 9660 files must be recorded in a continuous ascending sequence of logical blocks—called an *extent*—the location of extent fields (beginning at byte position 3) point to the location of the file.

Seeking a file can take as long as ³/₄ second, so having alternative methods to go from one file to another is very advantageous. The hierarchical files are lean but incomplete—parents know only where their children are and where their own parent directory is. The path table is complete but fat, with a record for each file on the disc. Figures 4.2 and 4.3 illustrate the difference between seeking a file within the same parent directory and seeking the file of a distant cousin.

TABLE 4.4 Directory Record Layout by Byte Position (BP)

BP	INFORMATION PROVIDED
1	*Length of Directory Record:* describes the total byte-size of this record.
2	*Extended Attribute Record Length:* total byte-size of extended attribute record, if any.
3–10	*Location of Extent:* points to the first logical block where file is located.
11–18	*Data Length:* file size given in a combined least-significant-byte and most-significant-byte notation.
19–25	*Recording Date and Time:* when file was created (includes Greenwich Time offset).

26	*File Flags:* each bit within byte 26 is assigned specific information content as follows:
	first bit: 0 if file's existence is shown 1 if file is hidden
	second bit: 0 if file is not a directory 1 if file is directory
	third bit: 0 if file is not an associated file 1 if file is associated file
	fourth bit: 0 if file format is unspecified 1 if file if formatted per an
	                by extended attribute record extended attribute specification
	fifth bit: 0 if file has no special security 1 if file is protected
	sixth bit: always 0 because reserved for future use
	seventh bit: always 0 because reserved for future use
	eighth bit: 0 if this is final directory 1 if file has additional
	                record for file directory records

27	*File Unit Size:* zero unless file is interleaved graphics and audio.
28	*Interleave Gap Size:* zero unless file is interleaved graphics and audio.
29–32	*Volume Sequence Number:* "1," or else which disc file is on in a multi-CD set.
33	*Length of File Identifier:* describes the total byte size of a subsequent field.
34–	*File Identifier:* if file is not a directory (see second bit at 26 BP above), then this contains FILENAME, SEPARATOR, FILEEXTENSION, SEPARATOR, VERSION#; if file is a directory, then this contains an Identifier in characters (unless it is the first or second directory record in this directory, in which case "00" and "01" are reserved for self-reference and parent-reference (parent of root = root).
—	*Padding Field:* absent if length of file identifier is an even number; "00" if it is odd.
__–__	*System Use:* contents are not standardized [but see Rock Ridge discussion and note that this may be any length because the first field—length of directory record—determines where this ends (will include a padding field if necessary)]

In the case illustrated by Figure 4.2, the CD drive's read head has come to the end of File 1 and now needs to seek the beginning of File 2 within the same directory. This example can be compared to asking your mom where your sister is. Reading through all the many path table records would be a waste of time, because File 1 can go to its own directory (4) and find out File 2's location much faster.

In Figure 4.3, the drive's read head has come to the end of File 1 and now needs to seek the beginning of File 3, which is within a different directory. This example can be compared to wanting the address of your faraway cousin Harold, so instead of asking your mom, you call Great-Grandma Liz who keeps track of where *everybody* is. Directory 4 would have no information about File 3. Instead of scrambling around within the incomplete directory records, looking for the right directory with File 3's information, it is worth taking the time to

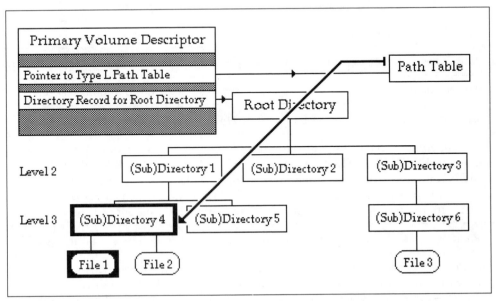

FIGURE 4.2 Simplified seek from File 1 to File 2 in the same directory.

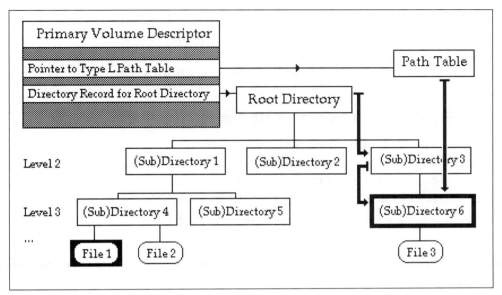

FIGURE 4.3 Simplified seek from File 1 to File 3 in a different directory.

go to the path table and find out how to go *directly* to the directory containing File 3.

Before leaving this discussion of maps and distant cousins behind, we need to mention the order that directory records must be stored in:

- • Records are sorted by their file names' alphabetical order, which is really their numerical ascending order as ISO 646 (similar to ASCII) d-characters: 0–9, A–Z, _.

- • The file name extension will be relied on as the next basis for sorting (also in ascending order), since many files may have the same file name.

  The file version is then turned to as a basis, but in descending order so that most recent versions appear first.

- • The associated file bit (the third file flag bit at Byte 26) is then used, also in descending order. This means that associated files (marked with a 1) will be organized before regular files (marked with a 0), the importance of which will become more meaningful in our discussion of Apple ISO 9660 extensions.

ISO 9660—It's Only the Beginning!

Imagine the stumbling blocks if there were as many different CD–ROM standards as there are graphic file formats. We can bemoan compatibility issues concerning CD–I, MPEG CD–V, or CD–R, but these issues are minimal compared to the mind-numbing array of over

WHY DO WE HAVE A STANDARD SUCH AS ISO 9660?

- So that data may be shared.
- So that results may be properly interpreted.
- So that data integrity may be assured.
- So that distributed production may happen.
- So that distributed processing may happen.
- So that accuracy may be assured and error trapping and correction may be interchanged.
- So that data configurations may be managed.
- So that data from different sources may be interchanged.
- So that parallel developments may occur.
- So that new hardware can easily adapt.
- So that uniform drivers may be written.
- So that an industry can achieve high credibility with its user base.

JOHN SANDS, 1990

80 incompatible file standards for graphics software—
graphic translation software is now becoming an industrial niche of its own. Since the biggest graphics, such as
IMAX Cineon frames, are about 100 MB, these problems are easier to solve with existing hard drives than
those that would be created by having a multitude of
650-MB-plus standards floating around.

Despite its static appearance, with strict maps of what
information may appear in what byte position, ISO
9660 has left itself plenty of room to grow. Several of
the areas reserved for future use have already been
seized upon by the Apple ISO 9660 and Rock Ridge
standards. These build upon ISO 9660's zoning foundation and add to it.

The extended attribute records that can appear at the
beginning of a file are also suggestive of a range of possibilities that have only begun to be explored, such as
improved use of interleaved graphics and audio for faster
streaming, and implementation of security restrictions
based on permission information. Permissions have
already made it possible to mass-distribute hundreds of
software titles in a locked format on CD so that a telephone call and a credit-card exchange get you a password
to unlock them. Even more important to the corporate
world is the impact of this for intracompany information
distribution now that CD replication can be easily accomplished on even a daily basis. Files can be restricted on a
need-to-know basis, but the same CD can appear in hundreds of in-boxes as easily as the daily supply of mail and
memos. The application use and (optional) escape
sequence fields at the end of the extended attributes
record can be any length at all, so future exploitations of
extended attributes are practically limitless.

Volume descriptors also come in various types, which
will be more fully utilized in the years ahead. After the

primary volume descriptor at the data bytes of Logical Sector 16, other 2048-byte volume descriptors can follow that have already been defined and yet left more than half empty so that they can be used in different ways:

- • 0 at 1 BP indicates that the volume descriptor is a boot record, allowing systems and applications that can read bytes 72 through 2048 to achieve special states.

- • 1 at 1 BP (as we have seen) identifies the primary volume descriptor.

  2 at 1 BP indicates a supplementary volume descriptor with bytes 1396 through 2048 reserved for future standardization.

  3 at 1 BP indicates a volume partition descriptor with bytes 89 through 2048 left unspecified for system use.

- • And here is the punchline:

  The volume descriptor set terminator must come at the end of these different kinds of volume descriptors, which must begin with the *primary* one at Logical Sector 16. The set terminator leaves bytes 8 through 2048 reserved for future standardization. So what is its specification at 1 BP? It's not four. No way! It is 255, so that numbers 4 through 254 can be reserved by ISO 9660 for the possible future standardization of hundreds of new volume descriptor types!

Those wishing to obtain copies of the actual ISO 9660 standard itself (a rather expensive 51 pages) may wish to contact:

Transaction Publishers
Rutgers University
New Brunswick, New Jersey 08903
(908) 932-2280

The publication is titled *Volume and File Structure of CD–ROM for Information Exchange,* ANSI/NISO/ISO 9660-1990, ISSN: 1041-5653. [It is identical in content to ISO 9660-1988 (ISO stands for the International Organization for Standardization). The 1988 standard was approved January 16, 1990, by ANSI (American National Standards Institute), and developed by NISO, the ANSI-designated Technical Advisory Group (TAG) to ISO Technical Committee 46. NISO may be contacted at NISO—National Information Standards Organization, P.O. Box 1056, Bethesda, Maryland 20827, (301) 975-2814.]

High Sierra

It's been said that everybody likes good laws and good standards, but nobody should see either of them being made. If the phrase High Sierra conjures up imagery such as the mountains surrounding Lake Tahoe, just put the High Sierra Casino in front of that backdrop and you've hit the nail on the head. The year was 1985, and industry giants assembled, impatient with the need for some standard of cross-platform conformity: Apple Computer, Digital Equipment Corporation (DEC), Hitachi, Microware Systems, Microsoft, Philips, Reference Technology, Sony, 3M, TMS, Videotools, Xebec, and Yelick. In short, the proverbial smoke-filled room.

What emerged from the 1985 Tahoe conclave of titans was a document titled, "Working Paper for Information Processing—Volume and File Structure of Compact Read-Only Optical Discs for Information Exchange." It appeared on May 28, 1986, authored by Lightbown, John Einberger (Reference Technology), and Chris Hamlin (Xebec), and edited by Howard Kakow (DEC), and was forwarded to the ISO for review. By 1987, pre-

liminary approval with a few minor changes was forth-
coming, but this was not soon enough for the competitive CD–ROM giants. High Sierra—the first attempt at
standardizing layout for compatibility between software
device drivers and CD–ROM drives from various manufacturers—was commercially implemented. Publishers
shipped discs in this format, and the acceptance of this
industry in its infancy was enormous.

By 1988, ISO published *Volume and File Structure of
CD–ROM for Information Exchange as Standard
9660*—two years is an almost unprecedented speed for
that international body's review process. The minor
changes to High Sierra consisted of the following:

- • Use of the CD001 standard identifier, as opposed
  to CD–ROM for High Sierra.

- • The offset from Greenwich Mean Time was added
  to the date and time fields.

  Several fields were added, such as the bibliographic
  file identifier (at 777 BP of the primary volume
  descriptor).

  Two directory record fields switched position, and
  largely trivial adjustments were made to the order,
  size, and type of volume descriptor fields.

- • Only one optional occurrence of the path table was
  permitted (instead of three).

As slight as these changes to the maps of byte position
were, they were sufficient to render the High Sierra
discs (already in use) unreadable.

By 1989, CD–ROM drives were shipped with drivers
that could read the new ISO 9660–compliant discs.
Because High Sierra had come flying out of the starting
gate, however, this was already too late for many users.
For example, DOS users were purchasing ISO discs

without having obtained the updated Microsoft Extensions (MSDCEX) version 2.0. Upon loading the newer discs, they would see the message: This is not a High Sierra disc. In the literature of the time, this is highlighted as an issue for developers, but it's just an historical anecdote now. Another anecdote is a client who threatened to punch John Sands' lights out (at the Microsoft 1990 conference) because of resentment at being pushed into the as-yet-unproven ISO standard.

As a draft version of ISO 9660, High Sierra is one of the success stories of the international standards process, but as an implemented standard High Sierra is now obsolete. Although some premastering software packages make a point of offering High Sierra as an option, it is no longer practical to master in this format. It would be better to help customers update their obsolete driver than to replicate in an obsolete format.

Apple HFS

File systems unique to particular product lines interfere with the industrywide goal of cross-platform compatibility while maximizing the utilization of the specific hardware's unique features. Any new device is free to specify its own formatting requirements, but this is often shortsighted in terms of social use of the technology and availability of titles and applications.

Apple and Macintosh users, as a group, treasure their hardware's intuitive interface with its adjustable windows and panoply of icons. The hierarchical file system (HFS, backwardly compatible to the previous MFS) supports this by specifying two separate file forks: a conventional data fork and a highly specialized resource fork that can be accessed by system calls to the resource manager.

Most of the Apple interface's unique features exist as resources in the resource fork with four-character labels, such as

ICON: 16 × 16-bit icons

ICN#: Displays unique file icons by a different method

CODE: Executable program strings used within the program

MENU: The menu line that appears along the top of the screen

STR: Character strings used within the program

This has allowed a flexible manipulation of files without having to change the contents of the data fork. For example, the MENU and STR resources have been changed in order to modify files for use in foreign countries. In addition to these resources, the finder also has available to it unique information about file type, creator and attributes.

UNIX UFS

The so-called UNIX file system (UFS) is actually a catchall term used to describe more than half a dozen different product-specific formats. UNIX users like to boast that their operating system predates DOS and has since grown to accommodate most of the power-user community. Silicon Graphics workstations, for example, all run on UNIX. But there isn't really one UNIX; rather, depending on the product line, additions to the core UNIX language exist that accommodate various special features of, for example, SUN versus Novell. The various file formats or CD formats that exist within the UNIX umbrella create a complex set of incompatibilities, sometimes even between different product lines of the same manufacturer. It should be noted here that UNIX people have some of the most powerful nesting instincts in the community of computer users: Devices will exist as subdirectories within the operating system, and paths nested a dozen levels deep are not uncommon.

Apple ISO 9660 Extensions

The Apple implementation of the ISO 9660 standard, which goes by the name Apple ISO 9660, is really an evolving standard representing whatever is state of the art for developers of ISO 9660 discs premastering on (for the most part) Apple hardware.

Apple has created extensions under which the system use area of the directory records (allocated but unused under ISO 9660) is put to use, and ISO 9660's built-in system of associated files is used to its fullest. Put simply, the contents of the resource fork will appear within an associated file (marked with a 1 at 26 BP file flags at the third bit); the contents of the data fork will appear as a nonassociated file (flagged by a 0 at the third bit).

The Apple finder was created so strictly with HFS in mind that enabling it to extract resources from an associated file is a process that is still undergoing improvement. Until recently, for example, icons or desktop windows always appeared at a given location and could not be moved (or in the case of windows, resized).

Specifically, the system identifier at 9 BP of the primary volume descriptor will specify the version of Apple extensions that is to be used, and then multiple extension fields may appear within the system use area of the directory records. These include the file type, creator, and attributes information that the finder requires.

The longer file names Apple users have grown so accustomed to, as well as other information such as version number, are used but may be truncated by DOS-specific hardware.

Rock Ridge

UNIX users generally love the UNIX environment and were very protective of it when ISO 9660 first arrived. The DOS-type file names and the restrictions to eight levels of directories appalled them. The melodrama of their emotional reaction to all this is best evidenced by the source of the name they used for the standard they developed in response.

The town of Rock Ridge is a creation of Mel Brooks' imagination in *Blazing Saddles*. It was threatened by a railroad planning to run right over it and was at first shocked that its protection was to be provided by the first Afro-American sheriff in the history of the West. But in the end, the town won. In the end, the Rock Ridge proposals enable UNIX users to keep all their cherished bells and whistles while still creating an ISO 9660–compliant CD–ROM. While these protocols are presently on their way to becoming an ISO standard of their own, products have already been released implementing this format by vendors such as Sun Microsystems and Hewlett-Packard.

The details of implementing Rock Ridge can be incredibly complex, addressing as they do a multitude of different UNIX operating environments. If you are

TABLE 4.5 Rock Ridge SUSP System Use Field Format

BP	INFORMATION PROVIDED
1–2	*Signature Word:* indicates type of SUSP Field: SP *System Use Sharing Protocol Indicator:* required in first directory record within the root directory, specifying adherence to SUSP protocols. ER *Extensions Reference:* specifies required extensions, if any. ST *System Use Sharing Protocol Terminator:* optional field to specify end of recording within the system use area. PD *Padding Field:* pads to end of logical block, if necessary. CE *Continuation Area:* pointer to logical block number where data continues.
3	*Length of System Use Field:* in bytes, allows drivers that can't read the data to skip it.
4	*System Use Field Version:* number of the version being implemented.
5	*Data:* may contain a wide range of different types of data.

premastering at home and you don't know UNIX, Rock Ridge is probably too challenging for you to implement. On the other hand, if you are a power user with UNIX experience and your target users will often have UNIX workstations, Rock Ridge is much more than a challenging CD–ROM format: Rock Ridge is a must. Its speed is eight times faster than UNIX UFS!

The Rock Ridge proposals are primarily the RRIP (Rock Ridge Interchange Protocol) and the subsequent SUSP (System Use Sharing Protocol). Like Apple ISO 9660, the system use area of the directory records is put to use and filled with system use fields. These are shown in Table 4.5. The application use area within the primary volume descriptor is also put to use, and directories of more than eight levels are permitted for UNIX users only. The longer paths are made possible by reassigning a UNIX level 9 directory back up to the top of the ISO 9660 directory structure, so that DOS or Mac users will access it as a high-level directory whereas UNIX users will view it as a deeply nested folder-within-in-a-folder-within-a-folder.

File names do not comply with the level 1 interchange restrictions but may be created so that they can be truncated by DOS hardware if DOS compatibility is a goal.

Updatable and Frankfurt

These CD formats allow multisession write-once discs to comply with ISO 9660. Updatable ISO 9660 requires the CD drive to be able to recognize that it is reading a multisession disc, in which case it goes to Logical Sector 16 of the outermost, most recent session to access the primary volume descriptor and directory structure for the entire disk. This information is updated from session to session so that the most recently recorded ISO 9660 directory information will be current.

The Frankfurt Group is more properly known as ECMA or the European Computer Manufacturer Association Technical Committee 15 working group. They have produced various proposals, most notably ECMA 168. This provides a complex yet flexible set of formatting conventions, using the system use areas (also exploited by Apple ISO 9660 extensions and Rock Ridge) and taking advantage of the multisession capability to record ISO 9660–required descriptors and records in their proper place after the multiple-session arrangement of files has been created.

Premastering Software and Hardware

Although the greatest efficiency of the compact disc format is in mass production, this is typical of any die-mold stamping process. The printing press has also been more efficient in high-volume production, but small presses and pamphleteers have used printing to achieve a special place in history.

A consumer or small-business entrepreneur cannot realistically envision gearing up for the mass production of discs, but it is possible and increasingly affordable to create a finished CD–ROM master (although I prefer to think of it as a finished premastered disc) either at home or in a small-business setting. Depending on your distribution goal, it may be adequate to simply burn a few dozen recordable write-once discs and then get them out to their target users. Even for a mass-market title, this permits a testing phase with substantial quality assurance advantages. At whatever point hundreds or millions of copies are desired, the recorded disc can be sent to a replication house, which will then base a glass master on it and take charge of the mass production at a low per-unit cost.

A powerful enthusiasm for CD–ROM desktop publishing is very justified, but it must be tempered with caution. An investment of under $5000 can now buy a CD recorder and the premastering software necessary to prepare a virtual image of the disc contents (which can then be written onto the disc). Be prepared for pitfalls, however, because it will still be years before do-it-yourself CD–ROMs evolve into real ease of use. In a decade, developing interactive multimedia and writing it onto your own CD will probably feel no more complicated than popping a VHS tape into your VCR—but that is not the 1995 reality.

Prerequisite Hard Drive Performance

The biggest reality check for people setting up their own CD–publishing workstations is the demands this places on a hard drive. It is no longer a question of hoping the drive doesn't crash or having a nice big hard disk with 40 to 400 MB on it, oh no! First remember that a CD–ROM stores over 650 MB of data, so at a minimum you need to be able to fit that as well as your premastering software onto your hard drive. Then, don't forget how audio and especially video can devour megabytes. If you are developing applications from scratch you'll have to store at least some of this in uncompressed digital form, so we're basically talking gigabytes, not megabytes. If you're doing your own video compression, you may even need extra fans and ventilation because your hard drive will be running hot!

When it comes to CD publishing, hard drive storage is at least a straightforward issue of having adequate capacity. The more important issue is the calibrated speed of your hard drive as it transfers the data that is to be burned into the recordable CD. This wouldn't be such a pitfall if people commonly anticipated it, rather than running out and buying a CD–R and extra giga-bytes storage and then being disappointed when their read-only-memory discs can't be read. Like fuel injec-tion in a car's engine, or how much pressure you apply when writing with a pen, your hard disk must supply data at a fast but steady rate so that the CD recorder can do its work properly (exact rate requirements will be device dependent). So make sure your hard drive is both fast enough and consistent enough before planning to use it for premastering. Related issues to watch out for are that your operating system runs without pauses and that your hard drive partitions don't give the rate (of the data stream) a case of the hiccups.

Formats and Name Filters

Premastering software packages range from low-end to high-end, with many different features available. Your first concern should be whether the operating systems of your target users will be supported by a package you are considering.

The high-end packages will often support a variety of formats, and there are cases where ISO 9660 is not the automatic answer. If you are distributing a DOS-based Windows product on CD–ROM with data that is organized to interact with Windows' unique API puts and calls, you don't really need ISO 9660. On the other hand, if you have some power users targeted who are not running on DOS, they may possess emulators (which will run programs written for other operating systems' unique programming environments). At the other extreme, some target users may not have the drivers they need to read an ISO 9660 disc. This used to be a big concern and is much less relevant now, but it still should be considered as part of your mental checklist.

In most cases, ISO 9660 or Apple ISO 9660 will do just fine, but if your goal is a DOS-compatible disc written in ISO 9660 level 1 interchange format (with the $8 + 3$ naming convention), you'd better be sure you've given your files names that comply with the standard. Remember that ISO 9660 is more restrictive than DOS. For example, if you put a hyphen in a file name—that's illegal. If you position a file out of alphabetical order (that is to say: ISO 646 ascending order), your file might be unrecoverable. For example, the CART really does come before the HORSE alphabetically, so if your directory records list the HORSE file first, the CART could get lost. When the seek reaches HORSE, the driver can conclude that it has already passed any files beginning with C (without finding CART), so it stops seeking.

Fortunately, many premastering packages offer filters that ensure that you can only enter names that are compliant. Some packages also organize directories in the correct alphabetical order. Unfortunately, since filters are features, these may only be included on packages that up their sticker price accordingly. A limited budget may force you to do without most of the features you want. Your genuine needs as a user may dictate that you raise more money before purchasing a package that satisfies them. You also might be scared off from packages that are loaded with features because, as a user, you might find it harder to operate within a high-end environment.

Let's look at the trade-offs involved with an affordable, single-format product with no name filters: Corel CD Creator ($249 for Version 1.0). The list of features Corel's product does *not* offer reads a lot like the list of features that other products do offer, but these other packages almost all cost over $1000 and many cost over $10,000. Low-end products, however, often offer advantages uniquely geared to a mass market that their more expensive competition simply do not possess (e.g., ease of use). CD–Creator uses a Wizard to walk you through the premastering process, leaving very little control in your hands—but if your hands don't really know what they're doing, that's a distinct plus!

As a learning tool to get acquainted with ISO 9660 while actually premastering recordable discs, Corel CD Creator is an incredible software deal. Novices who want to jump in should consider using this to get started. If you're on a very limited budget, you could purchase the Corel package ($249) and an adequate external hard drive (about $1000 per gigabyte, not counting the port/scuzzy connectivity issue). Then you would be able to deliver the hard drive with your finished data on it to a replication house and get a CD back for under $200. This is probably not your fantasy of CD publishing, but it's a respectable start!

It is better to evaluate premastering software packages after you can clearly distinguish your needs from your desires, so that you don't spend too much money on extra features. Don't forget that the software you buy is not just something you'll use—it's something you're going to have to learn. While you're learning, competition is driving prices down in the real world, and you'll be able to make better informed buying decisions later.

Geography and Optimization

Welcome to the world of high-end features, filled with such jargon as

Geographic control: The freedom to arrange and rearrange file locations.

Virtual image: Computerized model of an actual disc in which file location is supported by a geographic database.

Disc simulation: This essentially makes your hard drive run about ten times slower, so that you can performance test your virtual image as if it was a real CD–ROM. (Advanced software simulates the various seek times of different drives [between 1/4 and 3/4 second] and also allows simulation to be toggled off to provide image on the fly.)

Hole detection/compression: Finding gaps between files where nothing has been recorded (unallocated memory) and rearranging the virtual image intelligently to close those gaps (so that files are contiguous while remaining organized within geographic control parameters).

In addition to these aspects of high-end use, there is the quality of the reports that your software will generate for you, describing what you have already done or what the software proposes to do for you (for example, providing separate file lists according to disc address location or directory structure).

More mundane features, many of which might be critical to your needs, include

Support of desktop features: Control over screen color selection, mouse input, how display windows function, etc.

Batch-processing capability: Lets you set up a .BAT file to handle repetitive tasks (e.g., replicating several dozen CDs) with minimal user interaction. (Other efficiency features are the ability to call up a recorded series of keystrokes and the ability to tag a group of target files on which an operation is to be performed.)

Prevent file fragmentation: This is a requirement of ISO 9660, so once you have geographic control, you need your software to make sure you don't misuse it.

Name-filters toggle: It's great to have name filters (discussed above), but you should be able to turn them off if you want to (for instance, when backing up your own hard drive onto an archive CD–R).

Partition capabilities: The ability to make or remove disc partitions and the ability to span them.

Multiple-disc premastering: Working with more than one virtual image database at the same time.

Data security options: Comprises several different aspects of support, including the ability to hide or unhide files, and the ability to use binary editing for password insertion.

Binary input/output: Binary data transfer between the hard disk and CD–R drive is faster than copying one file at a time. (Another helpful feature is display of transfer duration and time elapsed.)

Tagging target files: Specifies multiple files on which an operation is to be performed, as opposed to having to command the operation separately for each file (one at a time).

Audio and mixed-mode: Ability to include 44.1-kHz audio on separate tracks.

Multisession support: Both read/write ability and quality of reports.

Support for different media: CD–R and tape formats (such as Exabyte and DAT); also, comparison of copy with original data.

These tools and capabilities should not be allowed to distract from the fact that optimization is essentially an art. Laying out your files and records across the geography of the disk so that seek times are optimized and the CD runs well requires perseverance, intuition, and a great deal of testing of various alternatives. For a long time, the established wisdom was that the files most frequently sought belonged closer to the hub of the CD, but this was based on the read-head technology that used to return to the hub for every seek. Now that read heads may move inward as well as outward, an alternate strategy involves locating most frequently seeked files closest to the center of the CD's recorded spiral. This creates a hot spot equidistant from the innermost and outermost extremes, so that every file on the disc is closer than they would be when using the closest-to-the-hub method.

Whatever the strategies of optimization used, a salient advantage of premastering yourself is that you can test and test again. The importance of this cannot be overemphasized. Too many CD–ROMs have been pressed in large batches only to reveal some critical problem or inefficiency of performance. The record album business once coined the phrase: It ain't final 'til it's vinyl. The commitment you make to premastering in all its aspects—and it's a big commitment—will allow you to proceed to the glass master stage knowing that you have produced an excellent CD–ROM.

chapter 5

Compression Basics

There is a Russian proverb, "When you see a bear dancing, you don't criticize its steps." The dancing bear is a commonplace of Russian circuses, and the idea is to just stare at it with amazement, appreciation, and a sense of humor. Some examples of data compression are very unsatisfactory. In the quest for efficiency, short-cuts are taken that produce poor results. But if compression is like a dancing bear in 1995, just give it a few years and it will turn into a ballet dancer.

Compression reduces the massive data streams required for video graphics down to manageable sizes. In addition to CD–ROM applications, other applications such as on-line services, cable boxes, and video conferencing are just a few of the areas where ever-increasing use of compression is inevitable. Although the need for compression is most obvious with video, it can apply to all kinds of digital data: audio, software, and so on. Compression has become like the weather—it's always going to be with us. Of course, you might not notice it if the weather is pleasant outside, but bad weather will really get your attention.

There are a lot of compression schemes available, but two sponsored by the International Standards Organization (ISO) have been in the public spotlight:

> *JPEG* ("jay-peg"): The Joint Photographic Experts Group was first out with the leading standard for compressing graphic information within a single frame, called *intraframe compression.*

> *MPEG* ("em-peg"): The Motion Picture Experts Group, influenced by JPEG, is still in the process of establishing the leading standard for compressing multiple frames (called *interframe*) and audio. Among other things, this allows the CD format to try to give VHS tape a run for its money.

Time factors and image-quality issues surround the consideration of all schemes of compression; for example,

> *Real time*: Decompression with no noticeable time delay.
>
> *Symmetrical/asymmetrical*: Describes whether or not compression and decompression take the same amount of time to accomplish. Asymmetrical compression can take hours per frame.
>
> *Lossless/lossy*: Whether the decompressed image quality shows no perceivable degradation compared to the original image. Lossy compression is very efficient but can result in a poor-quality image (this is where the dancing bear enters the picture).

We deal with these more fully in this chapter and Chapter 6. When you reach the end, you still won't be qualified to follow the arcana of a JPEG conference, but you will be able to approach compression in a well-informed way, whether you're buying and learning to use a new MPEG board for your home computer or developing a CD application for publication.

Where Is the Dancing Bear Dancing To?

True efficiency is a delicate balancing point between established methods that are approaching obsolescence and newer techniques that have not yet fully proven themselves. Technological progress passes through a series of machines or tools, arriving at designs that are optimal for their time of invention but become obsolete through a process of artificial evolution.

In 1995, low compression works well but high compression does not surpass the quality we've come to expect from our popular analog technologies. Depending on how fussy you are, 4-to-1 compression (4:1) or even 25-to-1 compression (25:1) is very good, but achieving higher rates of compression involves the loss of so much data that the results are like a dancing bear.

The X-15 test pilots introduced the phrase "pushing the envelope" into the English language. It originally described what they were paid to do: fly an experimental jet so aggressively that you achieve maximum performance, reveal the design's shortcomings, and avoid the failure of a crash and burn. This aggressiveness, which drives all technological progress (see Table 5.1), often results in failure. Luckily, poor compression doesn't kill anybody (medical radiology has to stick with lossless compression for X-rays).

Technological aggressiveness is known to produce ridicule, as described by the Gershwin song "They All Laughed." Most schoolchildren have been exposed to a standard lesson on how impractical the automobile was when first introduced: Cars were noisy, noxious, and hated. At the beginning of this century, paved roads were rare and amateur automobile enthusiasts would go out in volunteer work gangs to build them. Even decades later, however, when the phrase "Get a horse!" was an established object of scorn, the idea of the automatic transmission was so revolutionary that people laughed for weeks at the announcement that "Someday cars will shift gears by themselves."

TABLE 5.1 Technological Progress

Technological Progress		
CONCEPTUALIZATION	REALIZATION	DISSEMINATION
Proof of concept, a demonstration/ experimental model	A succession of commercial products	General use by the public

Looking at technological progress as proceeding from conceptualization through realization to dissemination, we can say that data compression is still in its early realization phase. Computers are only now entering the public dissemination phase, and phenomena such as the Internet are a natural result of this. The present excitement about CD–ROM is because it looks like it might get out of the middle ground of realization, but predictions for its broad dissemination remain speculative. Thirteen million CD–ROM drives or even twice that do not establish it as a technology in use by the general public, certainly not in comparison with cars, planes, phones, televisions, and so on.

So where is our dancing bear going? Because compression spans all data processing technologies, its success is not linked to the future of one particular kind of device. Data compression is going to the top. Low compression already works very well, and high compression will steadily benefit from many different research focuses that exist today in mathematics and the sciences. High compression holds the promise of making most of our data processing much more powerful without requiring proportionate innovations in the hardware. If you haven't laughed at poor examples of high compression, you just haven't seen what's out there . . . but once upon a time the automatic transmission was pretty funny, too.

Before Compression, How Big Is the Digital Data?

Digital audio data is described in Chapter 3. It is primarily a product of the sampling rate, the bit resolution, and monophonic versus stereophonic sound. Although audio compression exists, the option of sampling at lower rates frequently renders it unnecessary. As for digital video data, you may have read colorful descriptions of it as huge, monstrous, or massive. Such accounts often avoid the math that describes the actual size of the data by saying "trust me." All that's involved, however, is simple arithmetic to confront some actual data sizes instead of relying on "sailors' tales" and exaggerations. Although video imagery does overpower many home computers, manufacturers know they must develop more powerful hardware to support consumer enthusiasm for colorful full-motion graphics.

A PIXEL PRIMER

A pixel is not a pixie,
but a sprite is made of pixels.

Sonic the Hedgehog is a sprite. So are the Super Mario Brothers. If you stare at these game sprites, you can see that they are made up of little blobs of color. Each of these little points of color is a pixel.

A pixel is a picture element is a pel,
but it can be any size or color.

These picture elements, called "pels" for short, are component parts. You could actually dedicate a whole computer to each one. You can pick any number of colors to choose from for each one, even a trillion more choices than the eye can distinguish. A one-pixel picture would be a picture of a blob, but you could make it too small to see or as big as a house.

The finer your resolution,
the more commitment you've got to give it.

The screen image is composed of a certain number of pixels in a line going from left to right, and then the count of how many lines you have stacked on top of each other. The more pixels you cram in there, the better your resolution. But the computer has to use its memory to keep track of them all (that's why they call it a "bit map"). Ever commit to more than you could live up to? In a movie with a certain number of frames flashing by every second, a resolution with fine enough detail can overload any computer.

TABLE 5.2 Uncompressed Block

8	× 8	*Resolution:* each block contains only 64 bits.
	× 1	*Color:* you can't get simpler than monochrome.
	× 15	*Frames:* a flickering 15 frames per second.
Total =	960	bits (÷ 8 = 120 bytes) = **120 bytes/second**

As a starting point, let's examine a tiny specimen of raw video data. Later on you'll encounter the word block used to describe a small section of pixels (picture elements) 8 across by 8 down (see "A Pixel Primer" on page 106). These are handy small units for JPEG and MPEG standards to perform their fancy number-crunching on. We'll use a block here, keep it black and white, and assume a frame-per-second (fps) rate of only 15 in order to illustrate the arithmetic of calculating video data size (see Table 5.2). While a monochrome block such as this isn't going to stress out anyone's home computer, it's also practically useless.

• • You can double the frames to get a VHS standard (which is really 29.97 frames/second, but we'll call it 30).

• • You can add more colors to the example and multiply by the number of bits required (it goes by powers of 2, so 8 bits yields 256 colors, and 16 bits give 32,768 colors, which is actually 215 but one bit goes unused).

But the way frame-per-second rates and 16-bit color affect the total data size is nothing compared to the number of bits/pixels used for the screen resolution. An 8 × 8 block is really tiny.

• • If you multiply each side by 10 for an 80 × 80 image, you'll probably get something a little bigger than a postage stamp (as a rule of thumb, since the

TABLE 5.3 Uncompressed "Postage Stamp" Video

80 × 80	*Resolution:* a lot smaller than half a screen.	
× 16	*Color:* 32,768 colors are cheap compared to resolution data.	
× 30	*Frames:* VHS quality.	
Total =	3,072,000 bits (÷ 8 = 384,000 bytes) = **384 KB/second**	

number of pixels doesn't automatically determine the size of the image), but you'll have to multiply your total by 100.

The 120 bytes/second in our example are hardly anything, but multiplying that by 100 to get 12 KB/s is a big jump. Multiply all of these changes together (see Table 5.3) and you get 384 KB/s. That's some data-intensive postage stamp!

You can see why CD–ROM technology is so helpful for video storage. Compression can work miracles—compressing by factors of over 100 (written as over 100:1)—but there is no avoiding the large size of computer video data. Lets look at how many seconds of our uncompressed postage stamp example would fit on conventional storage media (each frame = 0.0333 seconds):

800 KB floppy disk	2.07 seconds
1.44 MB floppy disk	3.74 seconds
40 MB hard drive	104.17 seconds— over 1 minute
200 MB hard drive	520.83 seconds— over 8 minutes
650 MB CD–ROM	1692.70 seconds— over 28 minutes

Please remember that this is just a theoretical example, illustrating some of the basic arithmetic involved in calculating video data size. Using compression, a CD–ROM can contain 74 minutes of high-quality audio and visual data. Using more lossy factors of compression, a CD–ROM can contain hours of video. Our calculations do show, however, that the high storage capacity of CD–ROM is such a large improvement over other storage media that it makes computer video a practical possibility.

The actual standards, such as JPEG and MPEG, that will deliver computer graphics and video to your home are to be treated more fully in Chapter 6. For now, suffice it to say that such standards are always occupying a difficult middle ground, attempting to be as faithful as possible to the visual image without overwhelming the very limited power of the home computer.

A popular example is 5 MB/s to digitally emulate VHS (see Table 5.4), followed by a moaning and gnashing of teeth over the fact that few home computers are powerful enough to accommodate this data rate. This isn't stopping video CD from being on the Christmas lists of the very near future (it achieves a quality I find personally better than VHS although not quite as sharp as laserdisc). Then there are the naysayers who carp that beating VHS is a pathetic goal; this may have some justice for technophiles, but from a commercial viewpoint it is an effete perspective.

TABLE 5.4 Uncompressed VHS Equivalent

342 × 240	*Resolution:* each screen contains 82,080 bits.
× 16	*Color:* each screen bit can have 32,768 colors.
× 30	*Frames:* 30 frames per second is the VHS standard.
Total =	39,398,400 bits (÷ 8 = 4,924,800 bytes) ≈ **5 MB/s**

At the present moment, the main limiting factor is the speed at which the computer's bus can transfer data from the storage medium to the computer's central processing unit (CPU). If you've discovered, as millions of consumers have, that you need to buy more RAM for your computer to run the hot new CD–ROM titles, it is because the data must come across the bus in highly compressed form (usually no more than 154 KB/s) and then decompress rapidly in the CPU. More RAM gives the data the room it needs to spread out to its uncompressed size for display on the screen. So we can assume that the need for faster buses and more RAM is going to have to be met. Apple's NuBus broke new ground, and Intel is coming down the highway with a much more powerful bus, but this still doesn't get around the limiting factor of single-speed CD–ROM drives having a set data rate of 150 KB/s.

On-line users cope with an additional set of bottlenecks: Everyone wants the faster data rate of ISDN phone lines, but even so, is your modem good enough? New cable delivering even broader bandwidth, or satellite broadcast in the future to set-top boxes, will all hit ceilings of what data rate they can reliably deliver.

As Far as the Eye Can See

The point of video compression is that bottlenecks and technological limiting factors are not going to go away until the capacity of human visual perception has been artificially matched.

Color

Visual color capacity is often stated as being equal to 24 bits per pixel (sometimes called *true color,* also referred to as *millions of colors*). Our VHS example used 16 bits, or thousands of colors, and this is often used for digital entertainment; 8-bit color, or hundreds of colors, is typical of the installed base of Super-VGA home computers at present. Clearly there is a big difference between 256 colors and millions of colors! Even the statement that human vision is equivalent to 24-bit color is contested, for example, by proponents of the newer 32-bit color game systems who allege that there is a subjectively noticeable improvement (theoretically there shouldn't be). These numbers are complicated by the existence of very effective logarithmic means of color storage (as opposed to linear means) in the 8- to 10-bit range, with 10-bit log color being considered the equivalent of 24-bit linear color.

Resolution

Visual resolution capacity has been estimated with numbers as high as 2000 pixels per linear inch of field of vision. Such theoretical results far exceed the largest frames being digitized today; namely, Kodak's Cineon process, which captures IMAX at a resolution of 4096 pixels by 6144 rows (using 10-bit log color, the storage per frame for this is about 101 MB). The following is a summary of just a few of the resolutions that are presently in use:

from 160×120 to 320×240	Standard range of Intel's reduced-resolution Indeo process
640×480 and 800×600	Common resolutions for home multimedia computers
768×512	Kodak's Photo CD base resolution, considered equivalent to a 35-mm photograph
1024×768 and 1280×1024	Common high-resolution standards

The International Consultative Committee on Radio (CCIR) has defined several standards that are relevant here: The ambitious 601 standard for high-definition broadcast at 720×480 and the standard image formats (SIF) for U.S. television (NTSC), 352×240, and international television (PAL and SECAM), 352×288 (288 maintains a constant data rate with 25 fps versus NTSC's 30 fps).

Frames per Second

Psychometric research indicates that the brain observes far more slices per second than the mind is subjectively aware of. Technophiles have begun to proclaim 100 fps as a goal, but that number has more to do with our decimal consciousness than any scientific motivation. The fact is that 24 fps for cinema, 25 fps for PAL and SECAM, and 30 fps for NTSC have proven subjectively adequate, although they undoubtedly could be improved on. The standard for complaint is 15 fps, which saw extensive use on home computers in the earlier, more primitive days of video compression. It is generally agreed that 15 fps is subjectively inadequate.

Now and Forever

Consumer demand will drive the hardware markets to match human visual capacity. Already the virtual reality industry has sprouted a branch that delivers high resolution as an alternative to three-dimensional video. Who wants to be stuck in neighborhoods like 72 dots per inch (dpi) when so much more is already available? But the journey will have to occur in stages, as is indicated by the CCIR standards. Video and still-image compression will be with us all along this path of technological development.

While massively parallel computers could be made to serve up Cineon IMAX frames at 24 fps with a throughput of over 2.5 gigabytes per second (GB/s), that is a goal only in the minds of hardcore graphics junkies. What will happen is that better compression and better processors will arrive hand in hand as we increase the mass dissemination of photo-realistic technologies. The day the processors get to where compression is hardly needed for video should be just about when motion-hologram reaches a realization stage—in other words, there's no getting rid of compression. But to come back to earth in the 1990s, what we have now is compression technology in which DCT-based encoding is well established and wavelet and fractal compression offer more promise but less consistently reliable performance. So read on.

What Kinds of Number-Crunching Are Used to Compress the Data?

Digital data is constituted by a series of 1s and 0s referred to as a *stream*. Each 1 or 0 represents a bit in either an on or off state, and so this can be referred to as either a *bit stream* or a *data stream*. By definition, a data stream is inherently meaningful and therefore almost certain to be nonrandom. This means it can be compressed by applying formulas to it.

A random data stream cannot be effectively compressed. Because it completely lacks repetitive patterns, describing a random stream by means of formulas would be equally random and wouldn't shrink it down into a smaller stream of bits. Luckily, real-world applications are rarely called upon to deal with such mathematical abstractions. A random bit stream would have no properties of internal coherence and would display as video or audio noise.

Various formulas can be applied to reduce meaningful data, and this is one of the great ongoing challenges of contemporary mathematics, such as Chaos Theory. Different techniques are being explored in both theoretical academics and practical engineering. For our purposes, the essential fact is that the underlying pattern of any meaningful data stream can be described in a more economical format than merely repeating the series of bits that constitutes it.

The very concept of a formula presupposes this essential fact: A line can be described by defining two end points and stating that they are connected by a line. There is no need to define every intermediate point. All scientific formulas reduce observable data into underlying patterns that repeat themselves.

Abbreviation is the simplest formula of all. If patterns repeat themselves, name them something shorter, make a list of what their names are, and then just call each pattern by its shortened name or abbreviation. This isn't theoretically exciting, but for engineering it can be extremely useful. The list of names and patterns constitutes a strictly defined look-up table allowing translation of a data stream back and forth, from its longer version to its shorter version or back again. On its simplest level, you can use 0×17 to describe a string of 17 zeros. Run length encoding (RLE) actually implements this basic process of abbreviation in both the JPEG and MPEG standards of compression.

The term *algorithm* is a more sophisticated way to describe applying a formula or formulas to data. In its most general sense, an algorithm can refer to any mathematical operation or series of operations that manipulate data. More specifically, *algorithm* has come to be used in computer science to designate separate units of processing that a program can perform. Although an algorithm might theoretically continue processing forever, such as calculating π to n decimal places, programmers create algorithms that perform useful, finite work. So when we ask: "What kinds of number-crunching are used to compress the data?" this can be rephrased as the question: "What sort of compression algorithms are used?"

Transformations

One of the most powerful mathematical tools to have affected twentieth-century communications is known as the Fourier transform. It has given rise to many different, related algorithms or transformations. One of these, the Discrete Cosine Transformation (DCT) is the first and primary algorithm to be applied by JPEG and MPEG to a frame of raw video data. A detailed mathematical description of the DCT is beyond the scope of this work, but a brief review of frequencies and the Fourier transform will illustrate some of the underlying concepts.

The sine wave is one of the simplest forms of electronic data, moving smoothly up and down in its S-shaped course (see Figure 5.1). The simplicity of sine waves means that they can be described very easily by mathematical formulas. A wavelength is one complete trip from zero up to the wave's peak, down to its trough, and then up again back to zero. This can also be called a cycle. The height of the wave, whether positive or negative, is called its amplitude. A sound wave is a good example, pulsing through the air as a simple pattern of particles set in motion. A sound wave's loudness is an expression of the amplitude or height of the wave.

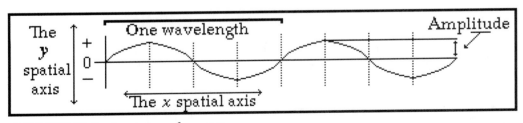

FIGURE 5.1 Anatomy of a wave.

Frequency is normally measured in cycles per second, called hertz and abbreviated Hz. If you've wondered what a MHz stands for (the M is for mega-, or 1 million), or Hz when it's used to describe the range of audible sound, it's just a measure of the speed at which these waves travel, whether they are sound waves moving through air, electronic sine waves passing through a wire, and so on. The amplitude remains unaffected by the frequency. Doubling the frequency means cutting the size of the wavelength in half so that there can be twice as many cycles per second. If the initial data is as simple as a musical tone, our ears actually perceive such a doubling as producing the octave above it.

When two frequencies are added together, they form a more complex pattern (see Figure 5.2). The amplitudes or heights of the waves are added together, obscuring the appearance each had separately as individual wavelengths. This process of adding together frequencies can be used to analyze any continuous signal or data into a list of separate frequencies that compose it. The Fourier transform provides the complex math that allows com-

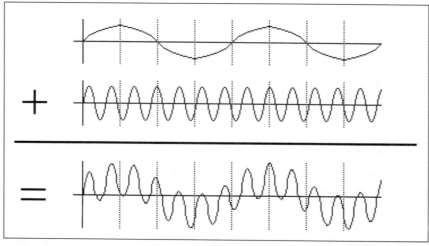

FIGURE 5.2 Adding sine waves.

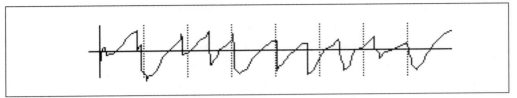

FIGURE 5.3 Continuous but choppy signal pattern.

plex patterns to be broken down into the individual separate frequencies that compose them.

The Fourier transform translates spatial data, such as coordinates on the x and y axes, into frequency data. In the case of a single sine wave, this is extremely easy. Thinking of it in terms of the digital data necessary to store a pattern, the frequency information is much more compact. Some very impressive jargon can be used to describe the data being brought over from the spatial domain into the frequency domain. The jargon is useful because the data must be manipulated according to different laws or principles depending which domain it is in.

Data or signals are often very complex (see the example in Figure 5.3). From a data storage standpoint, frequency data may or may not achieve compression relative to spatial data, depending on just how complex the spatial data is to begin with. Just as the randomness in data makes it more difficult to compress, this lack of pattern will also require more frequency data to fit the curve of an irregular complex wave.

The wave described by a set of x and y coordinates is treated as if it were a continuous wave, with no breaks in it, no jumps with empty space between them. This leads us into the discussion of quantization, which will be pursued later. For now the point is just that digital spatial data can be treated as continuous. This is the same principle as defining a line by its two end points.

The mathematical truth that a line has an infinite number of points on it does not stop engineers in their tracks. The quantities or discrete quanta by which something is measured or recorded will always produce a certain stop-and-go discontinuity in the real world. Mathematical transformations are made possible by the assumption that such data describes continuously connected spatial patterns.

Axes of Measurement

An irregular but meaningful pattern can be measured in greater or lesser detail. Screen resolution for video display provides an example of this. A 640×400 resolution does more than just provide four times the definition of a 320×200 image. Dependent on the image presented (e.g., a detailed landscape versus a simple geometric design), greater resolutions can allow meaningful properties of the data to be presented that will remain invisible at a lesser resolution. The Discrete Cosine Transformation evaluates these properties of visual data so that important detail, especially edges and boundaries, stands out numerically.

A two-dimensional image can be spatially analyzed along its horizontal and vertical axes. Analyzing the image's frequencies then results in determining mathematical values for horizontal frequencies and vertical frequencies. Figure 5.4 provides a crude but clear example of an image that has a higher vertical frequency than horizontal; in lay terms, the more lines you cross, the higher the frequency.

Full motion, in which multiple frames form a series of images in time, for example, 30 frames per second, can be added to this mathematical description by analyzing time as an axis, which is to say temporal frequency.

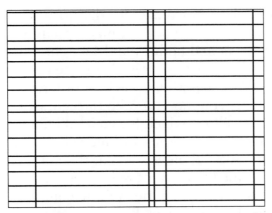

FIGURE 5.4 Spatial frequency example (vertical greater than horizontal).

Part of the nature of moving pictures is that much of the image stays the same from one frame to the next, causing the data that does change to appear to be in motion. This makes temporal frequencies very meaningful and therefore susceptible to compression. This is getting ahead of the discussion, however, except to establish what the axes of measurement are: horizontal, vertical, and temporal.

For a monochrome image, that's all you need. For audio digital data, the temporal axis is all that is significant. Color, however, makes life at least three times more complicated. There are various schemes for representing color digitally, but the most common of them break up the color data into three separate streams (less common is the use of true black as a fourth color). For example, 16-bit color might assign 5 bits each to red, green, and blue, leaving the 16th bit vacant. JPEG and MPEG use YC_rC_b, generally assigning 8 bits to Y and 4 bits each to C_r and C_b.

The YC_rC_b color standard is an interesting story in itself, involving perceptual quantization and backward compatibility issues. The short version of the story is just that $Y =$ luminance (also somewhat inaccurately referred to as brightness), and both C_r and $C_b =$ chrominance (as in color or hue), with C_r describing the red difference $(R - Y)$ and C_b describing the blue difference $(B - Y)$ from a norm. A common mistake is to guess that Y must stand for yellow, which for emitted light particles would mean a combination of blue and green. What the short story doesn't tell you is that the norm Y is composed of a specified balance of red, green, and blue color values. Clearly this is a much more complex way to encode color than simple RGB.

YC_rC_b was originally created as part of the NTSC standard for U.S. color television broadcasting, which was required to be backward compatible with black-and-white TV sets. The black-and-white sets could receive a complete image composed solely of the luminance (Y) information, ignoring chrominance. The color televisions could receive the full broadcast bandwidth, half of which was composed of luminance information (because the human eye is more sensitive to brightness than color). Of the other half, the red difference was given a bigger slice of the bandwidth than the blue difference so that the delicate range of flesh tones could be more accurately depicted. This is not the case with the JPEG and MPEG use of YC_rC_b.

Since color makes things three times more complicated, we will ignore it for the most part. The three streams are processed in the same way (although luminance still gets half the color bits). So henceforth we will refer to an image being analyzed spatially or temporally without regard to the fact that the same algorithms are performed in triplicate as part of the color processing. It's noteworthy, however, to see this balancing act of chrominance being sacrificed for luminance at such an essential level of measurement.

At the essential units of measurement for color, what we think of as "color" itself is subjected to a kind of lossy compression relative to brightness, as the chrominance data is quantized with reduced precision because of the nature of human perception. A comparison also suggests itself to the issue in audio digitization of at what rate (measured in kilohertz [kHz], or thousands of cycles per second) the audio data is to be sampled (e.g., 44.1 kHz or smaller). As we said at the beginning of this section, an irregular but meaningful pattern can be measured in greater or lesser detail. The decision of how much detail to use is bound to take perceptual issues into account.

The Discrete Cosine Transformation

The Discrete Cosine Transformation (DCT) was chosen by the JPEG and MPEG committees because it did so well in comparative tests. Different transformations, abbreviations, and quantizations of data were given trials and were also combined together in different sequences. So any theoretical explanation of why the DCT is the first thing used in JPEG and MPEG is abstract speculation. It's first because it was the contest winner. The DCT does, however, have qualities that relate to why it came in first place.

One way to describe a series of numbers is to state the first number and then state the difference ("now add 6 to that, then subtract 8") between that first number and the following numbers. This works very well for visual images (or even audio samples) because a turtle's shell or a can of cola will contain many color values that are very similar to each other. Of course, the big issue is what happens when you fall off the turtle and have to describe a background composed of a very different color. In a difference scheme of description, this sudden change of color will receive a conspicuously higher number, emphasizing where edges and boundaries occur.

Like other transformations, the DCT can be a powerful method of compression in its own right. Like other transformations, if data is extremely complicated or random then the DCT may not reduce its size at all. But unlike most other transformations, the DCT is a difference scheme that prepares the data for further compression by calling numerical attention to where changes occur.

Because the math of performing DCTs is challenging, the visual image must be broken up into smaller blocks. Otherwise, too much computational power would be consumed. A block size of 8×8—8 pixels across by 8 pixels down—was found to be ideal when the standard was originated (see Figure 5.5). Steady improvements in the computational power of home computers, however, now permit 16×16 blocks to be used by some machines. Even larger blocks may prove themselves faster and more efficient as increasingly powerful processors come into general use.

After analyzing the horizontal and vertical spatial frequencies of the 8×8 block, the DCT creates an 8×8 matrix of numbers or coefficients. The video data will continue to be represented by an 8×8 matrix during the quantization stage that follows the DCT, after which it will be encoded into a linear bit stream. Because the linear order is significant, we present it here, but the information won't be translated into linear form until after quantization.

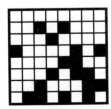

FIGURE 5.5 Monochrome 8×8 block example.

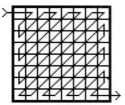

FIGURE 5.6 Zigzag order for block coefficients.

The numbers in the matrix are read in a diagonal zigzag pattern, starting in the upper left-hand corner and concluding in the lower right-hand corner (see Figure 5.6). The first, upper left-hand square is assigned a number that serves as an average for the whole matrix. Note that this is different from its being the numerical average of all 64 numbers. Rather, the information it represents, pertaining to lower frequencies that characterize the block, is an average of all the information in the block.

For a very powerful and lossy compression, the upper left-hand corner can be taken by itself and the other 63 pieces of the puzzle completely omitted. JPEG and other standards give this as an option, but of course an image composed of 8×8 blocks that are uniform for all 64 pixels will display as a very choppy image. Any edges that aren't straight up or straight across will present a very jagged appearance.

The zigzag along the block proceeds from the lower frequencies up to the higher, so the lower right-hand corner contains the finest resolution of detail. Because such detail often contains a heavy amount of random noise information, omitting the lower right-hand block can be to advantage in certain cases.

Along the zigzag path, the numbers often present small gradations of difference, such as: $[0, -1, +2, -1]$. Part of the logic of the quantization step will be to reduce such small gradations to a series of zeros. Keep in mind that these zeros are not neutral information, they are repetitions of the numerical value arrived at by the preceding positive or negative difference. For example, if you start with a value of 128 and then follow it with a series of differences such as [MI60, 0, 0, 0, 0, 0], then the five zeros actually have a value of 68. The difference of −60 jumps the 128 down to 68, and then the zeros express the fact that five additional pieces of the 8 × 8 block will continue to contain that value of 68 with no change.

The shape of the zigzag pattern itself maximizes the chances of encountering strings of zeros, or else data that can be readily changed to strings of zeros. As the path travels away from the upper left-hand corner's lower frequencies, it increasingly encounters finer detail in the higher frequencies, which can be quantized to zeros. Encoding the data a row or a column at a time would not take advantage of this inherent symmetry within the block.

By increasing the series of zeros, the second stage of quantization will prepare the data for efficient abbreviation within the third stage's run length encoding (e.g., 0×17 = zero repeated 17 times). So we might say that the particular value of using the Discrete Cosine Transformation in the first stage of compression is because it calls attention to where data can be efficiently lost or omitted. Emphasizing changes and differences produced by edges and boundaries, the DCT equally calls attention to broad areas containing very little change. Perhaps the essence of lossy compression is that most very small changes can be replaced with data showing absolutely no change. Because no change can be represented by a series of zeros, and these can be crunched effectively using run length encoding, the particular value of the DCT can be considered to be the accurate way it tells us where we can replace our meaningful data with zeros.

Perceptual Quantization

Quantizing reduces the precision of data by rounding it off. This process of approximation deliberately sacrifices finer details in data in order to achieve a simpler view of the big picture.

A basic method is to divide a set of numbers by a divisor and then store the results without the remainders; for example, [56, 74, 31, 12] could be divided by 8 and stored as the smaller numbers [7, 9, 3, 1].

A related method is place shifting and entails dropping the lowest digit(s) of a number. For example, [14, 17, 16, 11] could be represented by [1, 1, 1, 1]. To repeat this example in binary notation: [1110, 10001, 10000, 1011] could be represented by [1, 10, 10, 1] (in decimal, that would be 8, 16, 16, 8).

The loss caused by quantization is offset by whatever advantages accrue from the resulting simplification of the data. In general, the only reason for rounding is so that tasks involving calculations can be made easier. For any set amount of computing power, easier calculations enable more such tasks to be computed per second. Given the imbalance between the large size of visual digital images (as discussed earlier) and consumer computer power, it is inevitable that much of that data will be sacrificed by means of lossy schemes of quantization.

Efficient quantization is achieved by providing just enough detail in the data so that human perception is satisfied with it. This runs up against several obstacles:

- • *Limited precision of perceptual modeling*: Human perception is only understood up to a point.

- • *The data-dependency issue*: The mathematical breakdown of data based on perceptual criteria is highly data dependent.

• • *"Just Add Human"*: Aesthetic human judgment is inherently required at one or more stages of the quantization process.

Before elaborating on these, we can treat some simple examples of perception-based reduction of data precision.

The rule could be stated as, "Don't waste computational power on information that humans can't perceive. Although three-dimensional modeling has only distant bearing on this discussion, it provides a good illustration because the eye cannot see all the polygons contained in a three-dimensional model. In the early days of virtual reality efforts, researchers struggled to get three-dimensional data-intensive models up and running on what, by present standards, was relatively primitive hardware. One important solution (still in use) was to give only visible portions of the model detailed rendering. Although the whole model would remain stored in abstract mathematical form, only those portions of it that were visible would be allocated the memory necessary to provide a satisfactory visual image.

The easiest example of imperceptible data to relate to is audio masking. We all relate to the presence of background audio noise in the course of our daily lives. Our brains can filter our auditory perception in order to focus on the coherency of one of two (or more) competing audio signals. But if there is a jet plane taking off right overhead, we're out of luck. Conversation is impossible in the front rows of a rock concert, causing attendees to experience breakthroughs in their ability to read lips. There was even a broadway show titled *You Know I Can't Hear You When the Water's Running*. Analysis of digital audio reveals the patterns of these competing audio signals. When a mathematical model of perception determines that one signal effectively masks the other, the digital data for the inaudible signal can be deleted.

Perceptual quantization is not as simple as "Delete audiovisual data that people cannot see or hear." More accurately, it is only that simple in extreme cases such as seeing around corners or hearing a pin drop while a train goes by. High compression rates will often require sufficient quantization to produce noticeable image degradation, and this is where the dancing bear of our chapter title comes in. Truly efficient perceptual quantization must erase detail without going too far, but its algorithms are limited by both their own structure and the structure of the data, so the obstacles we have listed are an inherent part of this process.

Limited Precision of Perceptual Modeling

Human perception is only understood up to a point. Some major points are clear and can be easily stated, but their application remains tricky when it comes to finer points. For example, the human eye is more sensitive to gradations in luminance than chrominance (see Figure 5.7), so color gradations may be eliminated to a greater extent than differences in brightness. But uniform fields of color can result in annoying banding, as strips or bands of one color take on clear boundaries that are at odds with the content of the image.

If a sunset looks like stacked bands of colors with perceivable boundaries, this conflicts with our intuitive sense that a sunset should show a steady progression. So for any given image of a sunset, at which mathematical points should the algorithms conclude that more data should remain? Those points would be different for different types of sunsets, and there would be an interaction with the luminance data that is hard to satisfactorily analyze.

Another example is that human perception is less sensitive to changes at higher frequencies of audio and video than it is to changes at lower frequencies. Objective

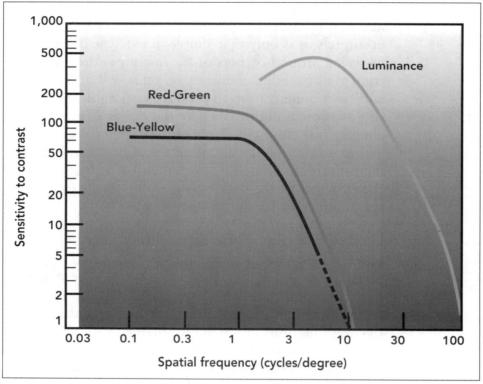

FIGURE 5.7 Human eye more sensitive to luminance than chrominance.

measurement of audio and video frequencies is quantitatively different from the way human perception analyzes these phenomena. For example, with light intensities, if you double a given value and then double it again, these two jumps will be perceived as increasing by an equal amount. Objectively the second jump is twice as big as the first, but perceptually, because the ratio of each jump is identical, they will be perceived as changing by the same amount. Imagine then some minimal increment in the lowest perceptible frequencies. Since it is the ratio of that increment that is significant, pursuing the same ratio to make incremental steps up to the highest perceptible frequencies will result in quantitatively bigger and bigger steps. Auditory and visual sensitivities do not all follow this simple ratio, but sensitivity still declines as frequencies increase.

So higher frequencies can be quantified so as to eliminate more detail than lower frequencies, but where does this leave great reds and purples? Although this problem first asserted itself with feature films transferred to VHS for home video, the problem is even more acute for compressed video on CDs. Filmmakers become very attached to the colors they choose, and it is a little-known fact that some filmmakers have been avoiding purple or careful gradations of red because the transfer is unsatisfactory to them. Of course, if they knew exactly what color gradations would be unaffected by compression (or transfer) processes, the filmmakers could restrict their palettes accordingly.

Perceptual models especially run into trouble when different ones piggyback on top of each other, which is referred to as *stacked coding* or *multiple-coder chaining*. This strikes many as a distant fear, but with the types of digital transmission multiplying (e.g., from studio to transmitter, from satellite to dish, across telephone lines or cable lines, etc.), different coding technologies are being introduced specifically adapted to the requirements of different signal links. Recording or retransmitting, if it involves an additional pass through compression-decompression, can cause different perceptual models to clash so as to produce very conspicuous artifacts.

Even a single perceptual model might seriously degrade information that is passed through it a second time, and whether or not it does so is data dependent in ways that are frequently unpredictable. This is why it is almost always a bad idea to extensively reedit lossy MPEG material. Although frames can be decompressed, cropped or otherwise altered, and then recompressed, this is one of many fast tracks to Artifact City.

The fact that degradation and artifacts are both data dependent and unpredictable is the basis of our stated obstacle that human perception is only understood up to a point. If human perception were more fully understood, then the mathematical models for perceptual quantization would be more successful at minimizing degradation and artifacts. If the specifically data-dependent aspects of this were more fully understood, then the results would be more predictable and adaptive algorithms could adjust accordingly, submitting different categories of data to more appropriate schemes of quantization.

It is our contention that the dancing bear of high compression has come to life as yet another artifact caused by the inadequacy of current schemes of perceptual modeling. Of course these schemes would not be inadequate if our collective quest for efficiency weren't driving us to use as much compression as we can possible get away with.

The Data-Dependency Issue

The mathematical breakdown of data based on perceptual criteria is highly data dependent. Perceptual criteria, expressed as formulas or algorithms within a model, will treat different kinds of observed data with varying degrees of success. The conspicuous degradation that constitutes an artifact can be considered as a kind of collision between data and algorithm—instead of passing smoothly through the algorithm, the data goes *splat!* and winds up looking or sounding like a mistake.

Although the way we've worded this obstacle amounts to a tautology, it points out the need to apply different kinds of algorithms to different kinds of data. This is already done by perceptual models, but it needs to be done better.

It is easy to blame limited computational power for the clumsy results of today's adaptive quantization algorithms, but it is not fair to use our processors as scape-goats. Computer graphics professionals with fine arts training are all familiar with the underlying realities that different kinds of images present to human perception. In a nutshell, the way we perceive the *Mona Lisa* is different from the way we perceive an African mask.

The future of perceptual quantization must lead us toward the intelligent application of different algorithms to different kinds of images. The judgment of which algorithms are suitable will require improved mathematical analysis of the kind of image as a precursor to applying one out of a larger selection of quantization formulas to it.

The most obvious example of this problem is jaggies: the conspicuously staircaselike appearance bit-mapped graphics gives to curving lines. Bit mapping represents vertical and horizontal lines without artifacts, but some jaggedness is inevitable for the representation of curves. Of course the practical solution is to switch over to vector tracing as an alternative to bit mapping, but regardless of what solutions are applied to the data, this is a problem of the "something must be done" variety. The future of interactive multimedia will be driven by the search for solutions to such data-dependent, subjectively unacceptable present-day problems.

"Just Add Human"

Aesthetic human judgment is inherently required at one or more stages of the quantization process. It is in the nature of interactivity that subjective assessments of quality will be made by users for every element of an application. To the degree that criteria of quality can be mathematically applied to data, processors can run multiple experimental trials of different techniques and then apply those criteria to the selection of a preferred technique. But aesthetic human judgment is not going to be moved over to the Department of Mathematics anytime soon.

When it comes to the visual degradation of an image, you cannot rely on automatic processes. Like proof-reading a text document, human inspection is an inherent part of ensuring that the data is in a useable form. Since the data dependency of quantization can lead to surprising results, there is an artistic element in the assessment of how well specific lossy quantization techniques have worked on specific sets of data. Some harsh results of the application of perceptual models may be considered to improve an image's essential usefulness in context, whereas some mild degradations of line or color may feel utterly unacceptable.

Compression is a necessity, but that other great parent of invention, trial and error, has a major role to play. Television programming already reflects many artistic and directorial uses of lossy quantization, in dramas, advertising, and music videos. Perceptual modeling and quantization is not yet considered a field of art, but as more models develop with different aesthetic properties, it probably will become one.

Data Abbreviation

Although data abbreviation is theoretically simpler than dealing with the frequency-domain or perceptual models, this type of compression is sometimes called by the most intriguing name of them all: *entropy encoding*. The idea behind this is that once you've assigned the shortest possible names to the repetitive patterns in the data, the potential for shrinking it further has been completely dissipated. Since strict look-up tables (LUTs) or some other form of extra data bits must be created to translate or unabbreviate the data stream, there comes a point where trying to shrink it with additional passes through the data would not be advantageous.

Run length encoding is easy to implement when identical data values occupy large parts of a stream. We gave an example earlier of using 0×17 to describe a run of zeros that is 17 zeros in length. If the data does not contain long runs of identical values, then this technique is not particularly rewarding.

Abbreviation schemes can use fixed-length or variable-length codes depending on whether the format of the abbreviations assigns all codes an equal length as opposed to some of the codes being longer than others.

In 1952, D. A. Huffman created "A Method for the Construction of Minimum Redundancy Codes" (Proc. IRE, 40 (10), 1098–1101, 1952). His concept can be summarized by stating that a Huffman code assigns shorter abbreviations to more redundant patterns and longer abbreviations to less redundant patterns. This can have two disadvantages: Very random data can produce some very long abbreviations, and the data stream must be statistically analyzed after a first pass before the encoding can actually take place (on a second pass).

If a Huffman look-up table is custom-created for an individual data stream, then it is the most minimal form in which that data can be represented. Its actual performance tends to be in the order of $1.5 : 1$ to $2 : 1$, but this is very data dependent. It is a common practice to use predefined Huffman look-up tables that are generically useful, and these can be custom-created to apply to several different but specific data streams. The goal of generic LUTs is to reduce the amount of storage required to record both the data stream(s) and the associated LUT.

The Huffman algorithm works by creating a binary tree with a 0 and 1 at the bottom, and then an additional 0 and 1 branching off of each of the previous nodes, and so on. The statistical probabilities of pattern redundancy in the data stream determine how this set of branches is formed. An unlikely pattern will find itself nested at the end of a long path that is a branch of a node, that is a branch of a node, and so forth. The unlikely pattern's code word will actually be the pattern of zeros and ones that provides a map or path, starting at the bottom of the tree, to the pattern's unique address at the end of many branches (e.g., 00000001). A statistically likely pattern, on the other hand, will have an address involving very few branches (e.g., 1 or 11).

Arithmetic encoding refers to several patented methods that improve slightly on Huffman when generic Huffman LUTs are being used. It divides up a number line based on probabilities. Divisions of the line, as defined by their upper and lower bound, are used to create the codeword for each redundant pattern. It is possible to accomplish this with only one pass through the data stream, which can make it faster than Huffman encoding as well.

Encoding and Decoding in the 1990s

The preceding review of compression basics emphasizes those techniques that are best established to be effective at the present time. Using DCT, quantization, and abbreviation in sequence is currently the preferred method for encoding JPEG, individual frames of MPEG for which all information (as opposed to partial) is contained in the frame, and also the H.261 video-telephone-conferencing standard. Decoding is then accomplished by reversing the sequence: expanding the abbreviated data, multiplying the quantized data to restore the correct frequency values, and bringing the DCT frequency data back over into the spatial domain.

It is important to note that when quantization is reversed by playing it backward, this only accomplishes the restoration of useable frequency values. Information that was killed off during the lossy-quantization encoding process can never be restored from the compressed data. Since the quantization was encoded using a divisor, which stripped off the data contained in the remainder portion of the quotient, reversing the process will be equivalent to having rounded off the original data. In other words, if you once quantize the *Mona Lisa*'s smile into a straight line, you can never get the smile back again by reversing the quantization.

There are other mathematical techniques of compression, notably the use of the Discrete Wavelet Transform (DWT) or fractal equations. Although these are likely to eventually surpass DCT-based encoding in the amount of compression that they can accomplish, their implementation has not yet achieved the success and reliability of DCT-based encoding. It is possible, however, to compose graphic data with DWT or fractal compression in mind so that the use of these techniques will be extremely successful and mathematically more powerful than DCT.

This general reliance on DCT-quantization-abbreviation is what has led to the mistaken impression that MPEG contains frames of JPEG. It would be more accurate to say that MPEG (I-frames; see Chapter 6) uses the same general sequence of compression techniques as JPEG, but the two standards differ in implementation.

Since JPEG and MPEG are defined as decoding standards, there are radically divergent levels of quality with which they can be encoded. In the crudest sense, this explains why an affordable MPEG board, whatever its marvels, will give you a compressed product that is inferior to what service bureaus can generally accomplish for you by encoding the same information by means of more powerful hardware and software.

This brings us to the misimpression that these standards make unique hardware demands. No special hardware is required to either encode or decode JPEG, MPEG, or most other compression standards. A special chip, such as the famous C-Cube MPEG chip, can be mass-produced and installed on a board so that hardware with limited power can efficiently and affordably decode and/or encode. Without the special hardware, any hardware will do, provided that it is a sufficiently powerful data processor to handle the algorithms without hanging up.

The next important concepts are temporal frequency and motion compensation, which are covered in the MPEG section of Chapter 6.

Compression Standards

Having explored general principles in Chapter 5, "Compression Basics," we can now review working standards for compression encoding and decoding—or codecs for short. This is a very dynamic area, both commercially and technologically, so we are attempting an overview that will not be swiftly invalidated by time.

Be aware that news about compression comes from different sources at different speeds:

- • Commercial vendors achieve the highest rate of hype per second, reaching the marketplace first with claims that are not so much exaggerated as wishful.

- • User groups (especially on the Internet) lag behind PR press releases, but reflect the real-world performance of products (and distribute freeware).

- • Expert papers, articles, and books are generally less narrow in coverage than other sources of information, but are still limited by the authors' scope of expertise.

In short, trust everybody and nobody. Some narrowness of perspective is inevitable with any source of information, but compression technology is steadily improving.

Of course, you can only keep an open mind until it's time to make a purchasing decision. At this critical juncture, ask yourself: "*Why* do I need to know?" The nightmare answer to this question is that you are about to start a two-year development cycle for a video-intensive game that has to be cutting-edge when it comes to market. If this applies to you—lots of luck!—give us a call. However, we hope this does not apply to you, and you can break your needs down into the following:

Ease of Use

Don't bite off more than you can chew when selecting a codec. If you need to do it yourself, make sure you can! Don't be embarrassed to settle for a slightly inferior, consumer-targeted package or a more expensive service bureau invoice. Getting the job done and the application finished is the priority.

Target Audience

We're mostly talking numbers here! The larger the size of your target market, the better the quality needs to be. The exception, of course, is computer-graphics professional groups, who will know exactly where you copped out (so quality has to be "to-the-max"). But if your audience is small, you can relax a little because you probably don't need to show off.

Cross-Platform Reliability

This is always the killer, as anyone who has paid for a quality assurance phase can tell you. If it doesn't decompress—you're dead! Make sure you choose a codec such that the system requirements meet your target audience's installed hardware (software too, although you might be able to supply this) with a clean fit.

Playback Quality

Remember that higher resolutions, bit-color schemes, and frames per second can easily consume your audience's processing capability. Don't let your love of beautiful graphics push you off the path of practicality. Keep in mind what sort of monitors your audience is using because that's your quality ceiling.

High Versus Low Compression

Don't show off without a good reason; high compression is high stakes and high risk. Analyze the costs and benefits of using multiple discs, because squeezing pixels may be more expensive than spreading them out.

Depreciation Cycle/"Churn"

Remember that today's state of the art will be cheaper tomorrow. Don't commit yourself to a long-term investment unnecessarily, since the innovations in this area are fast and furious. A two-year depreciation is a good rule of thumb, and four years is huge! It seems that everything is obsolete by the time you buy it, so try to plan on replacing what you purchase in two years.

With the pace of compression innovation accelerating, asking yourself "*Why* do I need to know?" is the only way to get to the truth that you need. Progress means that what is true is changing. You should take a general interest in this area and enjoy the news of new products, standards, and capabilities, as well as the perverse pleasure of seeing promoters' claims get shot down and seeing experts rage over disagreements.

Warning: Remember that a bit is not a byte, and therefore a megabit is not a megabyte! This is not facetious. The general abbreviation for megabit is Mb or Mbits, but there are many times when publications erroneously use MB for megabits or else confuse which is which entirely. If such confusion can slip by the editors of *Wired* or *New Media*, it can probably slip by you, too, so watch out. If you think in bytes and megabytes, just divide bit rates by 8 and you'll do fine.

We divide compression codecs into JPEG, MPEG, and other. This is not to devalue proprietary codecs, but there is a social side to science that has to be taken into account. International standards making is an expensive process, the costs of which are mostly spread out over the governments of the many participating nations as well as by companies who lend their R&D expertise, participating fully in the standards-making process. A 1991 estimate of the cost of ITU's CCITT committee (ITU has others) was between $1 and $2 billion a year (Richard Solomon, "HDTV: Technologies and Directions," SIGGRAPH '91 Panel Proceedings). This information becomes available to the general public and in turn influences dozens or hundreds of proprietary implementations of the standards.

Proprietary codecs are secrets, more or less. Some sketchy outlines become general knowledge, but the only way to gain in-depth understanding of proprietary codecs is to license them, at which point you become bound by nondisclosure agreements. This is good for business (supposedly) and pays back R&D costs, but it restricts both discussion and innovative improvement of these standards.

MPEG is the best case in point: It started on the sidelines, moved to the doghouse, and now has progressed to its present position as center of both abuse and hype. But some form(s) of MPEG will probably become the common codec(s) of choice, because everyone can discuss MPEG and how to improve it in an open forum. Of course, proprietary issues still apply to specific vendors' commercial implementations, but the quantity of information concealed by this is much less than when the entire compression scheme is proprietary in origin.

We discuss H.261 only in passing because its videoconferencing status gives it limited relevance to CD–ROM. JBIG is mentioned only briefly (under JPEG) because it is far from finished and small files with a few bits per pixel are only vital to CD–ROM when recording archives or indexes of graphics libraries. Wavelet (especially HARC-C) and fractal compression are treated briefly in closing as promising technologies.

JPEG

The detail lurking in almost every photograph is psychologically and numerically tremendous. Our eye filters out most of this information as our brain presents a coherent image to our minds. Of course a computer has to keep track of every bit of it. How else can it store a photographic image? If you zoom in on one of these images using a program like Photoshop, it's amazing to see how many little differences there are. What a chaotic panoply of pixels constitutes the image on a detailed level!

JPEG is not the ultimate compression scheme for two-dimensional images or all still pictures. Text and simple graphics of the arrow-and-box variety are used all the time, don't take up much storage memory, and for the most part don't need to be compressed. It's the great graphics in photographs and detailed commercial art that have been hard to get into computer applications because, uncompressed, they tend to eat up at least a megabyte of storage each. Calling them *continuous-tone* or *multilevel* images fails to vividly convey their complexity, but these terms do denote the gradations that the computer has to keep track of, one way or another.

Great graphics *in* applications is a goal that can been met satisfactorily by proprietary standards. But the vision behind JPEG goes much further: toward the "exchange of images across application boundaries" (Gregory J. Wallace, "The JPEG Still Picture Compression Standard," *Communications of the ACM*, April

1991, 34 (4), p. 31). Graphics people have been in a position of "digital envy" as they looked out on a world increasingly wired for the exchange of documents containing text and crude sketches. It is almost impossible for kids today to remember the old days, when having a text document that looked like a printer did it was a big deal. Now text and sketches go everywhere around the world with a quality that varies between a finished look and good-enough, but continuous-tone graphics, such as photographs, don't get around much and when they do it's mighty slow.

The Joint Photographic Experts Group envisioned a standard that was completely flexible as to the details of file structure or the organization of color data and at the same time offered clear specifics governing a wide range of file transfer mechanics. To a certain extent this has made JPEG a "dreamer with one bad leg," because to implement even its simplest version has required that a common file structure be invented for it, while on the other hand the full scope of its 29 alternative compression methods are yet to be integrated within any single commercial (or freeware) package. This hasn't stopped people from using it: Silicon Graphics, for example, uses JPEG as its in-house standard, and there are thousands of JPEG images available on line (Internet, AOL, etc.). So first we will review what this suite of 29 different coding processes consists of and then get down to basics, discussing implementation details of its baseline coding process number 1.

General Categories

Let's get futuristic, just for imagination's sake, and picture people sitting at their terminals in a networked environment over which photographic images are regularly passed back and forth. Many similar environments already exist, but let's imagine one that's based on *high-*

quality images moving *quickly* back and forth. One constant that can't change is the larger a file, the longer it takes to transfer. So let's examine the shortcuts JPEG introduces into this process. One that we've already described is the time-intensive lossless transmission of an image with complete fidelity to its original, as opposed to sending lossy versions of the original—the greater the lossiness, the greater the degree of compression, and the shorter the time of transmission will be. Other shortcuts include progressive transmission and thumbnail-first transmission.

Most images are currently transferred sequentially, that is, starting at the first (top) scan line and then proceeding in ascending numerical order to the last (bottom) scan line. One disadvantage of this, especially in our imagined working environment, is that users frequently want to review a variety of images and reject most of them before arriving at the selection they want. These users also want a general idea of what the entire image looks like, and a sequential top-down approach forces them to wait until the bottom line is transferred before being able to glimpse the entire image.

The idea behind progressive file transfer is to get some essential top-to-bottom data to the user quickly and then build up the full depth of the image by adding more detail in stages. That way users can choose to terminate the transmission having already seen a partial version of it top-to-bottom, but without having to wait for the image's full detail to feed in from the throughput. The GIF image file format has already implemented a simple version of this by allowing scan lines to be transmitted out of order (e.g., odd scan lines first followed by even lines, or any variation), but JPEG's progressive schemes are considerably more complex.

JPEG assumes that users' processing power at their workstations will be adequate to keep recalculating the image as more detailed throughput streams in, so in a sense JPEG assumes that bandwidth will always be a bottleneck (a safe assumption). Although a networked environment strikes us as the most appropriate example for discussion, it should be kept in mind that bandwidth and throughput-rate issues also apply to a single computer interacting with a dense storage medium such as CD–ROM. Another noteworthy environment is tele-operation of robotic vehicles, such as space probes, where the data rate is low and the user may want to send instructions to the device without waiting for fully detailed pictures to stream in.

A thumbnail-first approach, more properly called *hierarchical*, stores multiple versions of the same image and transmits them least-detailed first to most-detailed last. This is similar to the way a Photo CD (usually) contains each photograph scanned in at several different resolutions. The effectiveness of this is based on the mathematics of storage, since the complete file need only swell to 133 percent of the size of its most detailed image. To use an extremely simplified example, look at the 8×8, 4×4, 2×2, and 1×1 grids in Figure 6.1. As you can see by the darkened areas in the 8×8 grid, these successively less detailed images only approach 33.3 percent of its volume.

The multiple versions of the same image stored in a hierarchical file may be transmitted either sequentially or progressively. Hierarchical JPEG envisions some really

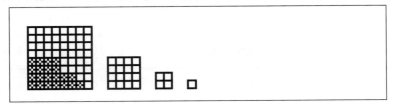

FIGURE 6.1 Hierarchical storage schematic.

big files, too detailed for many monitors to handle. The least detailed image will stream in very quickly and can be glimpsed as a thumbnail graphic, and a decision can be made as to what is the greatest desired resolution. Users without 1024×1024 monitors, for instance, can terminate transmission once they've received a 512×512 version.

Having expanded on lossy, progressive, and hierarchical processes in these general terms, we can now map out six categories of these (see Table 6.1). It might be handy to take a moment to consider each of these in turn, as a full enumeration of JPEG coding processes will involve several examples of each of each generic type.

Variations

The variations within these broad categories involve

- • The size of the color components (e.g., 8-bit or 12-bit)

- • The type of progressive coding used
  a. frequency-based (i.e., spectral selection) only, or
  b. frequency-based *and* rounding-off (i.e., successive approximation)

- • Two different techniques of lossless data-crunching (i.e., Huffman or arithmetic)

TABLE 6.1 Generalized Categories of JPEG

lossy sequential	hierarchical: lossy sequential
lossy progressive	hierarchical: lossy progressive
lossless sequential	hierarchical: lossless sequential

The discussion immediately following reviews several matters treated more fully in the preceding chapter. For a more systematic discussion, please refer to Chapter 5.

Color Components

It is no surprise that the nature of color data engenders a fair bit of confusion. There are a variety of digital approaches to color. Some are necessitated by differing requirements, such as printing versus screen display, but many are just the product of a sort of natural flurry of mutation that has all of us living on various graphics Galapagos Islands. Both for political and practical reasons, the JPEG Committee avoided many hard-nosed decisions. In addition to not specifying a file format, there are other elements that may be necessary to an image which JPEG does not specify: color spaces, pixel aspect ratios, image dimension, and acquisition characteristics. This was actually part of their design goals, to keep the JPEG standard general purpose and not too restrictive.

For our purposes, the important thing is to distinguish 8 bits per pixel *within a color component* from the sort of general discussions one hears of "8-bit, 256 colors." For example, 16-bit color may mean 5 bits of Red, 5 bits of Green, and 5 bits of Blue (RGB) with one bit left over. Speaking in terms of the components, one would say that this is 5-bits-per-pixel RGB component color. A few of the many color schemes in existence are shown in Table 6.2. As you can see, RGB and YC_rC_b both have 3 components respectively, while CMYK is a 4-component color system. The number of bits per component in a JPEG coding process will be the number of bits assigned to each of the components in whatever scheme one elects to use (JPEG can accommodate almost any scheme).

If you think that we are belaboring the obvious, then you are fortunate to already possess a good understanding of

TABLE 6.2 Sample Color Schemes

RGB (SCREEN DISPLAYS)	CMYK (PRINTING)	YC_rC_b (BROADCAST & VHS)
Red	Cyan	Y = luminance
Green	Magenta	C_r = red color difference
Blue	Yellow	C_b = blue color difference
	BlacK	

digital color. Tom Lane, organizer of the Independent JPEG Group bemoans the occasional posted images he sees described as 256-color JPEG. This is very nearly a contradiction in terms. The baseline (#1) coding process that is being used for such images is 8 bits *per component*, so RGB baseline is 24-bit color. Mr. Lane's best guess is that such images started out in GIF (which uses color look-up tables with up to 256 entries) and then were brought into JPEG, but he discourages thinking of JPEG in terms of the number of colors.

So thinking about JPEG in terms of the number of bits per component, with up to four components, we may say

Lossy coding processes are either 8 bits or 12 bits per component.

Lossless coding processes may be anything from 2 bits to 16 bits per component.

The 2-bit to 6-bit range is what can be expected for crude boxes-and-arrows sketches. It is expected that JBIG will becomes the standard of choice for such images (despite the fact that the algorithms for it *are* big and accordingly calculation intensive). JBIG is not quite final enough yet to generate the usual boom of implementations that happen right before a standard is officially finalized. A 12-bit (or more) image is incredibly faithful to the original. It is anticipated that such images will be confined to professional specialties such as medical radiology (X-rays) or satellite-photo analysis.

JPEG does not require that all its color components be of the same size. The prime example is YC_rC_b. It is common practice to organize the Y luminance information into groups of four and then assign one unit of Cr information and one unit of Cb information to the group. Although all three components still use 8-bit precision in JPEG, this spatial allocation of the information achieves a 2:1 compression automatically if RGB images are converted into it (see Figure 6.2).

Progressive Coding

Before proceeding to our discussion of progressive coding processes, a brief recap of several compression basics is called for. An 8×8 block of pixels within a single component [Fig. 6.3(a)] is analyzed by means of the Discrete Cosine Transformation (DCT). What results is a series of spatial frequency data ranging from the lowest frequency (the DC coefficient, which must be first) up through the highest frequencies (as represented

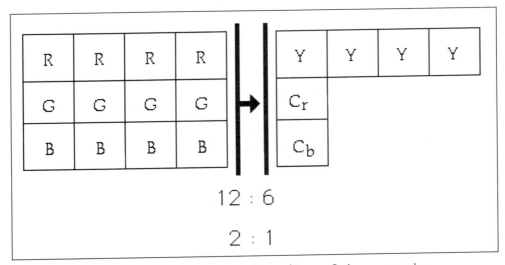

FIGURE 6.2 RGB-to-YC_rC_b conversion achieves 2:1 compression.

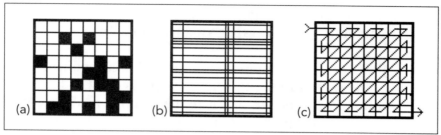

FIGURE 6.3   Reviewing compression basics.

by 63 AC coefficients). An example of spatial frequency is Figure 6.3(b), in which the vertical frequency is greater than the horizontal frequency. So what started as an 8×8 matrix of purely spatial data is transformed into an 8×8 matrix of (spatial) frequency data. The lowest frequency (DC) is in the upper left-hand corner and is the simplest summary of the spatial conditions in the block. The 63 coefficients (ACs) with increasingly higher frequencies will be quantized and then reorganized into a linear stream of data by following the zigzag pattern shown in Figure 6.3(c).

What this all means for JPEG is that you can slice and dice this data in order to determine which stages the image will go through when it is decoding progressively. Figure 6.4(a) shows an 8×8 block of a single color component that has been digitized with 8-bit precision. Figure 6.4(b) stacks the 8-bit coefficients with the lowest-frequency DC on top. Assuming that the normal zigzag pattern is followed, each row of this tower will have progressively higher frequencies the lower you go. One thing this means for compression is that you could just lop off some of the bottom (highest frequency) rows and all you would sacrifice are the finest details, many of which are invisible to the naked eye.

It is intriguing that one of the singular aspects of JPEG is that you do not have to follow the normal zigzag pattern. Until human aesthetics is better understood, what makes for successful compression will retain a certain mysterious element. What works for one image does not necessarily work for another. There is a general sense that although the lowest frequency is structurally vital for a foundation—beyond that who knows? It's all very image dependent. A certain group of the middle frequencies might capture more of the essence of the image than a procrustean approach that only uses the same number of lowest-frequency coefficients and then chops the rest off. That would work, but which would work best? It must depend on some taxonomy of image types that is not understood yet (in fact, compression could be used as the empirical tool by which to observe and discover these).

Frequency-based progressive JPEG is illustrated by Figure 6.4(c). The correct term for this is *spectral selection*. Assuming that one wants all 64 coefficients (and that the normal zigzag order is used), one can decide where one wants the several progressive passes through the image

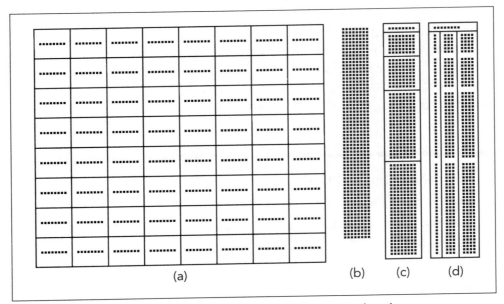

(a) (b) (c) (d)

FIGURE 6.4 Spectral selection and successive approximation.

to occur. Once again, the lowest-frequency DC must be first (and solo; one of the reasons this must occur is because a difference scheme relates all the DCs in an image). Now I must confess that I favor using 1 to represent the first in a series for the sake of this book; programmers often use 0 to represent the first in a series because this has practical advantages, but I don't believe that this serves the purposes of communication here (since programmers regularly foul up their if-loops with counting from 0, even they get confused by it). So in our example of Figure 6.4(c), the progressive stages go like this: 1, 2–7, 8–16, 17–36, 37–64. On your screen you would see the image blocked out and then filled in with four increasingly detailed stages. Although the last of these stages contains the most data and would take the longest to recalculate, it would show the least change in the image because it only added the finest level of detail.

Rounding off progressive JPEG is illustrated by Figure 6.4(d). The correct term for this is *successive approximation*. Once again, the DC is first and solo. After that, you can go chop-chop-chop and decide which of the less significant bits to either hold back on for later progressive stages or else eliminate entirely to achieve higher compression. For any readers unfamiliar with this (and who didn't read our discussion of quantization in the preceding chapter), this kind of bit dropping works as follows:

Take the number 76,493,516.

Break it in half and throw away the bottom piece.

Keep the top piece and, if you need to use it, multiply it by 10,000.

You get 76,490,000, which is pretty darn close.

Four numbers take up half the space of 8.

So you lost some detail (3516 to be exact), but you did achieve compression!

In Figure 6.4(d), we take one pass using only the most significant bit, then a second pass with bits 2 to 4, and a final progressive stage containing bits 5 to 8. One thing that is shown in the illustration and is in fact quite true is that this bit-dropping may contain several stages of spectral selection (the converse is not true—spectral selection may not contain successive approximation). Remember that these coefficients apply to the entire block, so Figure 6.4(d) really shows 13 stages of progressively feeding in the data for an image, as spelled out in Table 6.3.

As with our spectral selection, the delivery by successive approximation of the biggest packet of data—that contained in the 4 least significant bits, or stages 10 to 13 in the list given—will take the longest to recalculate yet

TABLE 6.3 Example of Spectral Selection Within Successive Approximation

1.	DC first and solo	coefficient 1	calculate image, then. . .
2.	First bit only	coefficients 2–7	recalculate image, then . . .
3.	"	coefficients 8–16	"
4.	"	coefficients 17–36	"
5.	"	coefficients 37–64	"
6.	Add bits 2–4	coefficients 2–7	recalculate image, then . . .
7.	"	coefficients 8–16	"
8.	"	coefficients 17–36	"
9.	"	coefficients 37–64	"
10.	Add bits 5–8	coefficients 2–7	recalculate image, then . . .
11.	"	coefficients 8–16	"
12.	"	coefficients 17–36	"
13.	"	coefficients 37–64	at last . . . the final image.

will show the least change in the image because it only adds the most detailed level of detail.

Interleaving

While we are on the subject of slicing and dicing up the data, this seems like a natural point to bring up interleaving. The goal of letting the user see progressive stages of the complete image as quickly as possible can only be effectively achieved if the several color components are interleaved together. JPEG provides a mechanism to do this by (for DCT) combining 8×8 blocks (called data units in this context) into regions with specified horizontal and vertical dimensions. These regions are then pipelined together as a minimum coded unit (MCU) in the throughput. (Predictive JPEG defines a single sample as a data unit, whereas DCT interleaving uses the 8×8 block.)

The restriction that an MCU may only contain a maximum of 10 data units means that only a segment of the range of images that can be handled by JPEG will be capable of being fully interleaved. For RGB (we are assuming DCT), JPEG can interleave 3 blocks from each component into an MCU (a total of 9 blocks). For YC_rC_b, 4 blocks of luminance plus 1 C_r and 1 C_b is the most that makes sense (a total of 6 blocks), since an MCU with twice that would be over the maximum limit. However, JPEG will allow widely disparate component sizes, some of which exceed what can be fitted within the MCU allotment of 10 data units. To pick an extreme but mathematically suggestive example, imagine one component that is sampled at only 10 percent of the resolution of another component. The appropriate ratio of data units in regions for these two components would be $10:1$, so it would be impossible to interleave these together in an MCU because the combined total is 11.

All of JPEG's 29 coding processes allow interleaving as an option. In the event that a component's sampling rate makes it unsuitable for interleaving, it is possible to single out one or more components for noninterleaved treatment. So JPEG images may be interleaved, noninterleaved, or a combination of the two.

Huffman and Arithmetic Encoding

Having reviewed 8-bit and 12-bit sampling rates as well as spectral selection and successive approximation, we now follow our program to review Huffman and arithmetic encoding. In Chapter 5, we refer to these as *data abbreviation algorithms*, whereby a data stream may be losslessly crunched into a smaller stream, but new data is created in the form of a table that lets one decompress and expand the data stream to its original size. It's rather like using a codebook in which frequently occurring words are assigned short identifiers. The scheme works well, but don't lose the codebook.

Although it is possible to employ a general-use Huffman table, this abbreviation scheme works best in a two-pass process: one pass to analyze the frequency of pattern recurrence in the bits and then compose an ideal encoding/decoding table, then a second pass to perform the encoding itself. Arithmetic schemes, on the other hand, work on the fly in a single pass. Statistical measurements of applying both schemes to the same data consistently favor arithmetic techniques (although Huffman is *theoretically* ideal), so as a practical matter arithmetic coding processes are preferred.

The mechanics of arithmetic encoding and table composition are proprietary, patent-protected processes. Of the 10 patents governing it, one is held by Mitsubishi and several are held by IBM and AT&T, respectively. High-end JPEG users may find licensing a worthwhile investment, although low-end users pray that these giants will liberate arithmetic techniques from their royalty-constrained prison. At any rate, as you will see, JPEG gives you a choice in all except its baseline number 1 coding process.

JPEG—The Big Picture

Without further ado, and postponing our discussion of lossless JPEG's mechanics, we now present the 29 coding processes of JPEG (see Figure 6.5). As you can see, it is indeed a suite of processes, all of which are unlikely to be encompassed within a single implementation or application in the near future. While the figure does little to distinguish number 1 from number 2, there is in fact a world of difference. Extended sequential DCT JPEG number 2 permits more tables to be carried for reverse quantization and expansion of the Huffman encoding, and many other complexities besides. Baseline 1, on the other hand, is like number 2 with default settings for all the little features. Baseline was designed to be easy to use by the computer-literate community, and it is finding incredible acceptance.

A brief review of the history behind this broad-ranging standard is appropriate. The need for a compression standard for color images was realized as far back as 1982. A working group of photographic experts was assembled under the ISO and other groups to begin laying the groundwork for such a standard, before time constraints due to market pressures caused a hurried or hasty adoption of an inferior standard.

By 1986, CCITT began working with previously standing committees to develop the standard we now know as JPEG. Several operating parameters were considered vital, and more criteria joined the parade along the way. Here's a brief synopsis of the goals of these pioneering meetings:

- • The standard would have to operate at 64 Kbits/s (not at all a random value—it's the speed of ISDN transmission).

- • The technique would have to be as lossless as possible, yet with excellent progressive compression.

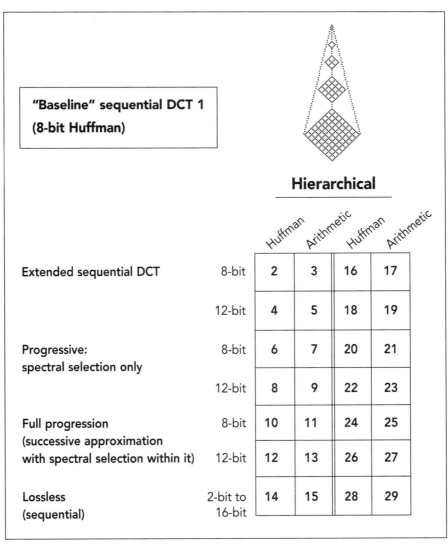

"Baseline" sequential DCT 1 (8-bit Huffman)

Hierarchical

		Huffman	Arithmetic	Huffman	Arithmetic
Extended sequential DCT	8-bit	2	3	16	17
	12-bit	4	5	18	19
Progressive: spectral selection only	8-bit	6	7	20	21
	12-bit	8	9	22	23
Full progression (successive approximation with spectral selection within it)	8-bit	10	11	24	25
	12-bit	12	13	26	27
Lossless (sequential)	2-bit to 16-bit	14	15	28	29

FIGURE 6.5 The 29 Coding Processes of JPEG.

- • Since teleconferencing was a possible use of the standard, lag time for the process had to be small. This is called *synchronous transmission* and is one of the items added to the wish list in the late 1980s.

- • The system has to be able to do its job in just one pass yet not rely excessively on buffering.

- • The system had to be fully functional regardless of the resolution of the original source.

- • Text content also had to be satisfactorily processed, which ultimately led to development of the JBIG standard.

- • The cost of implementing the system was also a major factor. The agreed norm was chosen as a 386 chip running at 16 MHz, able to decompress 64 Kbits per second. The advantage here is that it would allow for single-chip implementations.

- • DCT of 8×8 blocks. There were two reasons for this parameter: chip availability and the complexity of computation.

In April 1990, JPEG became ISO CD 10918. The standard continued to undergo revision until JPEG 8. It became an international standard in June 1993. JPEG is now copyrighted by ISO/IEC but in practice may be used free of royalties except those pertaining to the patented arithmetic data-crunching processes.

Lossless JPEG achieves a $2 : 1$ compression ratio. Desirable ratios for the DCT processes vary. The success of a given compression ratio for DCT is highly data dependent, so quality considerations must dominate the choice selected. Table 6.4 is a general guide to various ratios, but the deciding test must always be visual inspection of the results.

TABLE 6.4 General Evaluations of JPEG Compression Ratios

4:1 to 5:1	Visually matches original
6:1 to 10:1	Excellent match of original
11:1 to 16:1	Usually good enough in practice
17:1 to 32:1	Sometimes adequate
greater than 32:1	Possibly useful, but blocks apparent

JPEG can be implemented either in hardware or software and was intended to be embedded within other formats. Although it is very possible a JPEG decoder might not acceptably decode all possible renditions of a genuine JPEG image, this is the sort of implementation glitch that international standards may eventually be used to overcome.

Lossless JPEG Predictors

The DCT-based encoding processes were winners of a battery of competitive tests, but the design goal of achieving a lossless process worthy of inclusion remained. Almost as an afterthought, a predictive scheme was submitted and found to perform at about a 2:1 ratio with excellent consistency.

The concept underlying lossless JPEG is that one of eight formulas will be specified *in the data* to predict the content of a pixel (pixel X), after which the exact value of that pixel can be expressed as its difference from that prediction. So this is really a combination prediction-plus-difference scheme.

As shown in Figure 6.6 (sorry, but we're forced to call the first in the series 0 because that is its specified name), Selection 0 is an empty predictor, so that the value of the difference will be the full value of the pixel. Since pixel X is defined as being in the lower right-hand quadrant of four pixels, this may always apply to the first pixel in the first raster line of an image, but basically Selection 0 is only used in hierarchical mode (Figure 6.6).

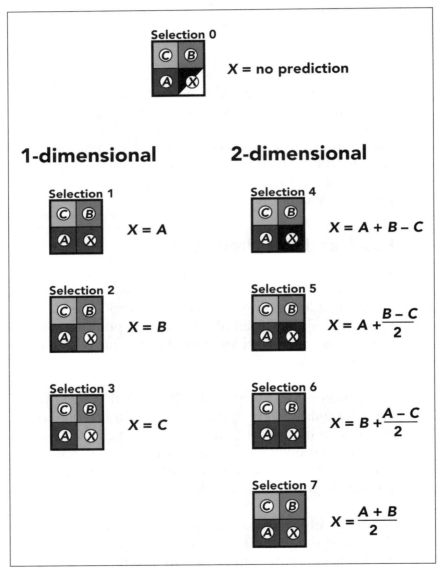

FIGURE 6.6   The eight predictor selections of lossless JPEG.

A similar restraint applies to the remainder of the first raster line of an image, because Selection 1 (repeating the preceding pixel) is the only other choice that does not take data from the raster line right above pixel X.

At the beginning of the second and following raster lines Selection 2 must be applied, and the fact that an A or C pixel does not exist does not pose a problem, since they are not required by the Selection 2 formula.

Selections 1, 2, and 3 are relatively straightforward one-dimensional repetitions of neighboring pixel information. Selections 4 to 7 are two-dimensional and more complex. Figure 6.6 uses grayscale values: A = 75 percent black, B = 50 percent, and C = 25 percent. In our examples, this causes pixel X to be composed of Selection 4, X = 100 percent or completely black; Selection 5, X = 87.5 percent; Selection 6, X = 75 percent, which happens to match A in our example; and Selection 7, X = 62.5 percent. As can be seen from this, Selections 4 to 7 will be most useful when a steep gradient of change affects the values of adjacent pixels.

Selections 1 to 7 form such a compact scheme of predictors that (with the exception of the first raster line and first pixel of all subsequent raster lines) all seven formulas may be applied to every pixel in order to determine which selection will result in the smallest difference value.

While 4:1 or 5:1 JPEG is adequate for the naked eye in almost any situation, lossless JPEG has many specialized uses. X-rays are the standard example, but of course many images must be faithfully transmitted and may potentially be subjected to visual inspection under magnification. If the data is sufficiently valuable, none of it may be sacrificed. Although a 2:1 compression ratio is hardly dramatic, it is certainly very useful. Doubling storage capacity is always a benefit (because someone somewhere will only have to spend half as much money).

The File Format Issue

Vendors rush in where standards committees fear to tread. The politics and practicalities of defining unique file formats for JPEG were more than the committee could take on. By December 10, 1991, C-Cube Microsystems brought out Version 1.01 of JFIF (JPEG File Interchange Format), having pooled information from every major vendor who was getting on the JPEG bandwagon. Although this is a simple and stripped-down implementation of JPEG's possibilities, many users are wildly enthusiastic about it and hope to see it become more widely adopted. Its two most notable restrictions are that it uses YC_rC_b 24-bit color (8 bits per component) only and requires that the pixels in each component be treated as evenly distributed or centered within that component.

The Aldus-led cooperative venture TIFF (Tag Image File Format) produced Version 6.0 in June 1992, which was intended to give adequate support for JPEG compression. In practice—namely, implementations/applications—all the bugs aren't out of what is now called JTIFF yet, but once users stop encountering minor glitches or difficulty-of-use dilemmas, the JTIFF format is bound to become fully supported by almost all developers of graphics applications (at least to the same extent that TIFF is).

Apple PICT and QuickTime support JPEG by putting a PICT header in front of the JFIF data format. Although full-motion JPEG has been attempted by several other means, full QuickTime support for JPEG-compressed images comes as close to guaranteed decodability as you're going to get. Besides videoconferencing applications, many developers prefer motion JPEG because it does not involve interframe compression (very lossy for frames that are made dependent on other, less-lossy frames). Bear in mind that QuickTime runs on Windows and can be implemented on ISO 9660–compliant discs using Apple Extensions, so JPEG video on CD–ROM is a part of everybody's future.

PostScript Level 2 and IIF (Image Interchange Facility) also support JPEG (at least its DCT processes). Handmade Software's .HSI format is the most notable of several proprietary file structures that use some JPEG but cannot readily be exchanged over application boundaries.

For those interested in journeying into the forest of graphic data structures and inspecting the individual trees, we can recommend two handy guides: *Graphics File Formats, Reference and Guide*, by C. Wayne Brown and Barry J. Shepherd, Manning Publications, 1995; and *Encyclopedia of Graphics File Formats*, by James D. Murray and William vanRyper, O'Reilly & Associates, 1994. It is an accepted fact of digital life at this point that there are too many graphics file formats and that they all seem to be multiplying and changing all the time, so if you want to journey in—good luck! By introducing many readers to this unnecessarily complex field, these books train people who can help solve the problem and reduce the multiplicity (dare I say fecundity) of graphic data structures.

For those of you whose needs are more basic, get online. The reason the Independent JPEG Group's list of frequently asked questions (FAQ) includes so many answers about converting GIF files is because thousands of users are out there doing it, so join in. You can probably get to the JPEG FAQ by whatever standard indexing search mechanism you normally use (that's how we did it). The FAQ suggests you get it from the news.answers postings archived at rtfm.mit.edu. If you have FTP, you can retrieve it (it's in two parts) as /pub/usenet/news.answers/jpeg-faq/part1 and /pub/usenet/news.answers/jpeg-faq/part2. If you don't have FTP access, then send an e-mail to mail-server@rtfm.mit.edu containing the lines

send /pub/usenet/news.answers/jpeg-faq/part1

send /pub/usenet/news.answers/jpeg-faq/part2

MPEG

Interframe compression works along the temporal dimension. A pixel-to-pixel comparison between frames (for example, first pixel of the third raster line in two serial frames) is straightforward as a calculation, but it is impractical by itself to capture the underlying qualities that make the sampled data meaningful.

For one thing, discontinuities are often random because live video incorporates many insignificant image fluctuations that the eye filters out. Digital analysis of the captured data will have to painstakingly account for this noise and represent it with the same mathematical precision as meaningful data.

TABLE 6.5 Examples of MPEG Data Sizes by Frame Type

	MPEG–1 (SIF@150 KB/s)	MPEG–2 (601@500 KB/s)
I-frame	19 KB	50 KB
P-frame	6 KB	25 KB
B-frame	2.5 KB	10 KB

More important, the whole idea behind moving pictures is that the camera tracks some changing subject within a larger visual context (e.g., background) that remains more or less stationary. The illusion of motion is created by running these images rapidly in sequence so that the mind perceives them as if they were a single changing image. From the point of view of the content in an individual pixel, this means that, if it is incorporated in the changing subject of a series of images, the content's two-dimensional pixel address will be steadily shifting.

So two goals of interframe compression are to minimize the representation of meaningless noise and to track the motion of image subfields, as in giving the forwarding address for traveling pixel content.

Frame Types

Usually discussions of MPEG begin with a now-classic treatment of redundancy between frames, especially in the background. Although it certainly saves valuable space in the data stream not to reiterate redundant data, this is already accomplished to a large extent by preexisting raster technology. For example, when a sprite runs across a stationary background in a video game, the background data does not need to be reloaded every frame (except to fill in the vacated portions of the sprite's previous location). MPEG also takes advantage of this, but background redundancy by itself does not explain the thought processes behind MPEG's use of four different types of pictures or frames: I, P, B, and D.

The I-frame resembles JPEG in that it is intraframe (I stands for intraframe) encoded using 8×8 blocks and a DCT-quantization-abbreviation sequence. It would be an overstatement to say that the comparison ends there, but the myth that MPEG uses some frames of JPEG or contains JPEG has gone too far. They both approach similar data with similar strategies, and it would be fair to say that as the earlier standard, JPEG has been an influence and even an inspiration to MPEG's development. But the logic of JPEG's overall structure is confined to (multilevel) still images and their transmission. Adding the temporal dimension has presented MPEG with many more far-reaching opportunities and challenges (i.e., problems). Of course, if you want to create an I-frame in MPEG out of samples organized in a JPEG file format, you can certainly do so; this is one of the reasons why motion-JPEG works well for editing data that will later be compressed under MPEG.

To dispel curiosity at this point: P-frames are predictive, B-frames are bidirectional, and D-frames are composed of only the DC coefficients in a block. D-frames are therefore the most lossy; since they are reserved for special uses where such lossiness is acceptable (and other frame types are excluded), we will not discuss them further. We also postpone a full discussion of P-frames and B-frames until our discussion of macroblock types (see "Macroblock Types" later in this chapter).

MPEG video's inherently lossy goal is to kill visual data selectively. It does this by using an I-frame as a data repository, decimating P-frame content by killing off patterns that already exist in the I-frame (leaving the P-frame completely dependent), and then decimating the B-frame content of any patterns that already exist in either the I-frame or its dependent P-frames. If this sounds very hierarchical and oppressive, it is! Another myth of MPEG is that you can only capture the information from a single frame of MPEG if it is an I-frame to begin with. This is not true, but B-frames are highly decimated creatures and frequently hated because of it. On the other hand, at data rates below 150 KB/s, the temporal redundancy of B-frames can improve the signal-to-noise ratio (SNR) by as much as 2 decibels (which for a base-10 logarithm function is a factor of 100).

In the real world, relative sizes of the different frame types may vary wildly depending on what parameters are set and the quality of encoding equipment, but Table 6.5 provides two examples that convey the general idea.

This diminution of size is accomplished by the incompleteness of the P-frame and the B-frame data. A P-frame's data set can only be completed by referencing information contained in the preceding I-frame. A B-frame's data set relies on its bookends: the nearest I-frame(s) and/or P-frame(s) both preceding and subsequent to it in the data stream.

The reason people say that you can't capture a complete P-frame or B-frame is that these are organized in the data stream as incomplete but containing references (motion vectors to data in other frames). Once all the data required has come in as input, however, complete frame information is routinely assembled.

The complaint video editors have is that MPEG is a lossy process. Let's say a sequence of images has already been MPEG-compressed and you wanted to recut it so that the data in a B-frame would begin the sequence. Capturing and assembling the B-frame's data and then using it as an I-frame would reduce the quality of subsequent, dependent P-frames and B-frames (which would also have to be re-encoded to accomplish this) because the original B-frame was too lossy for this purpose. All that means for editing purposes though is, don't go into MPEG until you're ready. Once your edited footage is final, MPEG is excellent.

As a standard, MPEG governs the syntax and parameters by which a compressed audiovisual stream may be

decoded. A range of possible encoding strategies is left
wide open by MPEG. The familiar videoconferencing
standard H.261 (formerly known as p*64, where p is a
factor from 1 to 30 and 64 is 64,000 bits per second, so
transmission rates may be from 8 KB/s to 240 KB/s in
increments of 8) uses a DCT-quantization-abbreviation
strategy similar to MPEG (and JPEG) but was con-
ceived with real-time, symmetrical implementation in
mind. Although MPEG-1 can be real-time encoded for
low-bandwidth applications, the whole point of MPEG
was not that it would be easy to encode but rather that
it would decode with high quality.

Figure 6.7 shows one example of what MPEG calls a
group of pictures (GOP): a series of I-, P-, and B-
frames, which are displayed in one order but encoded
and decoded according to strict hierarchical order (I
first then P then intermediate B, then subsequent I or P
followed by intermediate B, etc.). To be more technically correct, the decoding sequence in our example of
open GOPs would decode the first I-frame followed by
B-frames 11 and 12 in the preceding, shaded frame, fol-

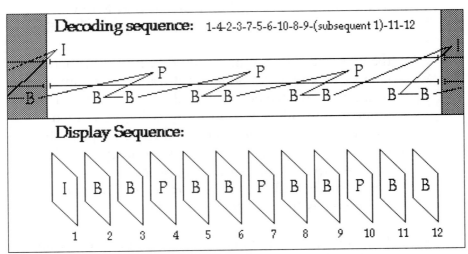

FIGURE 6.7   MPEG data order and display order contrasted.

lowed by P-frame 4, and so on. Open GOPs reference to frames in adjacent GOPs, whereas closed GOPs are entirely self-contained (self-referential). Although B-frames are thought of as needing bookend I- and/or P-frames (on both sides), it would be possible in our example to have encoded all the macroblocks of Frames 11 and 12 so that backward reference to P-frame 10 was all that was required. This illustrates that the real issues of how P- and B-frames function are elucidated by the macroblock types available to each type of frame, and not by generic statements about the frame types themselves.

As we will see by reviewing the range of macroblock-encoding choices available, MPEG is really an inherently asymmetrical compression standard for which quality is always bought by the effort put into encoding. This is not to say that real-time MPEG isn't good, but asymmetrical MPEG is what it's all about. If you're robbing P-frames and B-frames of their data and forcing them to feed on information previously passed through the data stream in order to become whole, then feeding them a well-balanced diet involves complex maneuvering. No wonder people hate B-frames: They are rarely encoded well enough to justify the effort of decoding them.

Macroblock Types

Behold the humble macroblock: four 8×8 blocks of the Y luminosity component forming a 16×16 area, one block of Cr chrominance component, and one block of Cb chrominance component. I-, P-, and B-frames have different types of macroblocks available to each of them. To zoom in on these macroblock types, let's start with an establishing shot of the larger landscape that surrounds them (see Table 6.6). The sequence, GOP, picture (or frame), slice, and macroblock layers of MPEG-1 syntax each have unique headers (MPEG-2 is more flexible;

TABLE 6.6 Six Layers of Syntax (MPEG–1 defined)

Sequence	The largest independent segments of the data stream; begin with identifying header followed by compressed GOPs; because a sequence contains GOPs with related visual context it is possible to define customized quantization tables and include them in the header (which also includes aspect ratios, picture rates, and characterizes the bit stream by bit rate and buffer size).
Group of Pictures (GOP)	Header required by MPEG-1 (but not MPEG-2); generally starts with an I-frame, followed by the subsequent P-frame, followed by B-frames, which are to be displayed as intermediate to the two, followed by the next P-frame, etc.; GOPs are designated "open" or "closed" depending on whether prediction-references are all contained within the GOP (closed); an example of an open GOP: final B-frames would have references to predictions contained in the I-frame at the start of the subsequent GOP.
Picture	The primary coding unit of MPEG; header specifies whether type is I, P, B, or D, and includes time reference so that display order is corrected from the encoded order.
Slice	One or more macroblocks sharing the same vertical position (specified in header); organized in ascending raster scan order, but a single raster line (or more correctly, vertical position) may contain more than one slice; header also includes quantizer scale permitting increased reduction of data for the slice.
Macroblock	Four luminance and two chrominance blocks $YC_rC_b = 3$ components) preceded by a header (Note: MPEG-2 permits different organization of components); the header is Huffman encoded along with the blocks and contains the following information: *Skip #*: increments address (by more than 1 if previous-frame(s) data is acceptable). *Type*: see Table 6.7. Quantizer scale: permits increased quantization. Motion vectors: horizontal and vertical (for P and B); backward (h, v) only for P; backward and/or forward (h, v) for B. Skip blocks: if previous-frame block(s) acceptable.
Block	Huffman encoded (note that MPEG-1 uses generic, fixed Huffman tables); no header; 8×8 (usually, but 16×16 implementations exist) block written to data stream in standard zigzag order (Note: MPEG-2 permits alternative order of AC coefficients).

for example, the GOP header is not mandatory). The five elements of the macroblock header convey a general sense of the issues in macroblock encoding.

The skip # and skip blocks areas in the macroblock header utilize the standard advantages of raster technology alluded to earlier for handling redundancy. If a subject is changing position against a stationary background, for example, the wallpaper in the room behind him does not have to be repetitively encoded and decoded. Such is not the case with motion-JPEG (at least its present implementations), wherein every frame is a discrete and complete picture. If previous macroblock(s) or even previous block(s) within the macroblock contain sufficiently identical information, the pertinent addresses can be incremented/skipped over, leaving the previous sample information in place (until a new frame requires fresh data in those segments of the two-dimensional image).

The quantizer scale area in the macroblock header is part of MPEG's multitiered system of quantization, which also permits adaptive quantization, since several different levels of alternative tables and degrees of quantization may be selected from. This is another feature missing from JPEG. In *JPEG Still Image Data Compression Standard* by William B. Pennebaker and Joan L. Mitchell (Van Nostrand Reinhold, 1993), the authors note that MPEG enthusiasts claim that "up to 30 percent better compression can be achieved with adaptive quantization" (p. 329) and propose suggestions as to how it could be added to JPEG (pp. 331–332). Under MPEG-2, even more sophisticated uses of quantization are standardized, as we discuss later.

The motion vectors area in the macroblock header is like a pointer that directs P- and B-frames where to go for their missing data. If the subject of a series of

frames is changing position, then the content of one
macroblock will more or less shift over to the address of
another macroblock (for example, panning across a
painting from left to right). This shift may be mathematically represented by horizontal and vertical coefficients.
B-frames never get referred to, but they have the greatest
degree of choice as to how they do the referring (bidirectional means forward, backward, or an average of both).
P-frames always refer backward. Although macroblocks
using these motion vectors are called *predictive*, in a
sense they are more like researchers in a library.

Predictive macroblocks are like a wanna-be society
matron who must suddenly acquire a knowledge of fine
art. She starts out not knowing much but knowing
where to look: Go to the library. After studying information on the subject, she can more or less get it down
pat. The specific shifts in motion vector(s) are like the
cards in a card catalog; they tell her precisely where the
book she wants is located, so she goes there and reads
it. To pursue this analogy with several questions:

- • How far afield should she search? The search
range for determining motion vectors during
encoding can be the most computationally
demanding part of the process. Distances of plus or
minus 1 macroblock in any direction only require
comparison with 8 other macroblocks, but a
search of distances 4 macroblocks in any direction
will require comparison with 80! (see Figure 6.8).

- • To what degree does she want to form her own
specific opinions instead of just slavishly reproduc-
ing what she reads? This gets to why they are
called predictive in the first place. If you code the
differences between a macroblock's samples and
those of the macroblock it is referring to, then you
get what looks like a standard prediction-plus-
differences scheme (e.g., lossless JPEG).

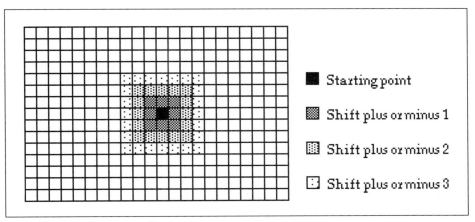

FIGURE 6.8   Search range examples.

- • How much does she want to get from a given book? This is the degree-of-quantization issue. Some books you can rely on and some you just want to skim. Skimming a book is like using a higher degree of quantization.

Now if you can forgive us the flippancy of our example, we can go on to the type area in the macroblock header. This area can be occupied by 16 of the 17 macroblock types in Table 6.7 (skipped macroblocks are not listed as types in the header, but it is useful to think of them as a type).

A first reaction to this incredible range of choices might be that you can see the difference between top-notch, service-bureau-encoded MPEG and what you're going to be able to get from a nice, affordable video-capture board. No human is going to adjudicate which kind of macroblock type to use on a one-to-one basis, so clearly MPEG has the potential for tremendous asymmetry, requiring the dedication of truly sizable computational resources. The shortcuts your user-friendly plug-in board is forced to use (because nobody wants to spend hours on each frame) result in an inferior data stream

TABLE 6.7 Macroblock Types (MPEG-1 defined)

I-frame	Intra-q	Intra-d				
P-frame	Intra-q	Intra-d	Pred-m	Pred-c Pred-mc	Pred-cq Pred-mcq	Skipped
B-frame	Intra-q	Intra-d	Pred-i Pred-b Pred-f	Pred-icq Pred-bc Pred-fc	Pred-ic Pred-bcq Pred-fcq	Skipped

Intra-q	=	Use scaled quantization table.
Intra-d	=	Use current quantization table.
		(Note: the sequence header permits Intra and non-Intra tables.)
Pred-c	=	Code the differences from the prediction.
Pred-m (without c)	=	Prediction is sufficient, do not code differences.
Pred-i	=	Interpolative, average the two referenced macroblocks.
Pred-b	=	Backward.
Pred-f	=	Forward (in display order; the subsequent I- or P-frame has already been encoded/decoded).
Pred-*c	=	Code the differences. (Note: Pred-mc is not a contradiction, it is a combination.)
Pred-*q	=	Adaptive quantization.
		At encoding, tests/trials different quantization settings:
		1. Non-Intra (if defined) or else Intra table supplied by sequence header.
		2. Increased quantization indicated by the slice header.
		3. Increased quantization indicated by the macroblock header.
		After determining which is optimal for encoding, the quantization factor selected is encoded along with the quantized data so that, during decoding, the data may be multiplied back to correct frequency-coefficient values.
Skipped	=	This is not a formally distinct type (does not appear under "type" in the macroblock header), but means that the skip # in the subsequent macroblock's header is incremented over this macroblock, so its values from the previous picture/frame remain unchanged.

(as far as content conversion is concerned). The good news is that however well your data is captured on the encoding side, decoding the MPEG stream will be relatively straightforward (although decoding interpolative B-frames is a real RAM hog).

A more considered reaction to the macroblock types, for those who have seen a lot of GOP illustrations, is that the conventional description of P- and B-frames has been seriously oversimplified. For example, one may see three

B-frames between two P-frames where the first goes backwards (its motion-vector reference), the second is interpolative, and the third goes forward. Although MPEG can be implemented with that kind of simplicity (by restricting the choices of macroblock types), it takes the guts out of the process to describe it that way.

Motion compensation for interframe compression is one thing. The way MPEG-1 introduced such versatile macroblocks (e.g., any frame type may have completely intraframe-encoded macroblocks, etc.) is another thing: It is a very powerful implementation of this technique. It also bridges the needs of both the home user with relatively minimal encoding requirements and the high-powered media vendors who require a high-quality platform to release digital video product. As beautiful as laserdisc video may be, it is an analog medium and laserdisc manufacture is considerably more demanding than pressing a digital compact disc. Considering the need for compression inherent in video data sizes, MPEG is a superlative answer.

MPEG-1 Constraints and MPEG-2 Directions

The Moving Picture Experts Group began work on MPEG-1 in 1988 and produced their committee draft in November 1991. The Draft International Standard (DIS) was final in March 1992 and became an International Standard (IS) in March 1993 (work on the audio portion was completed somewhat earlier). Now it is known as ISO 11172 Information Technology—Coding of moving pictures and associated audio—For digital storage media at up to about 1.5 Mbits/s.

The committee anticipated that many implementations of MPEG-1 would dispense with the low data rate. Specifications were issued for a constrained parameters bit stream (CPB), which would define applications that were in compliance with what was hoped would become common decoding characteristics of the standard (see Table 6.8). Almost at the same time, committee work began on developing separate standards governing higher bit rates: MPEG-2 and MPEG-3. As MPEG-2 made progress, its higher levels overlapped the HDTV uses MPEG-3 was intended to cover and MPEG-3 was dropped.

TABLE 6.8 Constrained Parameters Bit-Stream (CPB) Specifications

Maximum macroblocks per second = 9900

Maximum macroblocks per frame at 25 fps = 396   = 22 × 18

Maximum macroblocks per frame at 30 fps = 330   = 22 × 15

Maximum picture rate = 30 fps

Maximum horizontal size = 720 pixels = 45 macroblocks
Maximum vertical size = 576 pixels = 36 macroblocks

(which is big enough to accommodate CCIR-601 resolutions, but the data rate is too high so Standard Image Format (SIF) uses "quarter-screen" half-samples)

SIF horizontal size = 352 pixels = 22 macroblocks
SIF vertical size (at 25 fps, PAL/SECAM) = 288 pixels = 18 macroblocks
SIF vertical size (at 30 fps, NTSC) = 240 pixels = 15 macroblocks

(multiple-of-16 resolutions not required by MPEG-1, but mandatory under MPEG-2)

Maximum bit rate = 232 KB/s
(1.860 megabits/sec)

Maximum buffer size = 47.1 KB
(376,832 bits)

(To accommodate single-speed CD-ROM drives and common computer buffer sizes a common ceiling is less than 150 KB/s with a 40 KB maximum buffer, but many MPEG-1 implementations go for higher data rates (up to about 750 KB/s).

MPEG-2 has three parts: video, audio, and systems. Committee drafts were produced in November 1993, the DIS in March 1994, and the IS was approved in November 1994 as ISO 13818. Employing data packets (such as ATM) to transport higher transmission rates than MPEG-1, MPEG-2 fully addresses the need for interlaced video (which is broadcasting odd/even raster lines as separate fields, so 30 frames per second equals 60 fields per second) and covers a wide range of different resolutions and improved algorithms. In fact, MPEG-2 covers such a wide gamut of possible implementations that discussion of it generally focuses on what is known as Main Profile at Main Level (MP@ML). Table 6.9 puts MP@ML in its larger context of more demanding applications also addressed by MPEG-2. The levels define ranges of operating parameters; the profiles determine what algorithms and syntax may be used.

Although the maximum bit rates for each level are intended to be part of their definition, there is some latitude in practice regarding the resolutions. For example, the Grand Alliance agreement between influential vendors and institutions regarding HDTV includes MPEG-2 but employs different resolutions. Of course, if they want to build MPEG-2 systems, who is going to stop them from doing it the way they want to? Many vendors will pursue different routes along the overall map indicated by Table 6.9. It should be noted, however, that some limitations are inescapable, such as the MPEG-2 restriction on screen dimensions to multiples of 16 and the additional restriction that screen height for interlaced fields be a multiple of 32 (important to implementing the new macroblock type designed especially for interlaced broadcasting).

We haven't pursued the discussion of MPEG audio here because it's much less of an issue than the need to

TABLE 6.9 MPEG-2 Levels and Profiles (developments in flux)

	LEVELS			
	LOW	MAIN	HIGH-1440	HIGH
Image resolution (at 30 fps)	352 × 240	720 × 480	1440 × 1152	1920 × 1080
Maximum bit rate	500 KB/s (4 Mbs)	1875 KB/s (15 Mb/s)	7500 KB/s 60 Mb/s)	10,000 Kb/s (80 Mb/s)
Description	SIF consumers	CCIR-601	HDTV (European)	"wide-screen" HDTV
Simple Profile Like Main but no B-Frames	na/ (n/a = no development anticipated)	Software applications (with limited buffer-size)	n/a	n/a
Main Profile Like MPEG-1 without CPB constraints	backward-compatible uses (with limited monitors)	MP@ML Where the action is* (more than 90% of users)	(experimental) Cable, high-density CD	(experimental) Cable, high-density CD
Main + Profile Like Main with spatial and SNR scalability	n/a	(experimental) Broadcasting	(experimental) Broadcasting, cable, high-density CD	(experimental) Broadcasting, cable, high-density CD
Next Profile (European) Full scalability, option of different color component organization	n/a	(experimental) Broadcasting	Although development led by interests of European HDTV, uses may be far more extensive.	If implemented may go up to 12,500 KB/s (100 Mb/s)

*MP@ML yields an NTSC-quality image at 4–6 Mb/s) and a reliable high-quality image at 1000–1250 KB/s (8–10 Mb/s) reduce video data size. Left and right stereo channels were covered by MPEG-1 with several different operating modes. MPEG-2 adds left- and right-side/rear channels, a center channel, and even an additional channel for subwoofer special effects at about 100 Hz (called a .1 channel, leading to the assertion that MPEG-2 has 5.1 audio channels). It will also probably be possible to use other audio algorithms that are not backward compatible with MPEG-1—notably Dolby AC-3, which General Instruments plans to adopt in its cable set-top boxes. As any audiophile knows first hand, these are the sorts of mouthwatering extra features that keep vendors pushing improved hardware and keep buyers broke! MPEG-2 is full of such special features.

Whereas MPEG-1 kept things relatively simple in order to achieve minimal bandwidth compression, every stage and layer of MPEG-2 encoding is now replete with new features that can be implemented (encoding enhancements are not explicitly written into the standard; encoding is given great latitude provided decoding is compliant).

- • Modifying the DCT (using basis vector shaping) in conjunction with adjusting quantization matrices so that the decoded image will reconstruct as if the data were prefiltered/preprocessed (*encoding enhancement*).

- • Choice between progressive and interlaced line modes for the DCT.

- • DC-coefficient precision may be expanded to 9, 10, or 11 bits (MPEG-1 is 8-bit only).

- • DC and AC coefficients (both before and after quantization) may be directly altered based on optimization analysis (encoding enhancement).

- • Quantization is more flexible with a greater range of dynamic step sizes (0.5 to 56 instead of MPEG-

1's 1 to 31) and the option of downloading tables before each frame.

- • Stationary noise patterns caused by quantization errors made less visible by altering the timing of their appearance (encoding enhancement).

- • An alternative to the zigzag pattern for reading data out of block matrices and into a linear stream; this alternative is believed to make Huffman encoding more effective with interlaced fields.

- • An alternative Huffman table with superior performance condensing I-frame data streams (intra-VLC).

- • GOP header optional (mandatory under MPEG-1).

- • Automated assignment of frame types to content (adaptive testing). For example, I-frames can be automatically assigned to the first frame of a new scene (encoding enhancement).

- • The sequence header has expanded definitions of aspect ratios and picture rates (rates may define source, such as PAL or SECAM). (Also, data transfer and color-coding characteristics may be specified.)

- • Vertical and horizontal screen sizes now described by 14 bits; this allows sizes as large as $16,384 \times 16,384$ to be specified.

- • New macroblock definitions permitting different color component schemes and improved performance (the 16×8 macroblock) with interlaced video.

- • Motion vectors required to be at half-pixel accuracy (MPEG-1's optional full-pixel setting didn't work well).

- • Redundant (concealment) motion vector information may be added for error correction.

- • A host of additional methods for macroblocks to access prediction data (many of which are specially adapted to interlaced video, e.g., 16×8 motion compensation and field motion compensation), creating an enormously increased number of specific macroblock types.

All that and more "coming to a theater near you." It is evident why the future direction that MPEG-2 actually goes in is heavily dependent on investment decisions made by vendors as to how they want to develop implementations including combinations of these features.

We've saved the best for last: scalability. Different scalable modes are being developed for the Main+ and Next profiles, most notably spatial, signal-to-noise ratio (SNR), temporal, and data partitioning (with spatial and SNR techniques furthest along in development). These may improve error correction, the gradient of image degradation during live broadcast, and the ability for CCIR-601 displays to only receive an appropriately formatted portion of a wider HDTV signal.

- • *Spatial Scalability*: Low-frequency information uses fewer samples per inch for reduced spatial resolution (which may be adequate by itself for many applications). Higher-frequency information is then decoded with more detailed spatial resolution. During encoding, the higher frequencies may use low-frequency samples as predictions so only the differences need to be encoded. Useful with monitors of differing resolutions.

- • *SNR Scalability*: Higher-frequency data is lower priority and thus quantized more radically (increasing the SNR). Low-frequency data is coded at the same number of samples per inch but more precision. Low frequencies lay the foundation to which higher frequencies may add refinements to the image. Useful with receivers of differing processing rates and capabilities.

- • *Temporal Scalability*: Complete image data is given higher priority for every-other-frame/alternate frames. Lower-priority in-between frames use the complete data from the high-priority frames as predictions and record only the differences. Useful in stereoscopic video applications such as virtual reality LEBs (location-based entertainment).

- • *Data Partitioning*: The AC coefficients are assigned a priority break point in the slice header, creating two bit streams: a high-priority stream containing the DC and lower-frequency data, and a lower-priority bit stream containing the higher-frequency ACs.

This may seem like an awful lot of encoding for a standard that has very little product out there (so far), but one of the most exciting aspects of product soon to be released under the MPEG-2 standard is the enhanced playback it will benefit from over years to come. I'm not talking about improvements compared with other formats such as VHS or laserdisc, I'm talking about playing the same MPEG-2 video CD five years or ten years after its first release. Those of you who have listened to audio CD players using 18-bit or 20-bit oversampling know that these greatly enhance the playback of CDs recorded in 16-bit audio. Improvements should be even more marked with the artificial evolution of MPEG-2 playback devices because they will be pushing around a much more burdensome data stream. So the investment in high-quality encoding will reap rewards in improved playback long after MPEG-2 releases are first issued.

MPEG-4

Since MPEG-2 effectively covers high data rates, MPEG-4 goes in the other direction and covers bit rates not to exceed 8 KB/s (commonly expressed as 64 kilobits per second). It is expected that 6 KB/s will be the lower end of this very low bit rate and that resolutions may be about 177×144 with 10 frames per second. This is an opportunity for non-DCT technologies to be used, since major breakthroughs have occurred in many areas. At the convergence between what should work (mathematical breakthroughs) and what does work (performance testing), DCT methodology is not in the same cutting-edge position that it was a few years ago.

Whether the newer crop of promising algorithms and approaches can outperform DCT remains to be seen (let us repeat that the major advantage of DCT is the way it preps the data into frequency bands that subject themselves to quantization very reliably). An MPEG-4 seminar was held on July 20, 1994, in Grimstad, Norway, including experts on many diverse areas: psychologists; sensory physiologists; artificial synthesis of music, speech, and vision; digital graphics/animation; virtual reality; genetic algorithms, and so on. The chairman of the regional coordinators is J. Ostermann, who may be contacted at ostermann@tnt.uni-hannover.de for further information.

Other

JPEG and MPEG are only two prominent line items on a very long list of compression alternatives. As international standards, they each present forums for open discussion. They also represent a certain financial commitment to pursue development on the part of major vendors (like Sony or C-Cube) who have been thoroughly involved in the standardization process.

We expect JPEG and MPEG to occupy major positions of market dominance and heavy use in the next few years, although it is certainly possible that this will not occur. Popular understanding of these standards has entailed large areas of misconception and inadequate mass communication. We hope this work may exercise a constructive contribution to improving public (and developer) awareness. We would be derelict, however, not to at least mention some of the other methods of compression.

Before jumping in, we would remind you of the question we posed at the beginning of this chapter: "Why do you need to know?" That is not meant to be facetious or challenging. Many worthwhile new books have hit the shelves explaining how to use assorted proprietary formats to do your own multimedia video. Some of you may have already rushed out to buy Adobe Premier or the latest Macromind package. We do not mean to discourage or belittle any of that. Put it together and make it work. By all means.

Have you ever heard an area described by the phrase "It's very competitive"—only to discover that the intensity of competition was mind-boggling? That's what it's like out there for compression codecs, especially anything that can decode software only on a 386-or-better computer. It is almost impossible for books to be up to date three months after publication, although these books contain a wealth of information that merits thorough study even if some of it is less than current. The same is true for video packages or boards that you may buy and reading the documentation that comes with them. Concepts don't change as rapidly as facts (and some critics might allege that ISO standards change a lot more slowly than concepts), so the background to be gained from working with any good books, packages, or boards is bound to stay with you and grow as you keep up with current developments.

Find a newsstand that carries the major computer magazines and buy issues that contain comparisons or indepth discussions of digital-video product performance. Despite the delays of magazine publication, this is a necessary element of staying up to date. Remember, developers tend to get this stuff free, so you may find yourself swimming in periodicals before you know it (i.e., when you no longer have time to read them).

At the time of this writing, there is no full-screen 30 fps video that runs consistently across platforms without dropping frames. There are many handy, at-home ways to preprocess video so it will decode more handsomely despite having been compressed on affordable home capture boards, but right now there is no one package with a satisfactory range of preprocessing, and a little expertise on graphics file formats and assorted graphics packages is required to implement this. Digital betacams and CD–R drives are not common, and 1-gigabyte hard drives have only recently started costing $1000. Most of the general computer-buying public is still buying a computer off the shelf with only 4 to 8 MB of RAM and has no idea that they might have to spend that much money again on RAM chips if they want to create good video multimedia. It is 1995 and the new Microsoft Windows operating system still hasn't been released yet (with OLE and dozens of multimedia-friendly features). This message-in-a-bottle paragraph is written in the hopes that it will be incredibly funny by the time you are reading this, because we have hoped to give this chapter some long-lasting value.

Prime Venues: Microsoft and Apple's Quicktime

Many people are still laboring under the misimpression that Quicktime and Video for Windows are compression methods. Although packages generally contain some software-only encoding on-board, Quicktime and Video for Windows are operating system extensions that permit video coding and decoding to occur in a variety of file formats.

Quicktime is wonderfully cross-platform, whereas Video for Windows isn't. Microsoft's research and development has been targeted more on the anticipated Windows '95 or Chicago OLE operating system, instead of dedicating major resources to making Video for Windows more flexible. On the other hand, more computers in the United States are already running Windows than anything else (although developers continue to adore Macintosh), so cross-platform compatibility is not a big problem with Video for Windows (whereas it is Quicktime's lifeblood).

If you want to consider a range of video options and you are committed to either a Macintosh or DOS-based environment, call Apple or Microsoft and get the most recent list of file formats and popular compression methods supported by these products. Since most CD–ROMS are running on IBM-compatible or Apple multimedia PC's, these are the prime venues for anything you create to be displayed. If you are publishing, make sure you use one of the new adaptive color palettes so that when you display to 256 colors, they will be the colors you intend (as opposed to blues turning into reds because the number assigned to your blue is the same as the number assigned to someone else's red, etc.).

Champions and Contenders

Indeo and Cinepak are the two heavyweights who continue to battle it out. They both call intracoded frames *key frames* and call dependent, intercoded frames *delta frames* (for those of you who've managed to avoid calculus, the symbol D [delta] is used to describe how something changes). They both use vector quantization.

Indeo is the old-timer because of Intel's depth of experience with the DVI hardware-compression codec (since divested). Cinepak is the talented upstart that was greeted with enormous enthusiasm for its cleverness when it came out. "Better for low-motion video" used to be the established wisdom about Indeo, but since version 3.2 came out that has been much less true. Like heavyweight champions in boxing, Indeo has a lot of support behind it to keep it on top, or at least returning for contentious rematches. But Cinepak is an undeniable champion that may be expected to match or exceed any Indeo feature as they both continue upgrading.

Truemotion-S incorporates some vector quantization, discrete wavelet transformation subband encoding, and the power of one-pass arithmetic encoding. At the moment, many consider it the top contender because it handles sudden changes in types of content (music-video style or strobing effects) more smoothly than Indeo or Cinepak. It is also scalable to higher or lower resolutions, which is a tremendous advantage. Unlike the champions, however, its cross-platform flexibility has not been put through as many hard lessons. Sometimes it seems that "if the bus doesn't kill ya', the soundcard will!" If Truemotion-S can eliminate implementation glitches with its upgrades, it may have what it takes to be better than Indeo and Cinepak (not just in theory).

As for fractals, besides mentioning the company name Iterated Systems, there is only just so much to talk about. In contrast to unimpressive but very reliable methods such as Video 1 for Windows, fractal methods are like prima donna geniuses that are very impressive when they work, but it's hard to predict what they'll work for and when they will encounter something where it's as if they just don't want to work. Because fractal compression can achieve ratios beyond even wavelets (as high as 1000:1) and because fractally composed images are often very beautiful, it will be used and to good effect. But fractal implementations may remain a special area, off to the side of the multimedia mainstream, delivering breathtaking performances but only on occasion.

HARC-C with a Slingshot

Like virtual reality, hope has led to disappointment many times for true believers in compression technology. New contenders release fantastic announcements that rarely pan out when it's time for implementation. The big three—MPEG, Indeo, and Cinepak—sit side by side on Western Digital's WD9710 decoding chipset for one reason: reliability. Many former optimists who used to rave about this or that new codec no longer want to hear the words wavelet or fractal because they feel like they have been suckers in the past for promises which never came through (with the exception of Encarta's beautiful fractal compression). No currently available compression codec has killed the Goliath of high video bandwidth. So here is the latest contender, the latest David, and we'll see if it ends up buried or crowned when the dust settles.

HARC-C is a wavelet-based set of algorithms written in C language. The encoder is not fully automated yet, but the decoder only takes up 130 KB and can run on an IBM-compatible 486 without consuming 4 MB of RAM. For those of you who don't appreciate the meaning of this, that means HARC-C can be included on a CD–ROM just like Indeo and QuickTime implementations you probably already have sitting around in their jewel cases: The decoder is simply loaded during disc installation. As for its performance, see Figures 6.9(a) and (b), which show black-and-white prints of Mignard's

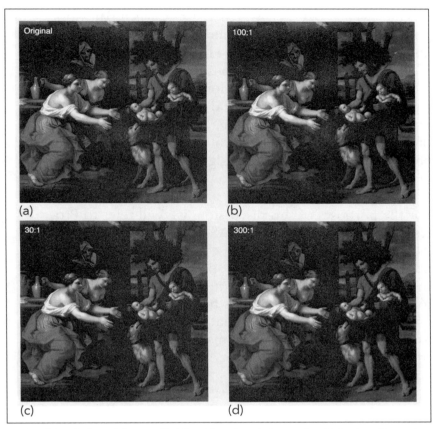

FIGURE 6.9 Mignard's *The Shepherd Faustulus Bringing Romulus and Remus to His Wife.* Which one was compressed at 300:1?

The Shepherd Faustulus Bringing Romulus and Remus to His Wife. Although (b) shows some minor degradation compared to (a), especially the babies' arms, it was expanded from a still image that was compressed at 300:1 (yes, that's three hundred to one). However well HARC-C delivers in the marketplace, that's a quality high-compression benchmark that is astounding for a little 130 KB slingshot of a decoder.

The Houston Advanced Research Center is developing and licensing HARC-C (check out their website at http://www.harc.edu/). The first public announcement of this new technology was March 1, 1995, when Ball Corporation's Aerospace and Communications Group announced its sublicense to use HARC-C for EarthWatch Inc.'s remote imaging applications (high-definition satellite-type photography cries out for this kind of quality high compression). HARC-C had been fully in development for several years before that, as P. K. Yuen worked on C language implementation of Charles K. Chui's newly discovered compression algorithms (both scientists are with HARC and also Texas A&M University).

For the purposes of this discussion, we will refer to Professor Chui's discovery as CHAS—the Chui HARC-C Algorithm Set. CHAS uses the continuous wavelet transformation to analyze the spatial data which is then compressed by applying different *spline* functions to it, different spline functions being used depending on the ratio of compression that is desired. While this is a wavelet-based compression scheme, CHAS is radically different from the DWT compression schemes now in use.

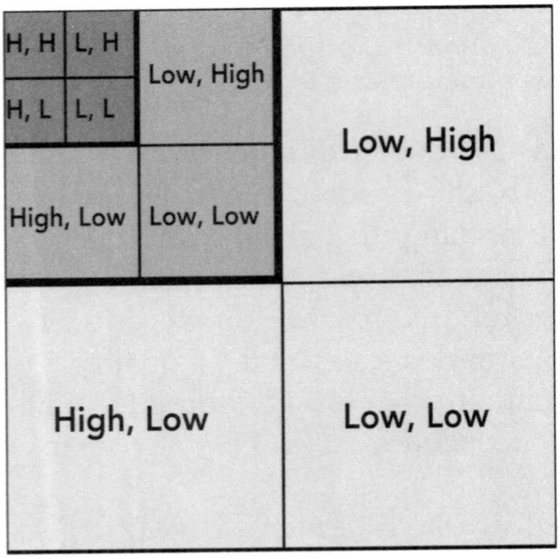

FIGURE 6.10 Standard process of decomposition quadrants.

The DWT (discrete wavelet transformation) uses a standard process of decomposition in which the spatial data is converted to frequency data (or vice versa) and the frequency data is assigned to quadrants (see Figure 6.10). The information in the High, High quadrant may then be put through the process again to describe the data more precisely. This may be done recursively until all the data is fully described, or it may stop at some acceptable level of approximation. Although codecs are available that use the DWT (such as Cap'n Crunch), when MPEG was running competitive trials (1988–1991), no implementations of the DWT were found to be as satisfactory as the DCT and so it was not used (among other things, the DCT's DC and AC coefficients could be quantized very reliably).

Professor Chui's breakthrough with the CHAS performs faster computations on the wavelet matrix with fewer operations per pixel than are required by the DWT. The wavelet organizes the data, but Chui's background in spline curves and approximation theory has allowed a radical new approach to determining what elements of the data can be acceptably sacrificed or killed off. For any given curve, running a spline curve through several pixels on that curve will provide an accurate or relatively lossy approximation of the curve, depending on how many pixels are used. Approximation theory provided Chui with fresh insights to construct algorithms governing where and how data would be lost so that (in our example) fewer pixels could be used more effectively.

While CHAS includes some rounding and therefore may be said to incorporate a quantization stage, the contrast with MPEG/JPEG quantization must be emphasized. Rather than relying on quantization of AC coefficients in order to kill off data that is deemed to be redundant, or unnecessarily detailed, the burden of data destruction is carried by the spline functions in CHAS. You can say that this is a much more precise way to delete parts of the data than previous compression schemes have allowed.

So it seems that HARC-C are the smartest algorithms presently available for killing off some data and storing what's left efficiently. HARC has routinely been performing 3 levels of compression on still images (30:1, 100:1, and 300:1) although it would be possible to select ratios in between these levels. (Even lossless compression can be performed at between 2:1 and 4:1, using the same algorithm.) Once intraframe compression has been performed, temporal frequencies can be analyzed for additional interframe savings of storage space. HARC-C reports that with 16-bit color, 640 × 480 resolution, and 30 frames per second, it clocks in with a 350:1 compression ratio with quality high enough to take on any challenger, even Goliath.

So is the world of international video standards about to be turned on its ear? Unlikely. Locomotives take a long time to slow down, and it is too soon to be able to determine whether CHAS should supplant the DCT. What is more practical is that every multiformat decoder or set-top box should include HARC-C's puny little slingshot, and then it can be a fair fight. It can even be hardwired into silicon chips more easily than larger, more cumbersome decoders, so why not welcome it on board. The digital video revolution needs all the high compression it can get.

Replication

Quick! Name the item in your house manufactured to the tightest tolerances? TV? No. Your wall thermostat? Wrong again. Here's a hint: This document is about compact discs.

Since the introduction of the compact disc some 13 years ago, the format has grown to become the leading music delivery system. Additionally, the various other CD derivatives such as CD–ROM, Photo CD, and CD–Video are well on their way to highly successful futures.

Part of the reason for the format's success must be credited to the following features:

- • A robust, dependable error-correction scheme, allowing for the most durable consumer delivery system ever.

- • Technical specifications that are easily adhered to by licensed manufacturers.

- • The total separation of disc content and subspecies from the manufacturing process. This allows the format to expand beyond the delivery of pure audio into the delivery of virtually any information that can be digitized.

- • Specifications that allow several manufacturing processes, both current and future, to compete for economic viability.

- • The advancement of sophisticated quality control devices that allow the manufacturer to efficiently check both the physical and the electronic parameters of the disc quickly and thoroughly. As a result the return rate for defective product is well below one percent, an astonishingly low level for any type of mass-produced consumer software (i.e., delivery medium: videocassettes, vinyl LPs, floppy disks, etc.).

CD Size, Speed, Optical Characteristics

The compact disc is one of the great marvels of twentieth-century engineering. In addition to being light, rugged, and small, the CD lends itself to mass replication at a moderate cost, even though the dimensions and tolerances needed rival those of semiconductor production.

Sitting within an absolute diameter of 120 mm, data occupies a 33-mm-wide area between the inner diameter of 50 mm and the outer diameter of 116 mm. When we include the lead-in and lead-out sections, the total area rises to 35.5 mm. Some quick math will show some impressive facts.

The track pitch specification calls for a value of 1.6 microns. Since the track pitch is equal to one track we can then compute as follows:

$$\frac{35.5 \times 1000}{1.6} = 22{,}188 \text{ tracks crossing a radius of the disc}$$

Because the track is a continuous spiral, we can compute the total track length as follows:

$$\text{Length} = 2 \times 22{,}188 \times \frac{35.5 + 46}{2} = 5.7 \text{ km or } 3.54 \text{ miles}$$

In this equation, the length of the spiral representing the track area is equivalent to the circumference of a circle, which is measured by the familiar formula $C = 2\pi r$ or πd. The track length is given by the total number of tracks (22,188) multiplied by the average circumference. The diameter in this equation is obtained by adding the width of the program areas including lead-in and lead-out areas (35.5 mm) and the maximum starting diameter of the lead-in area (46 mm). Halving this yields the radius, which is inserted into the formula as shown.

The storage of data is achieved by a series of pits and lands. A land is the absence of a pit. Pits are half a micron wide and can be injection-molded very successfully. To realize just how small a half-micron particle is consider these comparisons:

- • The prick of a pin is 700 times larger than a pit.

- • Five hundred atoms of hydrogen, end to end, would fit into the width of a pit.

- • The average fingernail grows half a micron in about seven minutes.

Looking at this from another perspective, a pit's proportions, or aspect ratio, are similar to those of a grain of rice. If one pit on a compact disc were the size of a single grain of rice, the proportional size of the total CD would be over 400 yards in diameter. That is the length of four football fields laid end to end.

This remarkable technology carries over to the player side. Consider that a CD player can find a specific starting point (our grain of rice) in less than a second. Players that perform this feat can be purchased for around $100 and will fit in your pocket or in the dashboard of your car. Discs can be manufactured for well under a dollar.

A CD might contain (depending on the running time) over 15 billion pits. Unlike LP records, CDs play from the inside to the outside. All these pits at a constant track pitch act like a diffraction grating. This accounts for the rainbow effect you observe when holding a disc.

Contrary to what you may have been told, pits and lands do not directly designate the 1s and 0s of binary code. Each pit edge, whether it is on the leading end or trailing end, is a 1. All areas in between are 0s. The disc's signal consists of not less than two 0s or more than ten 0s between pit edges. A pit can be only one of nine different lengths.

CDs rotate at constant linear velocity (CLV). This is necessary because the linear dimensions of the track are the same at the start of play as they are at the end of data. CD players regulate the rotational speed of the disc to maintain a constant clock rate of 4.3218 MHz. The CLV of any one disc is fixed, but CLVs on different discs can range from 1.2 to 1.4 meters per second. Players are oblivious to the difference, for they are concerned only with the constant bit rate previously mentioned.

Recalling our high school science days will assist us in understanding how light refraction enters into the picture. Remember that science experiment where a pencil is placed in a glass of water and appears to be broken? The wavelength of light changes and bends when it passes from one medium to another if these media have different refraction indices. The pencil appears broken because the change from traveling through air to traveling through water has bent the light.

The refractive index of air is 1.0 . The refractive index of CD plastic is 1.55. When the playback light beam transitions from air into a CD's plastic substrate, it slows, becomes bent, and focusing occurs. The light beam is focused to about 1.7 microns at the pit surface. The beam is over two times the width of a pit.

Land areas reflect almost 90 percent of the playback light beam back into the pickup. Remember that when the laser sees the pits from below they appear as bumps and are between 0.11 and 0.13 microns in height. There is a good reason for this dimension.

The wavelength of the playback laser light in air is 780 nanometers (nm). Once it enters the disc's plastic area

(remember that the refractive index of the plastic is 1.55)
the laser's wavelength changes to about 500 nanometers.
The height of the bump (pit) is approximately a quarter
of the laser's wavelength inside the plastic. Now, if the
bump's height is a quarter of the laser's wavelength, light
hitting a land area travels half a wavelength ($^1/_4 + ^1/_4$)
longer than light hitting a pit. A phase difference of half
a wavelength between light from a land area and light
from a pit occurs, causing cancellation. In summation, a
land area reflects light, a pit area scatters it. In practice,
to achieve a better tracking signal, the pits are just slightly shallower than the theoretical value of a quarter-wavelength, by a factor of about 20 percent.

The following table lists the dimensions that apply to
pit structures on a compact disc that achieve the
required signal for playback.

> Minimum pit length: 0.833 microns (1.2 m/s) to
> 0.972 microns (1.4 m/s).

> Maximum pit length: 3.05 microns (1.2 m/s) to
> 3.56 microns (1.4 m/s).

For all the precision involved in the manufacture of compact discs, we tend to take them for granted. Faulty new
discs are virtually unheard of, and the ones we've had
for awhile seem impervious (more or less) to whatever
torture we heap upon them. The format is incredibly
robust. As an experiment to judge the worthiness of a
CD–ROM, I once hung a bare disc from a tree branch—
and left it there for an entire year. Rain, snow, frost, and
sun faded the disc print slightly, but the disc performed
normally. There was some measurable degradation of
playback parameters, but the disc was still well within
the industry standards for those measurements.

Before you brand me as some sort of CD geek with too
much time on my hands, let me assure you that many

large CD manufacturing concerns have very sophisticated "torture chambers" that allow for the evaluation of measurable changes in the electrical properties of the disc as well as the ink used to print the identifying graphics and the lacquer sealant used to prevent oxidation of the aluminum. It is routine to test not only discs made in-house but discs from other manufacturers as well. Science is all very well and good, but the object of suspending a random disc from a tree was an attempt to give mother nature a chance to lock horns with this impressive piece of high technology manufacturing.

The pits on a compact discs are incredibly small. With some 15 billion (give or take a billion or so) pits on a disc, the precision required for manufacturing is very demanding. Fortunately, by adapting materials and processes used in other industries, CDs can be manufactured quickly and inexpensively. Although the disc itself may contain only about six cents' worth of raw materials, the machinery and manufacturing environment add a substantial cost to the finished product.

Testing CDs for Life Expectancy

Clever as the design and manufacturing processes of compact discs are, the medium is not impervious to everything. Here is a list of just some of the items that might affect the playability of a disc:

- • *Time*: The lacquer coating as well as the polycarbonate substrate can suffer from molecular breakdown.

- • *Temperature*: This variable can also degrade the lacquer coat.

- • *Corrosive solvents*: These can eat away at the lacquer until the raw aluminum layer is exposed.

Once exposed to air, aluminum will oxidize and
thereby give up its reflectivity.

- • *Mechanical stress*: Flatness and other factors may
  suffer from this if the stress is prolonged in either
  degree or time period.

- • *Ultraviolet, nuclear,* or *infrared radiation*: It takes
  less than 2 seconds for a microwave oven to render
  a disc unplayable.

- • *Handling*: Grime, scratches, and abrasions can take
  a toll over time.

- • *Acidic inks*: The ink used for cosmetic identifica-
  tion can, with time, eat through the protective lacquer coating and expose the aluminum. This was a
  common phenomenon in the early days of CDs
  (pre-1988), but is rarely seen today.

Of course, the prospects for a long life span can be
threatened even more if any of these factors are combined. The actual damage that can occur to a disc can
be classified as

- • Warping of the substrate.

- • Oxidation and/or corrosion of the aluminum layer.

- • Loss of disc transparency and discoloration.

- • A decline in the reflectivity measurement.

- • Increased birefringence.

- • An increase in the electrical noise level.

- • Delamination of the label and/or thin film layers.

- • Gouges, pits, and scratches.

When a disc begins to fail, the main signs are

- • *Loss of servo tracking*: The disc will lose its place
  and skip.

- • *An increase in error rate*: The time necessary to access data will rise dramatically.

- • *The disc jamming in the drive*: This is seen in severe cases of warping.

To a significant degree, disc performance is determined by four factors:

1. The access/playback software.

2. The data format of the disc (more on this later).

3. The alignment and design of the playback drive.

4. The physical parameters of the disc itself.

We'd be remiss if we didn't add a word or two here about some specific drive specifications. In practice, the performance of CD–ROM drives varies widely. No industry group or professional organization polices the final quality of drives. Moreover, testing equipment for discs is far easier to obtain and use than comparable equipment for the hardware used in playback.

Drives are either a three-beam or a one-beam type. Three-beam drives obtain a tracking signal from twin beams, one each to the left and right of the track. The single-beam types rely on the pits themselves. The multibeam type can overcome defects in playback more successfully than its counterpart, especially if the defect is specific to the read surface. On the other hand, single-beam drives play a wide range of HF signal levels far better. Obviously, both tracking and signal levels are of prime importance.

We now sidetrack for a minute and examine how the type of compact disc affects ease of playback (trust me, this does relate to disc quality). Let us take six types of compact disc and examine just what happens if the disc

is less than optimum. This table points up the fact that
the data structure of these six formats is widely diverse,
some formats having considerably more redundance
than others (see Table 7.1).

TABLE 7.1 CD–ROM Data Structures

DISC TYPE	BYTE	FIELD
CD–Audio	0 to 2351	User data
Mode 1 CD–ROM	0 to 11	Sync
	12 to 15	Header
	16 to 2063	User data
	2064 to 2067	EDC
	2068 to 2071	zeros
	2072 to 2351	ECC
Mode 2 CD–ROM	0 to 11	Sync
	12 to 15	Header
	16 to 2351	User data
Form 1 CD–XA/CD–I	0 to 11	Sync
	12 to 15	Header
	16 to 23	Subheader
	24 to 2071	User data
	2072 to 2075	EDC
	2076 to	2351 EDC
Form 2 CD–XA/CD–I	0 to 11	Sync
	12 to 15	Header
	16 to 23	Subheader
	24 to 2347	User data
	2348 to 2351	EDC

The "technique" various drives from different manufac-turers use can vary. For example, some drives look at EDC and/or ECC for every sector, but others consult those resources only when an error is detected. Not only must the accessible data be true and integral, but EDC and ECC must be policed to the same degree.

Here's an interesting fact (I use this fact to get free drinks, especially in the company of CD manufacturing people): Did you know that absolutely nowhere in the entire specifications for the compact disc format is the material from which the discs are to be made specified? Now, the discs you have are made out of an optical grade of polycarbonate, but they don't have to be. Some day in the future some materials or process breakthrough might lead to an economy of scale as yet unthought of. Some of these materials might be PMMA (12-inch laser discs are made from this material), certain grades of dicy-clopentadiene resin, and polymethyl pentene.

Today, injection molding is the preferred method of com-pact disc manufacture. But other methods are possible and many have even been tried. There are five other ways in which compact discs can be manufactured:

1. *Compression molding*: This was the most common method of making vinyl phonograph records. For various reasons (mostly speed of manufacturing), this method has not become popular.

2. *The 2P process*: This process uses a liquid pho-topolymer resin that is stamped and then cured with ultraviolet light. This process has proved eco-nomically feasible only in small runs.

3. *The photothermographic process*: This process turns out stamped and laminated product made from extruded polycarbonate film and sheet.

4. *Embossing*: In this process CDs are produced from a large roll of sheeted polycarbonate with aluminized mylar film. The process closely resembles that of a rotary printing press. A sheet of polycarbonate is unreeled, separated from a polyester interlayer film, and passed through a chemical softening process before the pit pattern is stamped on. Lamination is then applied before the discs are "punched" out. No clean room is needed.

5. *Photolithography*: In this process an ultraviolet light, photoresist, and an exposing process are used to put the CD pit stream onto a reflective coated plastic substrate by a contact printing process. Uncommercialized, due to the absence of a push-pull signal.

It is very possible that new research may give us more ways to make discs or that, through refinement or process evolution, one of the preceding methods might some day mount a challenge to the injection molding process, either economically or in speed of manufacture.

Regardless of the mode of disc manufacture, CD playback units must be able to recognize the presence or absence of a pit. More specific pit profiles will not and cannot facilitate better playback. A wide array of pit geometries will give equivalent playback. The playback process either works (satisfies the signal specifications) or it doesn't work at all. There is no such thing as "better" playback.

An obvious fact is that discs with pits that are sharply defined and have steep walls have a significantly higher point contact with the stamper and might be prone to a faulty separation when removed from the press. The condition known as *plowing* is prone to occur during the disc removal process. More than just cosmetic, this condition can cause significant loss of data.

CD-ROM Disc Manufacturing

Given the size of the pits that represent the data on a CD-ROM disc, manufacturing the discs requires a clean room atmosphere during all phases of the operation; contaminants invisible to the eye can obscure large amounts of data. For the same reason, extensive testing is undertaken during all phases of manufacture.

To make the CD-ROM disc, the data provider delivers the data on a suitable transfer medium (such as a CD-ROM Write-Once disc or 8-mm magnetic tape). The files and directory structures should either be defined for formatting on-site or preformatted by the data provider, in accordance with ISO 9660. Once the data is received, creating a CD-ROM disc requires eight steps:

1. Preparing a glass disc master.
2. Using a laser lathe and EFM to encode the data.
3. Creating stampers (dies).
4. Injection molding of the clear disc substrate.
5. Metallization of the clear disc.
6. Sealing the disc with lacquer.
7. Disc printing by pad, silk screening, or offset methods.
8. Packaging and shipping.

It Starts with the Glass

Whether laser-beam mastering is accomplished by dye-polymer or photoresist methods, life begins with a piece of precision glass called a *substrate*. (One current vendor, Del Mar Avionics, uses a different material—we'll cover them a bit later.) It is imperative, largely due to the fine dimensions involved, that the glass be absolutely flat, have a polished level surface, and possess precision dimensional accuracy. For this reason, "float glass" is the preferred starting point. In order to achieve the highest degree of exactness, molten glass is poured onto a bath of molten tin at 1000° centigrade. As it cools, the surface tension of the tin and the effects of gravity combine to assure precision flatness.

Such glass can be purchased with either one or two good sides. the platters can be reused many times, and if residual coating or surface particles become a problem, the option to repolish is always available. Usually, any chips, scratches, or other byproducts of human handling are the chief reasons for substrate retirement. The actual size of this glass substrate varies according to the actual brand of mastering equipment.

Whichever of the two major mastering methods (photoresist or DRAW) is used, the glass piece is washed and inspected for surface defects. The glass is first polished to optical flatness and cleaned by agitating it ultrasonically in a solution of de-ionized water and isopropyl alcohol. It is then inspected by laser while rotating. If the glass disc passes inspection, the actual mastering process can begin. It is at this point that the two methods begin to travel different paths. There are two types of mastering processes: photoresist and dye-polymer. We'll explain both.

A word or two needs to be said about vibration control during mastering, since such tight tolerances are involved. Both acoustical vibration and floor vibrations must be allowed for. A typical specification for vibration is less than $2.5 \times 10 - 3 = 10 - 2$ m/s2, from 0.25 Hz to 1000 Hz.

Laser-beam recording machines are wonders of engineering. Consider this: A typical pit is only 0.6 micron in width. The machines use an objective lens with a numerical aperture of 0.7 or 0.9 to condense the light and to generate an Airy disc of 0.5 to 0.7 micron, roughly the width of a pit. They have to image that spot of light onto the recording surface, then move it across the entire disc surface while keeping it in focus. The spot size is determined by matching the laser's power to the sensitivity of the coat material.

Laser intensity is controlled by an acousto-optic modulator, which is driven by the source encoder. Light can be transmitted only when the source encoder reposes in a relaxed state. When excited, however, the light is scattered. As the track radius advances, the rotational speed of the master is reduced; therefore the beam's velocity stays constant over the surface.

We all know that light gets dimmer and spreads out with distance. This fact dictates that the recording surface be as flat as possible. Variations in thickness of the coating on the glass will cause the focus to wander. To take this possibility into account, laser recording machines have accurate servo drives and a measuring system to make any necessary corrections. All this while the disc is turning at hundreds of revolutions per minute!

An Overview of Photoresist CD Mastering

Preparation of the Glass Master
Still further cleaning might be required with a mixture of isopropyl alcohol and de-ionized water. This wash

might aided by an ultrasonic vibration cleaning step prior to a final fluorocarbon wash. To further check for any irregularities on the surface, inspection is then carried out by focusing a laser beam on the rotating blank disc and making sure that reflective uniformity is present.

Discs meeting all these specifications are ready to have a layer of adhesive and then a layer of photosensitive material applied. Photoresist would not adhere well to the glass substrate by itself, hence the need for an adhesive, which can be uniformly dispersed at an almost unthinkably thin thickness. The adhesive used is either a silane coupling agent or a chrome film. Photoresist application is performed on a spinning application apparatus. It allows the thickness of the layer to be controlled as a function of both the rotational speed of the system and the viscosity of the photoresist itself.

Because the depth of the photoresist will determine the depth of the pits on the disc's data-bearing surface, the depth and consistency of the photoresist layer is tested using a laser to which the photoresist is insensitive. When it passes this test, the glass disc is oven-dried for stabilization. After this baking period, the master disc is ready to be used. However, it can be stored for a short period of time.

Just how can a simple layer of photoresist end up with pits of a largely trapezoidal shape? Well, as the writing laser focus on the cutting surface, it first affects the top layer of molecules. Next, it affects a smaller group of molecules underneath, then a yet smaller group, and so on, until it reaches the bottom of the photoresist. Remember that there is a layer of adhesive material below our photoresist but it is not sensitive to the laser's light. The development time for this method of mastering is extremely critical. If the development process is too short, insufficient material will be removed and the resulting pits will be too small; too much development will cause misshapen pits. The entire development process takes only 20 to 30 seconds.

Certain variables, such as the temperature of the developer and the temperature in the photoresist material itself can be compensated for by varying the development time. Normally test tracks are cut on the outside edge of the disc and monitored during development. In order to grasp just what fine tolerances are afoot here, consider this: Photoresist material is normally red in color, but when it is coated to the glass disc it is virtually colorless. In fact, it seems to have a green tinge to it!

Controlling the thickness of this resist layer, in which any defects would be carried through to all further discs, is done with an optical scanner and ellipsometer. Should any blanks not meet specifications at any of the checkpoints they may be returned to the polishing or coating processes and reused.

Cutting and Developing the Glass Master

The cutting of the glass master, which is produced from a customer's data, is done in rooms of class 10,000 air purity. The laser writes or exposes patterns of pits on the photoresist by transferring information from the master image. The disc is then developed; exposed parts are etched away; the actual pit structure of the finished disc is created; visual inspection for flaws and defects is carried out; and the disc is then electroplated with nickel. Examining this process in more detail yields better insight into the process.

The master is placed on a lathe and is then exposed with a cutting laser using Argon Ion ($D = 0.4579$ micron) or Helium-Cadmium ($D = 0.4416$ micron) wavelengths in order to form the spiral track of pits.

The information modulates the intensity of the lasers. The photoresist is sensitive to these wavelengths at relatively low power, and small pits are obtained without difficulty by using short wavelengths. The cutting laser moves from the inside to the outside as the disc revolves, exactly opposite to the cutting of a master for a conventional LP record. As track radius increases, velocity decreases, thereby maintaining constant linear velocity (CLV) and resulting in a longer playing time.

Light is absorbed in the exposed area, which changes the solubility. The height structure of the pits appears in the development stage when an alkaline solution dissolves the exposed photoresist. Monitoring with a Helium-Neon laser gives information on how development is progressing, indicates when to stop development, and allows a well-defined pit structure to be obtained. This development cycle lasts an average of 20 to 30 seconds.

In theory, a pit depth that would result in complete absorption of light, thereby distinguishing it from the reflective land, would produce the optimal data signal. This can be done by making the pit depth one quarter of the apparent wavelength of the laser pickup and by controlling the pit width so that the light intensity of reflections from the pit bottom and the surface are equal. In actuality the pit width and depth are altered a bit to beef up the signal. Since the disc will be read from the side opposite the label, pits appear as bumps from the readout side.

Although the explanation of the process you have just read might seem quite structured, many ancillary systems contribute to the success (or failure) of photoresist mastering. Here is a rundown of these areas:

- • *Glass prep station*: In this area glass masters can be reclaimed by stripping off any leftover adhesive or photoresist debris in an acid bath. Once this has been accomplished, recoating is attempted.

- • *Developing stations* and *curing ovens*: On the other side of the actual laser beam recording assembly one might find these areas. Additionally, a master disc player will likely be close by.

- • *Clean room*: Clean rooms are ultracontrolled environments that are designed to keep out dust, dirt, and other contaminants that can have deleterious affects on the mastering, plating, molding, and lacquering processes. Clean rooms are rated by the number of particles (ranging in size from 0.5 to 5 microns) that are present in a cubic foot of air during one minute. So a class 1000 clean room should have no more than that number of particles per minute per cubic foot. Air in rural areas can contain a million particles per foot. Urban area air can easily exceed five times that amount. Typical particles are items such as talcum powder, pollen, hair, microorganisms, and flakes of skin.

The dirtiest thing in a clean room? *Humans!* Even sitting in a still state, a human can shed 100,000 or so particles *per minute*. The same person engaging in moderate motion can give off over a million particles per minute. When walking at the leisurely rate of just 2 miles an hour it's possible to exude 5 million particles per minute. Obviously, the fewer humans in the clean room area, the easier job the air scrubbing apparatus has to perform. Because of our tight tolerances, glass mastering of all types is carried out in a class 100 clean room. Although modern photoresist systems are far less troublesome than previous incarnations, the human factor is still very important.

When the glass disc has been exposed, it is developed. The chemical developer removes exposed portions of the photoresist; the unexposed remains. Thus the glass disc now has a pitted layer of photoresist on it, with the pits corresponding to the times when the cutting laser beam modulator allowed the laser beam to hit the disc.

An Overview of Dye-Polymer Mastering

Dye-polymer (DP) optical recording cannot be classified as a new technology. The process has been used in read/write disc technology for several years. Both Pioneer and Kodak currently market systems using DP technology. It is, in fact, the very basis of the CD–Write-Once systems that are so popular today.

The dye itself is dissolved in a polymer solution. Dye-polymers are grain-free, capable of high resolution, and have no crystal structure. Like glass, they are amorphous.

The temperature of the 18M de-ionized water used for the final rinse of the glass is held constant to within $\pm 0.5°C$. The glass is held upside down during the coating process while the dye polymer is "squirted" on the disc from below. This method prevents any airborne particles from settling on the recording surface during this process.

In the dye-polymer process specific to compact disc mastering, the DP solution is spun directly onto a glass substrate without the use of an adhesive agent. Typical film thickness is 2100 angstroms ± 50 angstroms. The exact thickness is a function of the molding environment at the manufacturing site. A 1-liter bottle of DP solution can coat up to 50 discs, with up to 8 pieces of glass being prepped in 1 hour. After coating, the film thickness can be checked by the use of a light transmission meter (LTM).

The dye-polymer coating is very sensitive to the 488-nm wavelength of an Argon-Ion laser beam and absorbs the beam, causing a thermochemical decomposition process. The material in the cut area turns to gas (CO_2 and water vapor); since no real debris is generated microseconds after cutting, a Helium-Neon laser reads back the pits and provides a real-time readout of asymmetry, I_{11} amplitude, and (after decoding) an accurate block error rate. The focus of the Helium-Neon laser is set to the standard of an ordinary playback unit. After cutting, the master is placed in a forced air oven for thirty minutes at 100°C. This forced air is of class 100 purity. Baking has nothing to do with the sensitivity of the process. Its sole purpose is to remove any residual moisture on the disc. This insures that during the vacuum metallization stage, the nickel coating will properly adhere to the dye-polymer surface. Under moisture-free conditions metallizing can be delayed for up to 12 hours.

A proprietary program utilizing two-dimensional fast Fourier transforms for calculating predictable and accurate pit/bump profiles is implemented during the mastering process. There are two methods of entering the desired parameters for mastering:

As a mathematical model.

As an AFM output file.

The program simulates disc playback along a track containing both the longest (11 T) and the shortest (3 T) pits after 8-to-14 modulation. Thus, push-pull, I_3 and I can easily be ascertained for a specified profile. Usually, some production parameters must be adjusted in order to meet industry standards and specifications and to ensure that all variables interact properly. For instance, this program can quickly calculate signal amplitude when given a fixed value for push-pull.

One advantage of DP (dye-polymer) mastering is that a real-time servo-controlled feedback loop allows for adjustable control of asymmetry. If the asymmetry is held to a constant value, individual masters are virtually indistinguishable from each other. The feedback circuit is continuously variable from 0 to 20 percent. Controlling the asymmetry controls the pit profile, regardless of the thickness.

A concerted effort to adapt ultraviolet laser technology to photoresist mastering is afoot in Japan. Although both dye-polymer and photoresist mastering systems use visible light lasers for cutting, the fact that the 442-nm laser runs so close to the edge (photoresist will not react to lasers above 457.9 nm) has caused a renewed interest in ultraviolet (UV) lasers. Until now, lasers of this type have resided only in laboratory settings, no commercial applications have materialized. They're large, consume prodigious amounts of power, and are invisible to the eye!

An Overview of the Del Mar System

This unique mastering system is, more or less, an outgrowth of the high-tech military training materials and medical diagnostic equipment development background of the Del Mar Avionics Company of Irvine, California. Unlike the two other systems we've discussed so far, this mastering method does not employ glass substrates in its process. Instead, the end user of the system would use a precoated master disc with a precision 145-mm polycarbonate substrate obtained directly from Del Mar. The disc is 6 mm thick and 148 mm across, and is covered with a black plastic cover, which in turn is sealed in an airtight bag, which prevents environmental contamination. Shelf life is some 6 months. It is discarded after use.

The disc is pregrooved (a precise track is in place to facilitate the cutting laser's role). This laser cuts through the disc's cover and creates the pits along the preformed track. After cutting, the cover is removed and the master is processed in a standard industry manner. Since no on-site coating or glass recovery stations are needed, a space and economic advantage might be realized.

Electroforming

The master disc is coated with a 400-Å nickel or silver film to make it conductive. Then a coating of 99.99 percent pure nickel is electroplated over the first coating, to make a metal disc called a *father*. The nickel surface of the father, which was adjacent to the silver, is a mirror but negative image of the master disc; its lands (flat areas) correspond to lands, and its pits to spikes. Actual electroforming is begun at a slow rate so not as to "burn" the master disc. As the nickel buildup on the master increases in thickness, automatic control circuits increase the current to speed up the process.

The nickel's father's data side is inert due to passivation. When the father is electroplated, it produces another nickel part called a *mother*, which is an exact replica of the photoresist or dye polymer on the master disc.

This mother disc is used to create *sons*. The sons are copies of the father and are trimmed to size, punched with a center hole, and precisely backsanded to prevent "nodes" (surface irregularities), which would affect the smoothness and surface uniformity of the finished discs. We now have a plate that can generate tens of thousands of plastic replicas for market.

Intermediate Testing

Test pressings from the sons are submitted to bit-for-bit and block error rate (BLER) tests. Bit-for-bit testing compares 100 percent of the data on the disc against the original input data by comparing the bit streams of the two. Block error rate testing reads each sector and records how many require EDAC to correct errors—a good measure of disc quality.

Molding the Plastic Wafer

When the initial pressings from the sons test successfully, the stamping dies are ready for production. Pellets of polycarbonate (similar in appearance to rock salt) are blown into dryers to remove any moisture, a potential source of blemishes. They are then melted, and then molten polycarbonate is injected between the stamper and mold.

The faster and faster cycle times demanded by the ever-falling price of molded replicates have created a not insignificant pressure on the makers of polycarbonate material to formulate blends to allow more speedy manufacture. In the first few years after the introduction of the CD, cycle times were in the 15-second range. Today, they have achieved the sub-5-second range.

One method polycarbonate manufacturers have used to respond to the market is by increasing the MFI (melt flow index) to 65 to 70 g/10 min at 300°C. By way of reference, standard grades of polycarbonate have MFI figures in the 3 to 16 range. Heat stabilizing and agents to facilitate mold release are also added.

In addition to enhancing the purity of the plastic material, the goals of plastic manufacturers are to facilitate manufacture of discs that have minimal molecular orientation and residual stress. CD-grade polycarbonate is manufactured under clean room conditions, and even something as insignificant as the size of the finished pellets can affect the molding characteristics of the plastic blend. The smaller the pellets, the better the plasticizing time; however, pellets that are too small tend to clog valves and gather in "dead spots" in the distribution network. Typical figures might be a deflection temperature of 125°C under a 1.84-MPa load, flexural modulus of 2.1 GPa and Izod impact strength of 300 J/m.

One characteristic of polycarbonates that can cause trouble if not monitored is the hygroscopic penchant of the material. It is typical of these resins to absorb water, even from humid air. For best results, no more than 0.02 percent moisture content is acceptable. If this threshold is not held, residual moisture can attack the carbonate linkage of the polymer and bring about a defect known as chain scission. To combat this effect, raw plastic pellets are placed into hopper/drying units, usually for about 4 hours at a temperature of 2500°F. These units are designed to remove moisture from the atmosphere inside.

Optical-grade polycarbonate does not measurably degrade owing to its native inertness and, until recently, has been hard to recycle because of contamination by the aluminum, lacquer, and ink used in the CD making process. Recently, GE Plastics and Star Brite Industries of Darlington, Pennsylvania, have begun to actively solicit used polycarbonate for recycling .

The smooth surface of the polycarbonate is designed to protect the data-bearing surface while allowing light from the drive's laser to pass through. The surface adjacent to the stamper bears an exact image of the original pattern in the photoresist; it will be aluminized to provide a reflecting surface.

The first few generations of CD manufacturing equipment used a "batch" system. This means that each set in the process (molding, aluminizing, lacquering, and printing) was performed as a separate function, usually at a different position within the factory area. This was inefficient, to say the least. Batch processing meant transporting discs from one station to another, higher personnel requirements, and a higher rejection rate due to susceptible discs being exposed (and therefore vulnerable to damage and contamination). Total throughput of the factory floor was also limited.

With the advent of in-line systems, discs are often molded, metallized, and printed in a window of 10 seconds or less, thereby reducing contamination and increasing the percentage of acceptable discs. More important, the footprint of each station is dramatically smaller, allowing for more output per square foot of factory space. Space savings can reach the 40 percent range.

A cost saving is also realized because instead of conditioning thousands of square feet of air to class 100 clean room requirements, only critical areas of the disc-making process need to be maintained to this purity. This can be achieved by placing hooded air-cleaning devices over critical areas. By using positive pressure (downward) in the molding, metallizing, and lacquering areas, dirt and particle control can be maintained. For a yearly output of 10 million discs, a batch system might require over 900 m^2, whereas an in-line system with the same yearly output might take only 2.5 m^2 of space.

The increased demand for CD replication equipment has spurred an amazing refinement of robotic operations involved in the disc making process, specifically in moving discs from one station of operation to another. One such development has been the advent of carbon-fiber-reinforced epoxy articulated arms that weigh just 10 percent of the equivalent steel version. Such an advance allows for very fast and accurate movement. Other innovations include double cylinders, aluminum sliders, and linear bearings.

Cam robots even have a direct mechanical link to the stroke mechanism of the injection molding machine. This allows robotic movements that are precisely in sync with the opening and closing of the mold. A variable pitch system allows such robots to speed up and slow down. Further efficiency is achieved by placing the robotic arm that removes fresh discs from the mold outside the tool area yet inside the guard, thereby keeping the path of movement to a minimum. It's important to remember that the discs are still cooling when grabbed by the robot. By having an arm that handles the disc in four places instead of the normal two, distortion along the axial plane of the disc is reduced. Both electrical and pneumatic robots are used. The electrical type are almost twice the cost of the latter, but can be financially attractive for some functions. Electrical robots achieve smoother movements at high acceleration speeds than those of the pneumatic type; however, pneumatic robots are easier to service and have a high reliability factor.

Better servo motors have meant that a good power-to-weight ratio can be achieved along with low power consumption and excellent dynamic properties. Telescopic layouts have meant that overhead space requirements have been reduced. Robots can now remove a fresh disc from the press in less than a second. Robots excel in performing repetitive functions and reducing manpower requirements, but they can't "see" and therefore allow for functions or situations they are not programmed for. The use of robots has expanded from just the disc-manufacturing process to the packaging aspect of the CD business. Today, robots can open jewel boxes, insert printed material, correctly place both tray and disc, close the box, and shrink-wrap it.

Aluminizing the Disc

Although gold or silver can and have been used to metal-lize the polycarbonate, 99.5 percent pure aluminum is the normal choice. To apply it, the polycarbonate wafers are introduced into an anode/cathode chamber with an argon atmosphere. Applying a voltage through the argon excites its molecules, which impact and drive molecules from the cathode, an aluminum slug. The aluminum molecules deposit uniformly on the anode and the poly-carbonate wafer, a process called *sputtering*.

Coating the Data Surface

In order to protect the aluminum-coated data-bearing surface, a strong-sealing, durable lacquer is coated onto the metal surface. The disc is spun while the lacquer is dispensed on the disc's surface, centrifugal force being used to assure a consistent coating over the face of the disc. The disc is then sent to an ultraviolet light tunnel. The type of lacquer used is sensitive to UV light. This exposure causes it to cross-link and solidify. Ultraviolet lacquer exhibits better moisture absorption characteris-tics than the air-dried variety. After the lacquer is applied, the discs move into a quality-control system.

Printing and Packaging

The customer furnishes suitable negatives of camera-ready copy for cosmetic decoration of the finished discs. This decoration is accomplished on the lacquered side of the disc (in other words, the nonread side). Special inks are used in either case to ensure compatibility and inert behavior with either the lacquer coating or the polycarbonate. Inks that are too acidic may eat through the lacquer coating over time. If this happens, the aluminum becomes exposed to air and will oxidize, causing the disc to be difficult or impossible to read.

In years past, pad printing was the method of choice, and it is still used at some manufacturing sites. It has fallen from favor because of its lower resolution, about 85 lines, and silk screening is currently the most common method of disc printing. Offset printing is the system of choice for picture discs because it offers 150-line resolution, but the throughput is lower than silk screen: Offset does 50 to 55 parts per minute whereas silk screen puts out 70 parts per minute. An advantage to offset is a reduced cost of operation: Less ink is used and screens (there is one screen for each color used) last longer, about 10,000 impressions are possible. Disadvantages to the offset process are labor and added preparation work. Labor costs are higher because more training is needed for each operator. At times, colors are hard to stabilize and hold consistent.

Disc printing can be accomplished either *off line* or *in line*. In line means that the disc is printed immediately after lacquer coating. Off line means that after lacquering, the discs are set aside and printed at a later time. Economically, it would be ideal if all discs were printed in line; however, the process can vary in setup time. This means that injection molding, coating, and lacquering may have to be delayed until this setup is accomplished. In line is far easier if the disc print is only one or two colors. For complex printing jobs, extra discs are usually replicated to allow for quality-control acceptance.

It's safe to assume that more discs will fail printing quality control in complex jobs (three colors and up). For four-color or picture discs, customers must furnish a color proof that displays how the finished product should look. This print will aid factory personnel in determining how best to accomplish the print process (i.e., the specific order in which the ink colors are applied).

It is important that customers be strongly motivated to send in both color-separated laser outputs and a copy of the graphics file on floppy disc to the replication facility well ahead of the arrival of the data. These items should be inspected on the day of arrival and either judged suitable or not suitable for use. If these items are deemed unacceptable, the customer is contacted immediately with specific information regarding the judgment. Early arrival of these items will allow customers to resubmit the goods without impacting the delivery date of the discs.

At times, even though these items are physically acceptable, their nature may be such that they may produce disappointing results. For instance, too low a screen frequency can create an image that appears "posterized," and differing screen angles of the film and screen angles of the silk screens can cause a severe moiré effect. Again, prompt notification of the customer as well as a short education in the unique demands of printing on plastic help prevent delay of the order. New facilities should realize that fixing these problems on site is a chargeable task. The amount of revenue that can be generated can vary, but is usually enough to pay for a desktop publishing workstation and, depending on the size of the facility, a Linotronic machine to generate new film. Popular graphics programs such as Illustrator, Harvard Graphics, Corel Draw, Freehand, and others must be supported.

After the printing process is completed, the discs are moved into the packaging department, where they are suitably packaged and boxed for shipping. Jewel boxes remain a main source of packaging for compact discs. A typical jewel box contains some 85 grams of crystal polystyrene. Estimates put the amount of polystyrene used for jewel box manufacture in the Unites States in 1994 at over 33,000 tons.

Pressure from environmentalists has caused a rise in both pure cardboard and hybrid packaging. These packages, although pleasing to the "greenies" of the world, are very nonstandard in their configurations, and so difficult to automate. Larger companies such as Capitol and Warner Brothers make their own jewel boxes by injection molding. A three-machine system manufactured by Netstal can produce 22 million jewel boxes per year.

Thoughts on HDCD

With the advent of high-density compact-disc (HDCD) manufacture looming ever nearer, it is prudent that we step back and look at the entire manufacturing process. We do this with the idea that not only will both the art and science of disc replication be redefined, generation of a top-quality product will command a much more concerted effort in many areas.

Clearly, four distinct areas will be severely affected:

1. Glass Mastering
2. Injection Molding
3. Raw Materials
4. Test Equipment and Procedures

Processes and procedures will need to be reviewed and analyzed; the economic factors that will affect the manufacturing must be identified, implemented, and understood. High-density disc manufacture will greatly impact the injection-molding process, and that is the thrust of this section.

Current standards (Red Book) allow for a rather broad spectrum of signal amplitudes. It is easy to replicate acceptable product with as much as a 30 percent variation between the original glass master and a replicated part. This swing in the physical fidelity of a finished disc as compared to the original cut has proven to be most noticeable as a byproduct of accelerated cycle times.

The reduced pit dimensions, track pitch, and other criteria will not allow for such a wide swing of accuracy. Longer cycle times would seem to be an intrinsic part of our future. Without question, molding will have to be monitored with increasing vigilance, and constant attention must be paid to the end product.

The providers of glass mastering equipment would seem to face a daunting list of operating challenges, but before we proceed to discuss the various routes open to them and the stricter parameters they will need to meet, let us briefly look back at specific considerations encountered in the mass manufacture of the compact disc's closest antecedent—the analog laser disc—that affect both the cost and manufacture of that medium.

In marked contrast to CD manufacturing, the laserdisc format required pits with steep walls to achieve high contrast and reduce video noise. The average possible linear pit density was most ambitious—807 pits per millimeter. By comparison, standard CDs have only 238 pits per millimeter. In order to get a 40-dB signal-to-noise ratio in video playback, laserdiscs were required to hold the tolerance of their pit edges to about 50 Å. Compare this to the CD format, which has a tolerance of 1500 Å. This is a 3000 percent difference.

The steep pits and well-defined edges proved a real challenge to manufacture. Release of product from the stamper brought us face to face with a condition known as *plowing*, *staining*, or *clouding*. To this day yields in laserdisc manufacturing facilities are far below the yield of a typical CD facility. The lack of "draft" (the gradual diminution of thickness, diameter, or width given to a part so that the work can be easily withdrawn) is often cited as a cause for plowing. The need for a sufficient taper or draft on an injection molded item is well known. Molded parts with angles approaching 90°C are difficult to eject from the press and tend to have high stress levels.

The present CD standard has two large manufacturing advantages over the laserdisc format:

1. A far less critical pit density.
2. Pits with no specific shape or angle requirement, only the necessity that playback units recognize the presence or absence of a pit.

Plowing still occurs in CD manufacture, although it is almost always just a cosmetic defect. Only in the severest of cases has it been known to hinder playback. It is most commonly found toward the outside edge of a disc and is thought to be exacerbated when a disc begins cooling (therefore shrinking) while still in contact with the stamper. Plowing is neither an electrical or functional problem in the present CD making process.

The argument can be made that pits with steep, well-defined walls have more surface contact during the molding cycle than a shallower, more gradual pit, and so are less likely to release cleanly from the mold and therefore contribute to plowing. The significance of plowing in high-density molding will be covered shortly.

Mastering for High Density

On first glance it would seem that all that is needed here is a higher numerical aperture. Not so. It is going to take far more than that because the aspect ratio of high-density pits will change. In addition to the track pitch, the pit width and length will also be halved. The depth will change according to the wavelength of the playback laser. It is relatively simple to accomplish this by reducing the diameter of the recording light spot with a higher numerical aperture lens. Standard discs are cut with a spot diameter of about 55 meters. If a higher numerical aperture is used, a spot diameter of about 0.3 meter can be achieved. It is not yet clear what the playback wavelength will be dropped to (it is now 780 nm), but it likely will be somewhere between 635 to 670 nm. For our purposes, we'll assume the new wavelength to be 650 nm.

If so, then our pit depth will only decrease 17 percent. As you can see, we are rapidly migrating toward a deeper pit with narrower sides and steeper slopes, with a corresponding loss of draft. This fact, coupled with the huge increase in the number of pits should elevate the occurrence and severity of plowing to a level as yet undreamed of by most of us.

The Challenge

It is a very common practice these days to match certain mastering parameters to one's particular molding environment. The vagaries of the injection molding process can cause pit profiles to be of quite a different value than the metal mother. This value can approach a 35 percent difference in I_{11}, for instance. Although such differences present themselves in all facilities, the widest spread of such changes occur in plants that use presses from more than one manufacturer or presses of different age or models. Various CD signal specifications can overlap and thus constrain the pit profile of the replica (e.g., a trade-off between I_{11} amplitude and push-pull).

If you haven't investigated how your particular system can accomplish this, right now is an ideal time to start. Ideally, depth, width, and length should be able to be put under some sort of control, such as a servo system. An added plus would be the ability to determine what adjustments are needed in real time as the glass mastering is taking place.

Since a wide variation of pit profiles will give satisfactory playback (there is no "best" pit structure for playback) an additional item to be factored in is the ease of moldability of pit structure. Pits of a smaller size just might be affected by an amount of plowing that would be merely cosmetic on a disc with standard pits. Microscopy studies have shown acceptable product being made where the most important dimension, depth, is molded 30 percent smaller than the height of the bump on the stamper. This "shrinkage" is usually the greatest where the molding cycle times are the shortest.

In a molding facility, where cycle time is money, the presses will always be run at the fastest cycle time that will make acceptable product. Therefore, the shrinkage will be as large as the tolerances will allow. When high-density compact discs are made, all of the dimensions, and therefore the tolerances, will be significantly reduced. Consequently, the accuracy of replication of the pits must be higher, requiring longer cycle times.

The second area replication must deal with is the geometry (profile) of the bumps on the stamper and its ease of molding. The basic change in profile associated with all mastering methods is the change in aspect ratio (the ratio of height to width of the pit). As mentioned before, the width and length will be cut in half but the height will not. This means the pits must be more sharply defined with steeper slopes to achieve adequate optical resolution for good signal playback. In the photoresist method of mastering, steeper slopes are achieved by reducing the spot size, increasing the exposure, and reducing the development activity or duration.

With enough careful control, this change in profile can be easily achieved in the photoresist mastering process, but it causes serious problems in the subsequent molding of the replica, resulting in a substantial increase in the manufacturing cost of compact discs. The problems are manifested in a problem known as plowing *stains* or *clouds*, and are visible with the naked eye, resembling a roughly circular watermark staining the middle of the recorded area.

Because the photoresist mastering process forms the pits by chemical etching all the way down to the glass surface, the bottoms of the pits are always flat. Therefore, whenever the slopes are made steep, there will be a sharp corner at the bottom of the pit. When converted to a stamper, this sharp corner is prone to damage the sides of the pits molded in the compact disc at the time the plastic disc separates from the stamper. The damage is caused by the fact that the plastic disc has a large coefficient of thermal expansion (or contraction) and is cooling rapidly at the time the mold is opened. Therefore, there is a large radial shearing force at the interface between the plastic and the stamper. This force is released when the mold opens, causing the molded disc to shrink radially across the face of the stamper.

If the bumps on the stamper have sharp corners, there will be locations on the surface of the disc where the shearing force becomes high enough for the plastic to yield, causing the outer walls of the pits to be deformed or pushed away from the center of the disc. This deformation is visible to the naked eye because wherever the pits have been deformed, the pit area has increased, causing an increase in the diffraction efficiency of those pits. Your eye can easily see the shift in color caused by this local change in diffraction efficiency, which looks like a local stain. This is a common problem in manufacturing plants using photoresist mastering and has become much more troublesome in the efforts to produce high-density CDs.

In addition to the cosmetic defect caused by plowing, there is an increase in jitter, which can lead to higher BLER and, in extreme cases, loss of data, even on standard-density discs. On high-density discs, the tolerance for jitter is dramatically reduced, so high block error rates become a serious problem whenever plowing occurs. Current developmental work on high-density CD molding at a number of different facilities has shown a dramatic increase in plowing due to the steep slopes and sharp corners present on photoresist mastered stampers. To contend with this problem, typical cycle times have become more than double those of standard compact disc molding and the yield has gone down substantially. Again, these results indicate there will be at least a doubling of the manufacturing cost of compact discs using this approach.

Trials of high-density CDs manufactured with PMMA are also underway. PMMA is the plastic of choice for laserdisc manufacture. It is heavier than water but only half as dense as glass. The advantages of PMMA are two:

- • Cheaper than polycarbonate with excellent optical properties.
- • Low shrinkage and ease of moldability.

However, PMMA tends to absorb moisture and "dish," although the effect is reversible and not a factor except in the harshest of environments, such as an automobile.

chapter 8

Optical
Playback

Light has always been a fascination and delight for the human mind. The emerging optical technologies promise machinery that will make the Industrial Age appear downright medieval. The compact disc is a feat of precision manufacturing, but its utility emerges from the use of a "Buck Rogers ray-gun" to read it.

The photonic pulse from a laser-emitting diode travels through a chamber containing lenses, mirrors, other diodes, and a few moving parts. The light bounces against the pits of the compact disc, after which the light's modulation is a reflection of the subcode information on the disc surface. The photosensitive diode in the read-head assembly converts this flickering light beam into a pulsating RF signal (a pattern of electrons that represents the information of the data stream).

The day will come when this photon-to-electron conversion is unnecessary. Recent publications celebrate the independence of digital data from its carrying media. We might add to this that optical technology—in which the information travels at the fastest possible speed unburdened by the inertia of mass—is really the most appealing. Optical computing will eventually become standard, and photonic transmission will supplant electronic transmission as the basis of wired (as opposed to satellite) communication.

So where does the CD drive fit into all this grandiose talk? Front and center. As of this writing, over 92 percent of the world's lasers are in CD players. The playback assemblies that read compact discs are the first dissemination of the emerging optical technologies to the general public.

It is a well-known rule of mechanical engineering that the moving parts always get you into trouble (or break down). It is ironic that this old saw applies so well to CD playback: The spindle that rotates the disc and the sled on which the read-head assembly slides back and forth are the two main measures of a drive's performance.

In addition to these two servomechanisms (or moving parts), CD drives contain two fine-adjustment servos: one for focus and one to stay "on track." After discussing the servos, we will review other considerations, such as SCSI versus IDE logical drivers, the size of the drive's buffer, external versus internal drives, multidisc drives, caddies, and so forth.

Spindle and Sled Servomechanisms

The spindle turns the CD while the sled, on which the read-head assembly is mounted, slides along a track moving the objective lens closer to or farther away from the spindle (see Figure 8.1). An "objective lens" in a multilens observational apparatus is the lens closest to the object that is being observed.

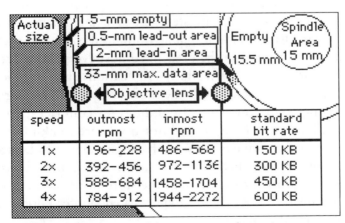

speed	outmost rpm	inmost rpm	standard bit rate
1x	196–228	486–568	150 KB
2x	392–456	972–113€	300 KB
3x	588–684	1458–1704	450 KB
4x	784–912	1944–2272	600 KB

FIGURE 8.1 Variable CD rates of rotation.

Writers alternately refer to the single-speed ($1\times$) constant bit rate as 150 KB/s, 153 KB/s, or 154 KB/s. If we multiply the 75 sectors per second by the 2048 bits that actually contain data in a CD–ROM's 2352-bit logical sector, then we arrive at the constant bit rate of 153,600 bits per second. This is the true number, so the conflicting 150/153/154 claims are just different ways of expressing this number in kilobytes.

Most writers for the general public use the convention (which is generally true for science) that "kilo-" equals 1000. According to this logic 153 KB is 153,600 bits truncated and 154 KB is the same number of bits rounded up.

On the other hand, CD–ROM standards are written by "computer-science types" who handle binary digital data all the time. The convention among binary data-handlers is to treat a kilobyte as 210 bytes—or 1024! Before you get too shocked by this unusual convention, imagine spending most of every workday operating in base 2. Digital professionals are inclined to think that base-10 counting is moribund and the result of evolutionary accident: "Had humans evolved with only one finger, we might have adopted binary more commonly, but there would have been a grave risk of causing offence when counting." (from *The Art of Digital Audio*, by John Watkinson.) If you divide the constant bit rate of 153,600 by 1024, out pops 150 KB/s, which is what is specified in the standard.

So double-speed drives, which are standard as of this writing, run at 300 KB/s and quad drives run at twice that. Triple-speed drives were introduced as an intermediate step, but their main achievement was having the popular "Rebel Assault" game optimized to run on them. These data rates are honored in the breach: Almost every CD drive is either a little faster or a little slower. Many publications run periodic lab tests of CD drives, and you can check the numbers yourself by purchasing one of a wide range of good software utilities for compact discs. This is why the most important thing to look for if you are thinking of purchasing a compact disc drive is a money-back guarantee! But, as we shall see, the goal of "faster is better" is affected by numerous different factors, so don't return your $4\times$ drive to the store just because it's running at 590 KB instead of 600. (Note: Expect to encounter kilobytes per second abbreviated as KBps.)

Variable Rotation Rate Achieves Constant Bit Rate

As discussed in Chapter 2, the consistent storage density along the compact disc's recorded track requires that the playback drive read the data using Constant Linear Velocity (CLV). For an audio compact disc playing start to finish, the adjustments this requires in the spindle's rotation rate and the sled's positioning are for the most part gradual. Even when skipping ahead to outer audio tracks, any slowness in positioning and rotation-rate adjustment may appear to be subsumed by the premusic pause. Whether the music is Allegro, Heavy-Metal, or Dance-Funk, listeners are prepared to expect a brief delay of several seconds before the music starts.

The constant bit rate for CD–ROM is less than that for CD–Audio because the logical sector was redesigned (under the Yellow Book standard) to store any kind of data instead of exclusively digital audio. If a CD–ROM is recorded in mixed mode so as to contain audio sectors (75 sectors per second, each with 2352 bytes of sampled data, equals 176,400 bytes per second), then even a quad-speed drive will generally slow down to 196 revolutions per minute to play the disc (although it could read/rotate faster and store future samples in the buffer). Video data, as well as audio, is defined by human perception in real time, but most categories of data that can be stored on a CD–ROM are not time dependent, so faster is better! The principle of reading data off the CD–ROM at a constant bit rate, however, using constant linear velocity, is essentially unchanged by this faster-is-better outlook.

Instead of constant bit rate, what you have is an average bit rate for sequential throughput. This is only achieved once the read head has locked onto a large file and can stay in position for a while reading it (honest, that's how they test this). Quad speed is a big advantage for large files, so for graphics and video users it can save hours of worktime (the extra expense of these drives is negligible compared to what warm bodies cost). Compact disc developers know they have to optimize their up-and-coming titles to 4×, so you can expect larger files in the future.

Access Time and Coordinated Functioning

Now back to the spindle and sled. *They have to work together.* The stream of data from the CD–ROM won't start flowing until the spindle is turning at the proper rate and the sled has positioned the read assembly under the correct logical sector to be read. For a short jump, the logical driver can just count sectors until it gets to a few tracks farther out or in, but this would be hopeless for a big jump in or out. Don't forget that the 1.6-micron track pitch specification means there can be over 22,000 tracks on a CD. So for big jumps, the spindle and sled have to "guess."

Successive approximation (the basic kind, not the JPEG kind) is a well-known algorithm for determining square roots, and it operates somewhat like guessing. Although Newton is credited with it, many schoolchildren feel they invented it themselves while taking tests. If you need to find an answer, sometimes the rough way is the fastest way, so you can guess, check your answer, guess again, check your answer, and keep on narrowing it down until you get it right. This is what the spindle and sled have to do repeatedly. A centimeter jump is over 6000 tracks, and even the fastest quad rpm of 2272 only checks out to about 37 turns a second, so it could take minutes to methodically count from point A to point B. Instead, the sled pushes off with its best guess, the spindle calculates the approximate rotational velocity at which it should be turning when the sled stops, the spindle adjusts the speed until the proper bit rate is achieved so that it's possible to get a read on the address, and then the whole process starts over again until the destination is finally reached.

Of course, this has been a *highly* anthropomorphic explanation. There are different kinds of sleds, some more traditionally mechanical, some using newer electromagnetic techniques that reduce friction, and some relying more heavily on a small-tilting mirror to make smaller jumps. There are different kinds of spindles, and clearly the most important requirement is a high-torque engine for all of the changes in acceleration that are required to reach the desired velocities quickly (and don't forget that kinetic energy is a function of velocity squared, so twice as fast means four times the energy). These design differences translate into variations in performance, but the logical driver (and its interface with the computer's CPU) is what issues instructions and guides the spindle to rotate at different velocities and the sled to occupy different positions.

When discussing data rates, we had the formally standardized 150 KB/s and its multiples to serve as benchmarks. No such standardization exists for consistently measuring how long it takes to get to the data. As we have shown, compact discs were designed to achieve enormous efficiencies of storage and manufacture. But the fact that the logical driver has to coordinate the sled and spindle as they play their guessing game is really a correlated inefficiency, and is partly to blame for CD–playback devices remaining relatively costly. It is also why CD–ROM drives have always been slower than hard disk drives, which move at a constant rotational speed (or constant angular velocity, CAV).

The access time required to get to the data before it can begin to stream out of the drive at a constant rate is commonly measured in milliseconds. Whereas hard disk drives will often have average access times of about a dozen or several dozen milliseconds, CD drives are so slow in comparison that one barely needs such scientific precision. It used to be that a CD–ROM single-speed drive might take a whole second of access time to get to the sector to be read. It is apparent why data rate and access time have had to be two separate measures of CD drive performance: If they were measured together, then an access time of one second would imply a data rate of zero! Access time of half a second became the norm for several years; a quarter-second access time is still more a common goal than a common achievement.

Clearly, what the CD drive has to accomplish during this access time is a complex process. Its description often borrows from hard disk drive technology:

1. *Seek time*: Read head repositioned to desired track.

2. *Latency*: Desired data rotates to the read head's position.

3. *Translation*: Data is read and transferred out of the drive.

This is inadequate to describe the CD–ROM process primarily because the constant linear velocity must be *very closely* approximated before any meaningful information can be read off the compact disc. The spindle can only estimate the approximate rate of rotation that should match the sled's new location. Performance improvements in this area have been achieved by including a position sensor on the read-head assembly, but since the margin for error is only 1.6 microns on either side (the track pitch), that only achieves a superior approximation.

This is a kind of settling-in period during which the rate of rotation is subjected to fine adjustments until CLV is attained for the new track position. A hard disk does not have a settling-in period because it spins with constant angular velocity (CAV), so reading may commence immediately subsequent to the read-head jump. See Figures 8.2 to 8.5 for a corrected, four-part description of the process.

A secondary fault with the hard disk description, one that is not corrected by simply adding the settling-in period, is that this simple model may have to be reiterated several times before the correct address is finally arrived at. So CD–ROM access time should be more accurately defined as consisting of a four-part process—seeking, settling in, latency, and translation—which must be performed either once, twice, or repeatedly through successive approximation until access to the desired data location is achieved.

Although the planned inefficiency of such a complex process may at first seem ludicrous, it makes sense to place the engineering burden on the playback device in order to optimize the efficiency of the storage medium. Audio collectors own hundreds of compact discs, but only need one or maybe several drives. Although CD–ROM collecting remains dauntingly expensive,

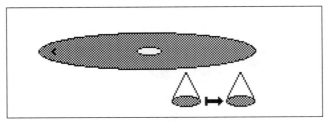

FIGURE 8.2   *Seek time.* Read head jumps to estimated position.

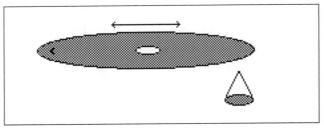

FIGURE 8.3 *Settling-in period*. Spindle adjusts speed to achieve readable data rate.

this is only because the price points so heavily reflect the costs of program development and content. When CD–ROM sales outstrip CD–Audio, their efficiency of manufacture will have allowed prices to fall at least as low as audio CD prices. A CD–ROM drive and MPC-2 computer will no doubt remain about as expensive as a very old used car, but this is tolerable considering that the home library of the future will contain gigabytes of affordable information and entertainment.

One prominent part of present-day reality is that you have to be very wary of CD-drive manufacturers' claims pertaining to seek time when looking to purchase a playback unit. Since there is no standard definition, many manufacturers manipulate their testing so that their numerical representations (e.g., 200 ms) will be superior to the competition's. The worst example is

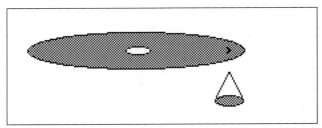

FIGURE 8.4 *Latency*. Waiting period while desired sector rotates into position.

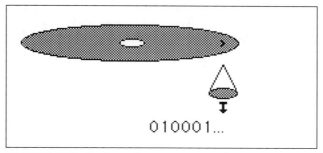

FIGURE 8.5 *Translation time.* A data stream
(e.g., 0100010010000100) is read and output from
the drive.

when it only describes a single read-head jump, sometimes across only a relatively short distance!

A standard measure of access time has been "1/3
stroke" for a jump across one third of the compact
disc's recorded radius, but even that may be abused by
parsing out pieces of the complex access time process.
Random access measurements are better if a large
enough statistical sample is used, but once again manufacturers may abuse this by defining random in whatever ways will make their milliseconds smaller than the
competition's.

Remember that "faster is better" applies as an overall
goal, but access time is only one element of performance.
There are quad-speed drives with loathsome access times
because the engines or drivers can't cope with the settling-in period. Even a good double-speed drive with an
access time slightly over a quarter-second may come with
a proprietary driver that isn't compatible with your existing computer system (or is compatible but will run too
slowly). Consult reputable periodicals that run objective
tests, and if you want to be really sure, buy a CD utility
program and don't take a drive home unless it comes
with a money-back guarantee.

Staying in Focus and on Track

The fine-adjustment servomechanisms that maintain focus and prevent track deviation are not used as manufacturers' selling points, but they are vital to the playback unit's engineering. In Chapter 2, aspects of playback were touched on that will be reviewed and explained more fully here. In particular, it is important to grasp some fundamentals of the nature of light.

Light waves can pass through each other. Because light particles have no mass, different light waves can pass through each other without collisions. The effect is conventionally compared to ripples in a pond moving out to the edge and then coming back again, so that inward ripples are now overlapping any that are still moving outward, creating a more complex pattern. This is similar to what happens when the laser light passes through the objective lens, bounces off the compact disc, and then is reflected (off a land) back down through the objective lens, having come back in the return direction.

Lightwave cancellation occurs when there is a half-cycle difference. If two ripples are staggered so that one ripple's highs match the other ripple's lows, and vice versa, then the "pond" may appear smooth. The light wave reflected off a pit is staggered in this way because the difference in height between pits and lands was designed to be a quarter-wavelength, so the light reflected off a pit will save itself the half-cycle round trip and the reflected light beam will be out of phase with the emitted beam. Because they are traveling in opposite directions, it cannot be said that these two exactly cancel each other out, but the net effect is about 90% cancellation, which is enough for the photosensitive diode to detect this as a distinction between light and no-light signals.

If the ripple image leaves you cold, an alternative is to imagine the lightwave as a series of pulses. If the returning, reflected beam sends back pulses that tend to fall between the emitted beam's pulses, then the end result would be smooth and continuous. The distinctively pulsing characteristic of the light would be lost, creating a relative effect of no-light, or nonreflectivity.

Light moves so fast that each individual bit is read as if the compact disc was not moving at all. For all practical purposes, the trip the light beam makes from the read head to the disc surface and back again happens instantaneously.

- • Even a quad-speed drive makes fewer than 20 million bit-reads per second [4.3218-MHz clock rate (for single-speed drives) $\times 4 = 17,287,200$ disc surface bits read per second].

- • The objective lens normally maintains a distance of about 1 mm from the bottom of the disc's polycarbonate, and the distance through the polycarbonate to the reflective metal layer is shorter than that, so the round trip is about several millimeters.

- • Light travels at approximately 300,000 kilometers per second or about 300 trillion millimeters per second. This speed is altered somewhat while the light is passing through the polycarbonate (because of its 1.55 refraction index), but the difference for our purposes is small enough to be ignored.

So the light has a "time window" of about a twenty-millionth of a second to travel a distance of about 3 mm. Since light travels about 15,000 mm every twenty-millionth of a second, the puny 3-mm trip isn't going to eat up much of the time window. For practical purposes, when the laser is shining on the compact disc and the lens is either receiving a reflection from the land or no reflection from the pit, the compact disc is standing as still as it does in our diagrams in Chapter 2.

Looking at the schematic illustration of compact disc playback (Figure 8.6), which portrays a cross section of a generic read-head assembly, our discussion of the fundamental nature of light lets us clarify two foundational facts:

1. Lightwaves pass through the objective lens in opposite directions simultaneously.

2. The position of the pits and lands on the compact disc may be treated as frozen in time because the laser bombardment process is extremely fast relative to the rotation of the disc.

The following discussion now takes on an unavoidably generic aspect because of design variances between different manufacturers' playback units. For example, our illustration shows a box that looks like two triangular prisms stuck together, labeled "Polarizing beam splitter," but although polarizing techniques improve beam splitting, they are not used by every manufacturer. For another example, between the beam splitter and the objective lens are two other lenses, the top one of which is labeled "Collimation lens"; these are both collimation lenses, which improve the parallel organization of the light beam, but (unlike the illustration) the bottom lens of this pair is placed below the beam splitter in many designs. Another generic aspect of this discussion will be our choice of focus and tracking servomechanisms to describe: astigmatic focus and three-spot tracking. These are appealing, high-performance choices in general use, but by no means are these the only engineering designs that perform these tasks.

Astigmatic Focus and Three-Spot Tracking

Looking again at Figure 8.6, we would ask that you mentally imagine three additional details (which would have made the graphic overcomplicated):

The actuator: Imagine that the barrel immediately surrounding the objective lens has the ability to move up and down (by means of an electrical coil surrounded by a magnetic field, such that a change in electrical charge will cause the lens to move upward or downward).

Two adjacent focused beams: The diffraction grating near the bottom of the illustration is skewed at a precisely tilted angle so that the series of lenses will produce two additional focused spots of light on the disc surface. Imagine one of these spots about 20 microns ahead of the main focused beam but shifted laterally to one side (by a small fraction of a micron), and imagine the other about 20 microns behind the main spot and shifted laterally to the other side.

Six fine-adjustment photodiodes: The destination of the reflected beam in the illustration is the photodiode to the right of the cylindrical lens. Imagine this as a cluster of four diodes arranged like a pie cut in four pieces, between two additional diodes, one on either side.

The fine-adjustment servomechanisms correct or compensate for two things that can go wrong even when the spindle and sled are doing their jobs perfectly: loss of focal distance and track deviation. Both of these are more or less natural concomitants of the extreme precision of the compact disc format.

Compact Disc Playback

CD playback is designed to take into account that no disc is perfectly flat. A vertical play of ±400 microns is allowed. More than 500,000 pits ate traveling past the laser's focal point every second.

When the laser beam is diffused and phase canceled, the playback unit reads this as a minus voltage condition (a zero). When the beam returns to the photodiode, it is a plus voltage condition (a one).

Pit

Pit

Pit

Land

Land

Land

Land

Protective layer

Reflective layer of aluminum

Pit

Clear Polycarbonate

Objective lens

When viewed from underneath, pits are actually bumps. The height of each bump is 1/4 of the laser's wavelength inside the plastic. Light hitting a land area travels half a wavelength (1/4 + 1/4) longer than light hitting a pit. This phase difference of the wavelength causes cancellation due to phase.

A thin layer of aluminum above the read surface reflects the laser beam and sends it on a return journey back to the photodiode.

The objective lens targets the two bands on the read layer of the disc. It also sends returning light back to the collimation lens.

Collimation lens

The collimation lenses adjust the line of sight for both the light and the dark bands. The bands are kept in parallel in both send and return modes.

This cylindrical lens increases the light's deflection and passes it on to the photodiode.

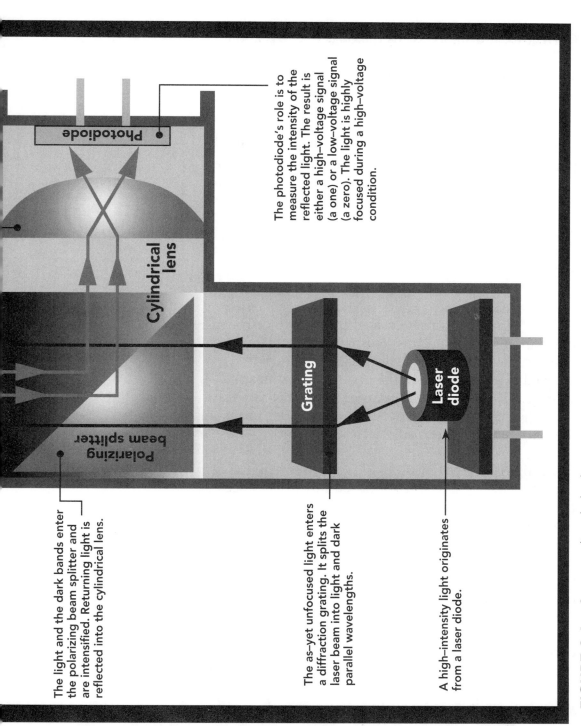

The photodiode's role is to measure the intensity of the reflected light. The result is either a high–voltage signal (a one) or a low–voltage signal (a zero). The light is highly focused during a high–voltage condition.

The light and the dark bands enter the polarizing beam splitter and are intensified. Returning light is reflected into the cylindrical lens.

The as–yet unfocused light enters a diffraction grating. It splits the laser beam into light and dark parallel wavelengths.

A high–intensity light originates from a laser diode.

FIGURE 8.6 Compact disc playback.

Correct focal distance keeps the objective lens about a millimeter away from the bottom of the polycarbonate. The red laser beam from the objective lens strikes the polycarbonate with a diameter of about a millimeter and then is refracted by the plastic down to a spot size of 1.7 microns. One advantage of this is that dust or scratches on the plastic that are significantly smaller than a millimeter may be practically ignored, because enough light passes on either side of them to form the 1.7-micron spot on the reflective layer. Remember that the distance has been calculated so that the lands and flat areas that separate adjacent tracks will be highly reflective, whereas the pits will reflect no light (or rather, very little light) back into the optical assembly.

Loss of focal distance occurs for two reasons, either because the disc has become slightly warped or because it is flapping while it spins (flapping is usually an issue only for the outer tracks). The maximum variance allowed is ±0.4 mm, and the objective lens must be able to move up or down in order to compensate for this. The actuator servomechanism, which performs this motion, must be informed which way to move.

The astigmatic focus method takes advantage of the fact that if the disc is too close to the lens, then the reflected light beams will be *divergent*. Conversely, if the disc is too far away from the lens, then the reflected light beams will be *convergent*. The cylindrical lens sends the light beam to the four clustered diodes in such a way that divergent, convergent, or parallel beams will produce distinctly different signals. The logical driver can then inform the actuator whether to move the objective lens up or down, and by how much, in order to maintain correct focal distance. It is interesting to note that one of the significant limitations to designing faster CD drives is overcoming the tendency of the actuator to resonate when making frequent adjustments.

It is easy enough to visualize track deviation because the pit width is only half a micron. With a 1.6-micron track pitch separating adjacent recorded tracks, that means there are 1.1 microns of highly reflective empty space on either side of the track. One metaphor that comes to mind is trying to ride a bicycle very fast along the yellow line in the middle of a road; what makes it fun is that it's challenging to try to stay on the line. Imperfections in the center hole that is cut in the CD or warpage that can occur during the disc replication process can cause track deviation of ±30 microns! That's a very curving bike ride. The engineering design of the servomechanism that adjusts for this may be similar to the actuator but at right angles to it, or else the spot may be moved laterally by means of a mirror right below the objective lens, such that small adjustments to this mirror will move the spot from side to side. As with the actuator, the track-following servomechanism must be informed which way to move.

The three-spot track-following method uses the two adjacent focused beams and sends them to the diodes on either side of the pie cut in four pieces. As shown in Figure 8.7, these spots are staggered laterally so that a deviation to either side will cause one spot to be completely off to the other side. Since the pits are essentially nonreflective, that means that the recorded tracks are much less reflective than the empty areas on either side (each 1.1 microns wide). If a pit is visualized as "black"

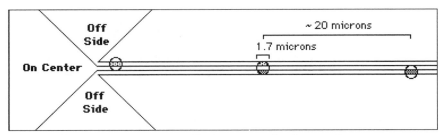

FIGURE 8.7   Positioning of "three-spot" adjacent beams.

and a land as "white," then these empty areas will also be "white," since they are on the same level as the lands; the recorded track will appear "gray" as the black pits and white lands run together and "mix colors." Track following does not analyze the diode information with the same clock precision that the data stream has to use, or the "gray" effect would not occur.

The feedback signals for the astigmatic focus and three-spot tracking servomechanisms are what allow the logical driver to recognize that an adjustment instruction must be sent to the servos (see Table 8.1 and Fig. 8.8).

TABLE 8.1 Focus and Tracking Feedback Signals

"ASTIGMATIC" FOCUS SERVOMECHANISM FEEDBACK SIGNAL = (A + C) − (B + D)	
Signal = 0	*In Focus*: The beam reflected off the compact disc is parallel and strikes all four diodes equally.
Signal > 0	*Too Close*: The reflected beam is *diverging*, so the cylindrical lens directs most of its light to A and C (through the lens' flat axis).
Signal < 0	*Too Far*: The reflected beam is *converging*, so the cylindrical lens directs most of its light to B and D (through the lens' convex axis.)
"THREE-SPOT" TRACKING SERVOMECHANISM FEEDBACK SIGNAL = E − F	
Signal = 0	*On Center*: The two additional track-following spots, E and F, are both focused on the less-reflective recorded track.
Signal > 0	*Adjust Toward F-Side*: Spot E is more reflective because it has wandered onto the space between adjacent tracks, which is on the same level with the lands and is likewise highly reflective. Lens should adjust away from the E lateral side and toward F, bringing E back on track (because the E-spot moves with the lens).
Signal < 0	*Adjust Toward E-Side*: Spot F is between tracks.

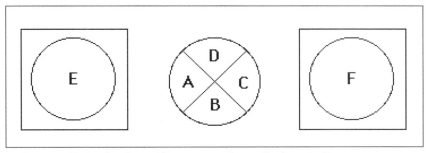

FIGURE 8.8 Six fine-adjustment photodiodes: A–F.

To review, the fine-adjustment servomechanisms for focus and tracking do not offer the sort of "faster-is-better" performance characteristics the spindle and sled do. Manufacturers are not going to go out and tout these servomechanisms with the enthusiasm they reserve for data rate and seek time. Having seen some of the engineering involved, you might think that they should!

One important lesson to be drawn from all four servo-mechanisms is that the following oversimplification has to be debunked: The computer instructs the CD drive to obtain a file or sector(s) of data that begin(s) at a precise location on the disc. The drive goes to the location, reads the data, sends it to the computer, and then awaits its next instruction.

In a way, that is a perfectly fine description. But this isn't some debating society where one person talks and then stops, and then the other person talks and then stops. The CD drive is more like the stereotype of a close-knit, big family where interruptions are regular, different activities are going on at the same time, and everyone has to work together very smoothly or things will bog down.

The CD drive has to be in almost constant communication with the computer in order to operate properly, and it interfaces through the logical driver. As we proceed to other considerations, you should bear in mind that lenses are inert, moveable parts need to be told what to do, and it is ultimately the logical driver that coordinates and enables the CD drive's optical playback technology to perform faster and better.

Choosing the Right Features

"Faster is better" exists in a context of system configuration, which is highly dependent on the types of applications and user requirements that come into play. One might say that the best CD drive is the one that will work best for *you*. Of course, much of the appeal of computer technology is the wide range of work it is capable of performing, but different system configurations are optimal for different *kinds* of work. A common approach to categorizing this is as follows:

Low end: For multimedia and CD–ROM, this involves older computers, usually without sound cards or speakers. Users are those who purchased their PCs when a 40 MB hard drive with 1 MB RAM was still considered a big deal. They want to upgrade to CD–ROM capability without buying a new computer.

Middle ground: The multimedia PC is upon us (MPC, but note that MPC-2 is the current standard). Increasingly, new computers include built-in CD playback, but many purchasers bought their computers without this. For example, a graphics artist with a 100 MB hard drive and 32 MB RAM who uses a SyQuest external drive and color scanner might want to add CD–ROM to access the many image libraries available, or just play new game titles.

High end: The sky is the limit here. A soundtrack composer will turn out the music for a movie in three weeks while sitting at a workstation filled with MIDI devices and assorted peripherals. Corporate LANs (local area networks) are increasingly including multiple-CD drives as a readily accessible means of storage and retrieval (often combining recordable CDs for in-house records with multiple-disc subscription services providing up-to-date statistical databases).

This range of real-world applications means that *compatibility* is the single most important factor when evaluating the different aspects of CD–ROM drives, both in the technical sense of data transfer and the nontechnical sense, which involves ease of use and appropriateness to the user's needs. So the first topic to cover is the interface that connects the computer to the CD–ROM and allows the logical driver to do its job. There are two main camps, each of them with salient advantages: SCSI-2 and IDE/ATAPI.

SCSI (pronounced "scuzzy") is the acronym for small computer system interface. The name is now most commonly associated with the peripheral controller board that must be installed for SCSI systems, but like any interface it is also a command language or set of common instructions that can be used in a wide range of different configurations. It began back when the 8-bit interface was common and earned some reputation for being difficult. Many manufacturers went their own way and created proprietary interfaces for their equipment, some of which were based on SCSI but with limited compatibility, others of which were entirely unique.

Integrated drive electronics (IDE) began in 1986 with the AT-attachable (ATA) interface for connecting the hard disk drive to the computer. As the future of CD–ROM technology showed promise, manufacturers wanted to use the already-installed IDE board as an alternative to incurring the additional cost of SCSI card installation. The problem was that the byte requirements for CD–ROM commands were longer than the commands used with ATA IDE. Vendors were attempting to work around this when Western Digital (which had originally developed IDE with Compaq) proposed that its solution become the new standard: the Packet command. This command permits the longer CD–ROM commands to be moved (within the byte requirements of ATA) by writing repeatedly to the data register without increasing the number of register addresses. This became accepted as "Enhanced IDE" and was formally defined in 1994 as ATAPI (AT Attachment Packet Interface).

The general rule is that IDE/ATAPI is easiest and cheapest for middle-ground users, whereas SCSI is best for high-end and low-end use. SCSI still has the low end because so many of the older machines either used it or can be upgraded with it. SCSI's high end is its own area of computer expertise and is steadily improving. SCSI-2, which is now standard, includes improvements such as a fast-speed mode for increased throughput, a wide-bus mode allowing a second cable for 32-bit transfer, intelligent seek-time minimalization, and so on. The Corel Corporation and its SCSI! product (utilizing Adaptec's ASPI [Advanced SCSI Programming Interface]) deserve special mention for bringing the benefits of SCSI both to the general public and to the widest possible range of peripheral hardware. The ASPI driver is able to work within this system with unusual flexibility. Although IDE/ATAPI falls short of SCSI-2's performance ceiling (for example, IDE supports only four peripheral devices but SCSI supports seven and permits chaining), IDE can also be expected to improve.

Unfortunately, although the logical driver is at least as important as any other consideration, it is hard to go beyond the statement that it must be compatible! Third-party drivers exist with advanced caching features and all sorts of bells, whistles, and promises. If you've got a half-decent drive with a lousy driver, these commercial drivers might be just the solution for you, but if you already have a good drive with a good driver, then most of these are as likely to hurt performance as help it, because they might attempt to control your drive in ways that are far from optimal for its unique character-istics. Companies like Plextor and Apple take notable pride in supplying drivers that fully exploit the potential of their drives, as do many other companies.

Other characteristics of CD drives can also be meaning-fully evaluated in terms of low-end, middle-ground, or high-end use:

Buffer size: If the buffer on your drive doesn't work well, you'll know it! Especially when video clips come through in sporadic pieces—64, 128, and 256 KB are the middle-ground range of choic-es; these are all pretty low, and a model with a 256 KB buffer won't necessarily outperform a model with a 64 KB buffer (e.g., Plextor's DM-5028). High-end users should probably spend the money on a 1 MB buffer, but middle-ground users should just evaluate the smoothness of video playback.

External or internal drive: Internal drives are very middle-ground unless some unique feature of an external drive has special appeal (such as RCA jacks for hooking up to a stereo amplifier). On the low end, external is the only option. For high-end users, installing an internal drive would be a waste of energy. Their system configuration is modular, and it must be possible to reconfigure it efficiently (also, power-user types like to drag pet peripherals to events like expo presentations or recording studio gigs).

Multiple-disc drives/jukeboxes: The idea of a 500-disc CD–ROM jukebox is mouth-watering but only useful for corporate and institutional high-end applications. One of the advantages of the CD is that it really is compact, so switching discs is not a big burden. Pioneer has an interesting line of choices, and other manufacturers are also wooing middle-ground users. There are middle-ground users who happen to use multiple-CD sets very heavily, and of course more and more applications are being released as multiple-CD sets (since 650 MG only gets you so far). Perhaps the most important question to ask if you are looking to purchase one of these is how many actual drives the model has, rather than just how many compact discs it can store and manipulate.

Caddy or tray: Tray is middle-ground; caddy is low-end and high-end. The big exception to this is middle-ground users with kids who will be touching the CDs, in which case the extra protection of the CD caddy is very good. Older and cheaper drives almost all used the plastic caddy containers, but middle-ground consumers have shown a strong preference for trays. A good CD tray facilitates disc switching, but watch out for CD trays that only extend out partially (increases risk of disc damage) or expose the read head's objective lens (increases risk of drive damage).

CPU utilization: Good drivers and drives, that work well together, make smaller demands on the CPU. For middle-ground users, avoid buying anything with higher than 40 percent CPU usage. For high-end users, a lower ceiling of CPU usage may be an important part of running certain applications, but the numerical value of that ceiling will depend on the system and the application.

RAM cache: Optimal RAM-cache utilization is another one of those specializations of computer expertise. Consumers may be duped into buying special cache software (or even hardware) that is inappropriate for their systems and will lower performance (and may force them to reload their operating systems). On the other hand, good caching can make applications run so much faster that even knowledgeable middle-ground users will optimize (change) how their cache functions as they switch from one application to another. So the keyword again is compatibility, and the details often vary for different applications. Many of the better drivers that come bundled with drives use some caching, and this is the best answer for the middle-ground user. High-end users try to use caching to the fullest whether or not CD drives are involved.

Multisession playback: So far, manufacturers' claims for "multisession playback capability" are sort of an inside joke in the CD–ROM world. Several drives have been advertised as having multisession read capability, but have been shipped with drivers that were unable to process multisession data! On the other hand, recordable and multisession CD is an area where a lot of progress is being made, and changes in the technological details are bound to produce future incompatibilities. Although our middle-ground example of a graphics artist would probably prefer to buy a drive that could read multisession Kodak Photo CDs, most middle-ground users do not need this capability.

In closing, although a purchasing decision is always caveat emptor (buyer beware), CD–ROM drives are steadily improving while slowly coming down in price. To repeat our best advice, check out objective comparison tests run by major computer magazines, don't be afraid to buy a CD utility that will let you run tests on your own, and always try to get a money-back guarantee. It's better to get good technical support with a product or to buy a drive that is packaged so that everything you need to set it up is already in there, but these don't have to be deciding factors.

CD drives are not completely optical playback devices. Some characterize them as opticoelectronic, which is more accurate. But to return to the sort of grandiose talk with which we began this chapter, emerging optical technologies are going to bring a radical change when we can manipulate most of our data without having to move particles with mass, subject to inertia. In such a futuristic age, the CD players and CD–ROM drives of today will stand out as historical landmarks. We can all look forward to high-density CD and what can be accomplished thanks to the development of a long-lasting blue laser. There are many landmarks ahead of us, but there's nothing like the first time. Today's CD players and CD drives are the first use by the general public of devices that optically read and manipulate (substantial quantities of) digital data.

Resource List

CD Manufacturing Facilities

Allied Manufacturing (WEA)
6110 Peachtree Street
City of Commerce, California 90040
Tel: 213-725-6900
Fax: 213-725-8767

Americ Disc Canada
2525 Rue Canadian
Drummondville, Quebec
Canada J2B 8A9
Tel: 819-474-2655
Fax: 819-474-2870

Americ Disc Florida
8455 Northwest 30 Terrace
Miami, Florida 33122
Tel: 305-599-3828
Fax: 305-599-1107

American Multimedia
2609 Tucker Street Extended
Burlington, North Carolina 27215
Tel: 910-229-5554
Fax: 910-228-1409

ASR
8960 Eton Avenue
Canoga Park, California 91304
Tel: 818-341-1124
Fax: 818-341-9131

Astral Tech Americas, Inc.
5400 Broken Sound Boulevard
Boca Raton, Florida 33487
Tel: 407-995-7000
Fax: 407-995-7001

BQC
2101 South 35 Street
Council Bluffs, Iowa 51501
Tel: 516-244-1568
Fax: 516-244-1573

Cassette Productions
4910 West Amelia Earhart Drive
Salt Lake City, Utah 84116
Tel: 801-531-7555
Fax: 801-531-0740

Cinram Canada
2255 Markham Road
Scarborough, Ontario
Canada M1B 2W3
Tel: 416-298-8190
Fax: 613-726-1609

Cinram USA
1600 Rich Road
Richmond, Indiana 47374
Tel: 317-962-9511
Fax: 317-962-1564

DADC
3181 North Fruitridge Street
Terre Haute, Indiana 47804
Tel: 812-462-8160
Fax: 812-462-8886

Denon Digital Industries
1380 Monticello Road
Madison, Georgia 30650
Tel: 303-791-5659
Fax: 303-791-5660

Distronics
2800 Sumitt Avenue
Plano, Texas 75074
Tel: 214-881-8800
Fax: 214-442-7552

DMI Anaheim
1120 Cosby Way
Anaheim, California 92805
Tel: 714-630-6700
Fax: 714-630-1025

DMI Huntsville
4905 Moores Mill Road
Huntsville, Alabama 35811
Tel: 205-859-9042
Fax: 205-859-9932

EMI Manufacturing
1 Capitol Way
Jacksonville, Illinois 62650
Tel: 803-522-9893
Fax: 803-522-3242

Europadisk, Ltd.
75 Varick Street
New York, New York 10013
Tel: 212-226-4401
Fax: 212-966-0456

EVA-TONE
4801 Ulmerton Road
Clearwater, Florida 34622
Tel: 1-800-EVA-TONE
Fax: 813-572-6214

HMG
15 Gilpin Avenue
Hauppauge, New York 11788
Tel: 516-234-0200
Fax: 516-234-0346

IBM
1001 W. T. Harris Boulevard
Charlotte, North Carolina 28257
Tel: 303-924-6300
Fax: 303-924-7191

IPC
9400 Jeronimo
Irvine, California 92718
Tel: 714-588-7765
Fax: 714-588-7763

JVC
2 JVC Road
Tuscaloosa, Alabama 34505
Tel: 205-556-7111
Fax: 205-554-5505

KAO Infosystems
41444 Christy Road
Fremont, California 94338
Tel: 510-657-8425
Fax: 510-657-8427

KAO Infosystems
1857 Colonial Village Lane
Lancaster, Pennsylvania 17601
Tel: 800-525-6575
Fax: 717-392-7897

METATEC
7001 Metatec Boulevard
Dublin, Ohio 43017
Tel: 614-761-2000
Fax: 614-761-4258

NIMBUS Manufacturing
State Road 629
Ruckersville, Virginia 22968
Tel: 804-985-1100
Fax: 804-985-4692

NIMBUS Manufacturing
85 East Bay Boulevard
Provo, Utah 84605
Tel: 801-375-6797
Fax: 801-374-8757

P & Q CD
5460 North Peck Road #E
Arcadia, California 91006
Tel: 818-357-4088
Fax: 818-359-4229

PILZ Compact Disc, Inc.
54 Conchester Road
Concordville, Pennsylvania 19331
Tel: 800-894-3472
Fax: 610-459-5958

Polygram
U.S. Highway 29
Grover, North Carolina 28073
Tel: 703-734-4236
Fax: 703-734-4280

Rainbo Records
1738 Berkeley Street
Santa Monica, California 90404
Tel: 310-829-0355
Fax: 310-828-8765

Sanyo Laser Products, Inc.
1767 Sheridan Street
Richmond, Indiana 47374
Tel: 317-935-7574
Fax: 317-935-7570

Six Sigma
PO Box 1418
Tacoma, Washington 98401
Tel: 800-451-5742
Fax: 206-926-0953

Sonopress
108 Monticello Road
Weaverville, North Carolina 28787
Tel: 704-658-2000
Fax: 704-658-2008

SONY
400 North Woodbury Road
Pitman, New Jersey 08071
Tel: 800-323-9741
Fax: 609-589-3007

Speciality Manufacturing (WEA)
210 North Valley Avenue
Olyphant, Pennsylvania 18447
Tel: 717-383-2471
Fax: 717-383-2165

Technicolor
3233 East Mission Oaks Boulevard
Camarillo, California 93012
Tel: 800-656-8667
Fax: 805-445-9558

Technidisc
2250 Meijer Drive
Troy, Michigan 48404
Tel: 313-435-8540
Fax: 313-435-7746

3M California
2933 Bayview Drive
Fremont, California 94538
Tel: 510-440-8161
Fax: 510-440-8162

3M Optical Recording
3M Center Building 223-5N-01
St. Paul, Minnesota 55144-1000
Tel: 612-733-2142
Fax: 612-733-0158

Triptych CD
1604 Tillie Lewis Drive
Stockton, California 95206
Tel: 408-271-7373
Fax: 408-271-7370

Ultra Media
2048 Corporate Court
San Jose, California 95131
Tel: 408-383-9470
Fax: 408-383-0806

UNI Manufacturing (MCA)
Highway 154
Pinckneyville, Illinois 62274
Tel: 618-357-2167
Fax: 618-357-6340

U.S. Optical Disc, Inc.
1 Eagle Drive
Sanford, Maine 04073
Tel: 207-324-1124
Fax: 207-490-1707

ZOMAX
5353 Nathan Lane
Plymouth, Minnesota 55442
Tel: 612-553-9300
Fax: 612-553-0826

CD-ROM Publishers

A6, Inc.
1050 South Cypress Street
La Habra, California 90631
Tel: 714-773-5412
Fax: 714-773-0562

Abacus Software, Inc.
5370 52 Street S.E.
Grand Rapids, Michigan 49512
Tel: 616-698-0330

ABC-CLIO
PO Box 1911
Santa Barbara, California 93116-1911
Tel: 805-968-1911
Fax: 805-685-5467 or 805-685-9685

Accurate Research, Inc.
1500 Wyatt Drive, Suite 10
Santa Clara, California 95054
Tel: 408-748-9988
Fax: 408-748-9989

Acuris, Inc.
931 Hamilton Avenue
Menlo Park, California 94025
Tel: 800-OK-ACURIS/415-329-1920
Fax: 415-329-1928

ADAM Software, Inc.
1600 River Edge Parkway, Suite 800
Atlanta, Georgia 30328
Tel: 404-980-0888
Fax: 404-955-3088

Advantage Plus Distributing, Inc.
211-C South Salem Street
Apex, North Carolina 27502
Tel: 919-362-8212
Fax: 919-362-8294

Afrolink Software
1815 Wellington Road
Los Angeles, California 90019-0653
Tel: 213-731-5465
Fax: 213-730-0653

AIMS Media
9710 DeSoto Avenue
Chatsworth, California 91311-4409
Tel: 800-367-2467
Fax: 818-341-6700

AimTech Corporation
20 Trafalgar Square
Nashua, New Hampshire 03063
Tel: 800-289-2884
Fax: 603-883-5582

Airworks Media
1400 North Woodward Avenue
Suite 169
Bloomfield Hills, Michigan 48304
Tel: 810-645-5730

Alan Rand Multimedia Group, Inc.
PO Box 400
Dayton, Indiana 47941-0400
Tel: 317-449-1000
Fax: 317-449-1727

Alberta Distance Learning Centre
Box 4000
Barnhead, Alberta
Canada T0G 2P0
Tel: 403-674-5333
Fax: 403-674-6561

Allegro New Media
16 Passaic Avenue
Fairfield, New Jersey 07004
Tel: 201-808-1992
Fax: 201-808-2645

American Best CD
44244 Fremont Boulevard
Fremont, California 94538
Tel: 510-623-0950

American InfoScience
1948-B South IH 35
Austin, Texas 78704
Tel: 512-440-1132
Fax: 512-440-0531

Andromeda Interactive, Inc.
1050 Marina Village Parkway, Suite 107
Alameda, California 94501
Tel: 510-769-1616
Fax: 510-769-1919

Application Software
144 Kiel Bay
Alameda, California 94502
Tel: 800-824-9572 or 510-523-0777
Fax: 510-522-1157

Ask Me Multimedia, Inc.
7100 Northland Circle, Suite 401
Minneapolis, Minnesota 55428
Tel: 800-275-6311

Asymetrix Corporation
110-110 Avenue N.E., Suite 700
Bellevue, Washington 98004
Tel: 800-448-6503 or 206-637-5828
Fax: 206-637-1504

AT&T Multimedia
2701 Maitland Center Parkway
Maitland, Florida 32751
Tel: 800-448-6727

Athana, Inc.
23955 President Avenue
Harbor City, California 90710
Tel: 310-539-7280
Fax: 310-539-6596

Attica Cybernetics Ltd.
Kings Meadow, Unit 2
Ferry Hinksey Road
Oxford, 0X2 0DP
United Kingdom
Tel: 011-44-865-791346
Fax: 011-44-865-794561

Automap, Inc.
1309 114 Avenue SE, Suite 110
Bellevue, Washington 98004
Tel: 206-455-3552
Fax: 206-455-3667

Avtex Interactive Media
2105 South Bascom Avenue, Suite 300
Campbell, California 95008
Tel: 800-895-4263 or 408-371-2800
Fax: 408-371-5760

Azam Corporation
1333 Lawrence Expressway, Suite 201
Santa Clara, California 95051
Tel: 408-296-0659
Fax: 408-296-2063

Azeus Systems Limited
1203 Cigna Tower
482 Jaffe Road
Causeway Bay
Hong Kong
Tel: 852-893-3673
Fax: 852-574-4952

Aztech New Media, Inc.
99 Atlantic Avenue, Suite 100
Toronto, Ontario
Canada M6K 3J8
Tel: 416-539-8822
Fax: 909-738-1961

Bayware, Inc.
1660 South Amphlett Boulevard, Suite 128
San Mateo, California 94402
Tel: 415-312-0980
Fax: 415-578-1884

Beacon Learning
125 Cambridge Park Drive
Cambridge, Massachusetts 02140
Tel: 617-661-0079
Fax: 617-661-0195

Berkeley Systems, Inc.
2095 Rose Street
Berkeley, California 94709
Tel: 510-841-5083
Fax: 510-841-5093

Biblesoft
22014 Seventh Avenue South
Seattle, Washington 98198
Tel: 206-824-0547
Fax: 206-824-1828

Broderbund Software, Inc.
500 Redwood Boulevard
Novato, California 94947
Tel: 415-382-4400
Fax: 415-382-4582

BT Interactive, Inc.
40665A North Calhoun Road, Suite 101
Brookfield, Wisconsin 53005
Tel: 414-783-2400
Fax: 414-783-2410

BTL Publishing
Business and Innovation Center
Angel Way, Listerhills
Bradford BD7 1BX
United Kingdom
Tel: 011-44-274-841230
Fax: 011-44-274-841322

Cambrix Publishing
6269 Variel Avenue, Suite B
Woodland Hills, California 91367
Tel: 818-922-8484
Fax: 818-922-8781

**Canadian Centre for the Development
of Instructional Computing**
3-102 Education North
University of Alberta
Edmonton, Alberta
Canada T6G 2G5
Tel: 403-492-3935
Fax: 403-492-3179

CD Technology, Inc.
764 San Aleso Avenue
Sunnyvale, California 94086
Tel: 408-752-8500
Fax: 408-752-8501

CD–ROM Source
5348 North Tacoma Avenue
Indianapolis, Indiana 46220
Tel: 317-726-0022

CD–ROM Strategies, Inc.
6 Venture, Suite 208
Irvine, California 92718
Tel: 714-453-1702
Fax: 714-786-1401

Center for Leadership Studies
230 West 3 Avenue
Escondido, California 92025
Tel: 619-741-6595
Fax: 619-747-9384

Chadwyck-Healey
Cambridge Place
Cambridge CB2 1NR
England
Tel: 011-44-223-311479
Fax: 011-44-223-66440

CIT Multimedia
2011 Auto Center Drive, Suite 105
Oxnard, California 93030
Tel: 805-485-1466
Fax: 805-485-3114

Claris Corporation
5201 Patrick Henry Drive
Santa Clara, California 95052
Tel: 800-544-8554 or 408-987-7406
Fax: 408-987-7558

ClassAct Multimedia
1121 South Orem Boulevard
Orem, Utah 84058
Tel: 800-235-3276 or 801-221-9400
Fax: 801-221-9942

**Communication and Information
Technologies, Inc.**
777 North 5 Avenue
Knoxville, Tennessee 37917
Tel: 615-673-5000
Fax: 615-673-0024

Compton's New Media, Inc.
2320 Camino Vida Roble
Carlsbad, California 92009
Tel: 619-929-2500
Fax: 619-929-2555

CompuMedia Technology, Inc.
46520 Fremont Boulevard, Suite 602
Fremont, California 94538
Tel: 510-656-9811
Fax: 510-656-9821

Compute Publications
1965 Broadway
New York, New York 10023
Tel: 212-496-6100

Computer Support Corporation
15926 Midway Road
Dallas, Texas 75244
Tel: 214-661-8960
Fax: 214-661-5429

ConnectSoft
11130 Northeast 33 Place, Suite 250
Bellevue, Washington 98004
Tel: 206-827-6467
Fax: 206-822-9095

Course Technology, Inc.
One Main Street
Cambridge, Massachusetts 02142
Tel: 800-648-7450 or 617-225-2595
Fax: 617-225-7976

CPV Interactive
1801 Avenue of the Stars, Suite 240
Century City, California 90067
Tel: 310-286-1001
Fax: 310-286-0530

Creative Multimedia
513 Northwest 13 Avenue, Suite 400
Portland, Oregon 97209
Tel: 800-762-7668 or 503-241-4351
Fax: 503-241-4370

Creative Labs, Inc.
1901 McCarthy Boulevard
Milpitas, California 95035
Tel: 800-998-5227 or 408-432-6705
Fax: 408-428-6611

Cyber Software International
7555 North Del Mar Avenue, Suite 203
Fresno, California 93711
Tel: 209-447-0108
Fax: 209-447-0208

DAariel Multimedia Publishing
825 Saturn Street, Suite 116-14
Jupiter, Florida 33477
Tel: 407-744-2546
Fax: 407-744-0988

Dae Kyo Computer
6F Kunja Building 942-1
Taechi-Dong, Kangnam-Ku
Seoul 135-280
Korea

Database America Companies
100 Paragon Drive
Montvale, New Jersey 07645
Tel: 201-476-2300
Fax: 201-476-2405

DataConcept GmbH
Hauptstrasse 88
D-90547, Stein
Germany
Tel: 011-49-911-96779-0
Fax: 011-49-911-96779-90

Davidson & Associates
19840 Pioneer Avenue
Torrance, California 90503
Tel: 310-793-0600
Fax: 310-793-0601

Deep River Publishing, Inc.
565 Congress Street, Suite 200
Portland, Maine 04101
Tel: 800-643-5630 or 207-871-1684
Fax: 207-871-1683

DeLorme Mapping
Lower Main Street
PO Box 290
Freeport, Maine 04032
Tel: 800-335-6763 ext. 064 or
207-865-1234
Fax: 207-865-9291

Diamond Entertainment Corp.
4400 Route 9 South
Freehold, New Jersey 07728
Tel: 908-431-0700

DIC Interactive
303 North Glenoaks Boulevard
Burbank, California 91502
Tel: 818-955-5400
Fax: 818-955-5696

Digital Directory Assistance
5161 River Road, Suite 6
Bethesda, Maryland 20816
Tel: 301-657-8548
Fax: 301-652-7810

Digital Impact
6506 South Lewis Avenue, Suite 250
Tulsa, Oklahoma 74136
Tel: 800-775-4232 or 918-742-2022
Fax: 918-742-8176

Digital Media Group, Inc.
5300 West 104 Street
Los Angeles, California 90045
Tel: 310-677-4880
Fax: 310-410-4088

Digital Playground
21630 Marilla Street
Chatsworth, California 91311
Tel: 818-773-4999
Fax: 818-773-8020

Disc Manufacturing, Inc.
1409 Foulk Road, Suite 102
Wilmington, Delaware 19803
Tel: 302-479-2500

Discis Knowledge Research, Inc.
90 Sheppard Avenue East, 7th Floor
Toronto, Ontario
Canada M2N 5W9
Tel: 800-567-4321
Fax: 416-250-6540

Discovery Network
7700 Wisconsin Avenue
Bethesda, Maryland 20814
Tel: 301-986-1999
Fax: 301-986-4827

Drive T's Music Software
124 Crescent Road
Needham, Massachusetts 02194
Tel: 800-989-6434
Fax: 617-455-1460

Drew Pictures, Inc.
246 First Street, Suite 509
San Francisco, California 94105
Tel: 415-247-7600
Fax: 415-974-6733

DSR Software, Inc.
5 Park Plaza, Suite 770
Irvine, California 92714
Tel: 800-455-4377 or 714-553-6581
Fax: 714-553-6585

Dynaware USA, Inc.
950 Tower Lane, Suite 1150
Foster City, California 94404
Tel: 415-349-4700
Fax: 415-349-5879

E.M.M.E.
14 Ferncliff Road
Cos Cob, Connecticut 06807
Tel: 203-869-6047

Edupro Ltd.
Diamond Exchange Building
Diamond Tower 10/F, Suite 1090-91
34 Jabotinsky Street
Ramat Gan 52521
Israel
Tel: 011-972-3-751-4533

Edutainment Group
13139 Ramona Boulevard, Suite E
Irwindale, California 91706
Tel: 818-338-5189
Fax: 818-338-9589

EE Multimedia Productions, Inc.
1455 West 2200 S. Suite 100
Salt Lake City, Utah 84119
Tel: 801-973-0081
Fax: 801-973-0184

Eidolon
5716 Mosholu Avenue
Riverdale, New York 10471
Tel: 718-884-7095
Fax: 718-884-1563

Electric Dreams, Inc.
13891 Newport Avenue, Suite 285
Tustin, California 92680
Tel: 714-573-2112
Fax: 714-573-0948

Electronic Imagery, Inc.
100 Park Central Boulevard South
Suite 3400
Pompano Beach, Florida 33064
Tel: 305-968-7100
Fax: 305-968-7319

EM Alternatives, Inc.
11520 North Port Washington Road
Suite 203
Mequon, Wisconsin 53092
Tel: 414-241-8513
Fax: 414-241-8514

EM Corporation
41 Kenosia Avenue
PO Box 2805
Danbury, Connecticut 06813
Tel: 203-798-2050
Fax: 203-798-9930

EMpower Corporation
PO Box 68125
Raleigh, North Carolina 27613
Tel: 919-847-4667
Fax: 919-848-0473

Erotica-ROM
8008 Dover Shores Avenue
Las Vegas, Nevada 89128
Tel: 702-228-9277

etrok
1550 N Fuller Avenue, Suite 305
Los Angeles, California 90046
Tel: 800-883-8765
Fax: 213-876-8169

Evergreen International Technology, Inc.
930 West 1 Street, Unit 102
North Vancouver, British Columbia
Canada V7P 3N4
Tel: 604-986-0121
Fax: 604-980-7121

Expert Software
800 Douglas Road, Executive Tower
Coral Gables, Florida 33134
Tel: 305-567-9990

Finney Company
3943 Meadowbrook Road
Minneapolis, Minnesota 55426
Tel: 800-846-7027
Fax: 612-938-7353

Fireflies
232 East Blithedake
Mill Valley, California 94941
Tel: 415-381-3463
Fax: 415-381-7571

Foresight Resources Corp.
10725 Ambassador Drive
Kansas City, Misssouri 64153
Tel: 816-891-1040

Future Vision Multimedia
60 Cuttermill Road, Suite 502
Great Neck, New York 11021
Tel: 516-773-0990

Gazelle Technologies, Inc.
7434 Trade Street
San Diego, California 92121
Tel: 800-237-6675 or 619-693-4030
Fax: 619-536-2345

Glencoe/McGraw-Hill
936 Eastwind Drive
Westerville, Ohio 43081
Tel: 800-334-7344 or 614-899-4451
Fax: 614-899-4451

Go Digital Magazine
1517 20 Street
Santa Monica, California 90404
Tel: 310-829-5457

Gourmet Video
13160 Raymer Street
North Hollywood, California 91605
Tel: 818-765-8720
Fax: 818-765-1250

Grafica Multimedia, Inc.
940 Emmett Avenue, Suite 11
Belmont, California 94002
Tel: 415-595-5599
Fax: 415-595-4144

Graphix Zone, Inc.
38 Corporate Park
Irvine, California 92714
Tel: 714-833-3838
Fax: 714-833-3990

Great Wave Software
5353 Scotts Valley Drive
Scotts Valley, California 95066
Tel: 408-438-1990
Fax: 408-438-7171

Grolier Electronic Publishing, Inc.
Sherman Turnpike
Danbury, Connecticut 06816
Tel: 800-285-4534
Fax: 203-797-3130

Gryphon Software Corporation
7220 Trade Street, Suite 120
San Diego, California 92121
Tel: 619-536-8815
Fax: 619-536-8932

Harmony Multimedia, Inc.
1116 South Bixby Drive
City of Industry, California 91745
Tel: 818-968-8486
Fax: 818-968-9683

Hewlett-Packard
2850 Centerville Road
Wilmington, Delaware 19808
Tel: 800-227-9770
Fax: 302-633-8901

Hopkins Technology
421 Hazel Lane
Hopkins, Minnesota 55343-7116
Tel: 612-931-9376
Fax: 612-931-9377

Horizons Technology, Inc.
3990 Ruffin Road
San Diego, California 92123
Tel: 619-292-8331
Fax: 619-292-7321

HQ Multimedia-Systeme GmbH
Feldmunnstrabe 68
D-66333, Voklingen
Germany
Tel: 011-49-681-50088-0
Fax: 011-49-681-50088-80

Humongous Entertainment
13110 Northeast 177 Place, Suite 180
Woodinville, Washington 98072
Tel: 206-486-9258
Fax: 206-486-9494

HyperGlot Software Company, Inc
6204 Baum Drive
Knoxville, Tennessee 37919
Tel: 615-558-8270
Fax: 615-588-6569

Hyper-Quest, Inc.
1718 Main Street, Suite 333
Sarasota, Florida 34236
Tel: 800-404-9737 or 813-365-9800
Fax: 813-365-8324

Ieman Business, Inc.
3rd Floor 2, Number 316, Section 5
Nan-King East Road
Taipei 105, Taiwan
ROC
Tel: 011-886-2-746-9958

Image Smith, Inc.
1313 West Sepulveda Boulevard
Torrance, California 90501
Tel: 310-325-5999
Fax: 310-539-9784

Imagination Pilots, Inc.
640 North Lasalle Street, Suite 560
Chicago, Illinois 60610
Tel: 312-642-7560
Fax: 312-642-0616

IMSI
1895 East Francisco Boulevard
San Rafael, California 94901
Tel: 415-454-7101
Fax: 415-454-8901

Individual Software, Inc.
5870 Stoneridge Drive, Suite 1
Pleasanton, California 94588
Tel: 800-822-3522 or 510-734-6767
Fax: 510-734-8337

INFOBUSINESS, Inc.
887 South Orem Boulevard
Orem, Utah 84058
Tel: 800-657-5300
Fax: 801-225-0817

Ingenio EDV-Software
Millergrasse 40
A-1040, Vienna
Austria
Tel: 011-431-597-3144-0

Inset Systems
71 Commerce Drive
Brooksfield, Connecticut 06804
Tel: 203-740-2400

Insight Software Solutions
PO Box 354
Bountiful, Utah 84011
Tel: 801-295-1890
Fax: 801-299-1781

Intellimedia Sports, Inc.
Two Piedmont Center, Suite 300
Atlanta, Georgia 30305
Tel: 800-269-2102 or 404-262-0000
Fax: 404-261-2282

Interactive Knowledge, Inc.
1100 South Mint Street, Suite 209
Charlotte, North Carolina 28203
Tel: 800-344-0055 or 704-344-0055
Fax: 704-344-1505

Interactive Multimedia Edutainment, Inc.
433 California Street, Suite 912
San Francisco, California 94104
415-393-1470
Fax: 415-393-1488

Interactive Publishing Corporation
300 Airport Executive Park
Spring Valley, New York 10977
Tel: 516-482-0088
Fax: 516-773-0990

InteractiveWare
1235 North Loop West, Suite 1120
Houston, Texas 77008
Tel: 800-723-3339 or 713-862-9800
Fax: 713-868-2622

Intermaginary Entertainment
255 Main Street, Suite 106
Venice, California 90291
Tel: 310-281-7031

InterMedia Interactive Software, Inc.
3624 Market Street, Suite 302
Philadelphia, Pennsylvania 19104
Tel: 215-387-3059
Fax: 215-387-3049

Interplay Productions
17922 Fitch Avenue
Irvine, California 92714
Tel: 714-553-6655

European Office:
71 Milton Park
Abingdon, Oxon, OX144RR
United Kingdom

Sources of CD-Write-Once Machines

Dataware Technologies, Inc.
222 Third Street, Suite 3300
Cambridge, Massachusetts 02142
Tel: 617-621-0820
Fax: 617-621-0307

Eastman Kodak Company
343 State Street
Rochester, New York 14650
Tel: 716-724-4000
Fax: 716-253-7443

JVC Information Products
17811 Mitchell Avenue
Irvine, California 92714
Tel: 714-261-1292
Fax: 714-261-9660

Meridian Data, Inc.
5615 Scotts Valley Drive
Scotts Valley, California 95066
Tel: 403-438-3100/800-767-2537

Microboards, Inc.
308 Broadway
Carver, Minnesota 55315
Tel: 612-448-9800
Fax: 612-682-9806

Optical Media International
180 Knowles Drive
Los Gatos, California 95030
Tel: 800-347-2664/408-376-3511
Fax: 408-376-3519

Philips Consumer Electronics
One Philips Drive
PO Box 4180
Knoxville, Tennessee 37914-1810
Tel: 615-475-8869

Pinnacle Micro, Inc.
19 Technology Drive
Irvine, California 92718
Tel: 714-727-3300/800-553-7070
Fax: 714-789-3150

Plasmon Data Systems, Inc.
165 Centre Pointe Drive
Milpitas, California 95035
Tel: 408-956-9400/800-445-9400
Fax: 408-956-9444

Ricoh
3001 Orchard Parkway
San Jose, California 95134
Tel: 800-955-3453/408-432-8800
Fax: 408-432-8372

Smart & Friendly
16539 Saticoy Street
Van Nuys, California 91409
Tel: 818-994-8001
Fax: 818-988-6581

Sony Electronics
Data Storage Products Division
3300 Zanker Road
San Jose, California 95134
Tel: 408-955-4947
Fax: 408-955-5169

Todd Enterprises
224-49 67 Avenue
Bayside, New York 11364
Tel: 718-343-1040
Fax: 718-343-9180

Trace Mountain Products, Inc.
1040 East Brokaw Road
San Jose, California 95131-2393
Tel: 408-437-3375
Fax: 408-437-3393

Virtual Microsystems
1825 South Grant Street, Suite 700
San Mateo, California 94402
Tel: 800-722-8299/415-573-9596
Fax: 415-572-8406

Yamaha Systems Technology
981 Ridder Park Drive
San Jose, California 95131
Tel: 408-437-3133
Fax: 408-437-8791

Young Minds, Inc.
1910 Orange Tree Lane, Suite 300
Redlands, California 92374
Tel: 714-335-1350
Fax: 714-798-0488

Labeling and Printing Equipment Sources

APEX Machine Company
3000 Northeast 12 Terrace
Fort Lauderdale, Florida 33334
Tel: 305-565-2739
Fax: 305-563-2844

Archon Company
7647 West Yucca Street
Peoria, Arizona 85345
Tel: 602-979-4451
Fax: 602-878-5791

Axiomatic Technologies Corp.
4995 Timberlea Boulevard
Mississauga, Ontario
Canada L4W 2S2
Champion Duplicators, Inc.
43301 Osgood Road
Fremont, California 94539
Tel: 510-651-1934
Fax: 510-659-0047

Costas Systems
5625 Brisa Street, Suite B
Livermore, California 94550-9271
Tel: 510-443-2332
Fax: 510-443-0450

Data Disc Robots
Monnet Strasse 2
52146 Wuerselen
Germany
Tel: 011-49-2405-69020
Fax: 011 49-2405-18696

DIC Trading U.S.A., Inc.
222 Bridge Plaza South
Fort Lee, New Jersey 07054
Tel: 201-592-5100
Fax: 201-592-8232

Dubuit of America
4042 North Nashville Avenue
Chicago, Illinois 60634
Tel: 312-282-9494
Fax: 312-282-2358

Duplication Equipment Brokerage
3830 South Windemere Street
Englewood, Colorado 80110
Tel: 303-781-1132
Fax: 303-781-1277

Gelardi Design
PO Box 2757
Kennebunkport, Maine 04046
Tel: 207-967-0679
Fax: 207-967-2820

I-O Solutions, Inc.
2999A Washington Street
San Francisco, California 94115
Tel: 415-441-9340
Fax: 415-563-0792

Kammann Machines
10 State Avenue
St. Charles, Illinois 60174
Tel: 708-513-8091
Fax: 708-377-7759

Labeling Systems, Inc.
97 McKee Drive
Mahwah, New Jersey 07430-2105
Tel: 201-529-5311
Fax: 201-529-8023

Langenpac Kyoto, Inc.
6154 Kestrel Road
Mississauga, Ontario
Canada L5T 1Z2
Tel: 905-670-7200
Fax: 905-670-5291

LSK Data Systems GmbH
Benzstrasse 15
D-64807, Dieburg
Germany
Tel: 011-49-6071-24077
Fax: 011-49-6071-24079

Lyrec Manufacturing A/S
PO Box 123
Skovlunde 2740
Denmark
Tel: 011-45-4453-2522
Fax: 011-45-4453-5335

Marubeni America Corporation
2000 Town Center, Suite 2150
Southfield, Michigan 48075
Tel: 810-355-6448
Fax: 810-353-2298

Media Automation
527 West 3560 South
Salt Lake City, Utah 84115
Tel: 801-288-0330
Fax: 801-288-0369

Mediaform, Inc.
400 Eagleview Boulevard
Exton, Pennsylvania 19341
Tel: 215-458-9200
Fax: 215-458-9554

Microcircuit Engineering Corp.
192 Rancocas Road
Mount Holly, New Jersey 08060
Tel: 609-261-1400
Fax: 609-261-1679

Netsal Machine, Inc.
20 Authority Drive
Fitchburg, Massachusetts 01420
Tel: 508-345-9400
Fax: 508-345-6153

ODME USA, Inc.
8000 Corporate Center Drive
Charlotte, North Carolina 28226
Tel: 704-542-5303
Fax: 704-542-5309

PILZ GmbH
Ingrid-Pilz Strasse 1
85402 Kranzberg
Germany
Tel: 011-49-8166-670270
Fax: 011-49-8166-670307

Roldex Industries
9980 Glenoaks Boulevard, Unit A
Sun Valley, California 91352
Tel: 818-504-6294
Fax: 818-504-6833

TECA-PRINT USA Corp.
10 Cook Street
Billerica, Massachusetts 01821
Tel: 508-667-8655
Fax: 508-670-6023

TETKO, Inc.
333 South Highland Avenue
St. Paul, Minnesota 55144
Tel: 612-733-3953
Fax: 612-736-1246

TRACE
1040 East Brokaw Road
San Jose, California 95131
Tel: 408-441-8040
Fax: 408-441-3399

Victory Enterprises Tech.
223 West Anderson Lane, Suite B-300
Austin, Texas 78752
Tel: 512-450-0801
Fax: 512-450-0869

Film and Video Sources

ABC News
47 West 66 Street, 6th Floor
New York, New York 10023
Tel: 212-465-4211

A.R.I.Q. Footage
One Main Street
East Hampton, New York 11937
Tel: 800-249-1940 or 516-329-9200

Action Sports
PO Box 301
Malibu, California 90265
Tel: 310-459-2526

Action Sports Adventure
1926 Broadway
New York, New York 10023
Tel: 212-721-2800
Fax: 212-721-0191

Adventure Photo & Film
24 East Main Street
Ventura, California 93001
Tel: 805-643-7751

Aerial Focus
8 Camino Verde
Santa Barbara, California 93103
Tel: 805-962-9911

Aeronautic Pictures
12021 Wilshire Boulevard, Suite 380
Los Angeles, California 90025
Tel: 805-649-9192

Airboss Stock Library
1230 Liberty Bank Lane, Suite 320
Louisville, Kentucky 40222
Tel: 502-425-8161
Fax: 502-425-8597

Alaska Stock Agency
PO Box 244082
Anchorage, Alaska 99524
Tel: 907-562-5245

Amazing Images/Shields Archival
6671 Sunset Boulevard, Suite 1581
Hollywood, California 90028
Tel: 213-962-1899

American Production Services
2247 15th Avenue West
Seattle, Washington 98119
Tel: 206-282-1776

American Time Lapse
3712 North Broadway, Suite 282
Chicago, Illinois 60613
Tel: 312-554-1234

Archer-Telecine Stock Film Libraries
PO Box 8426
Universal City, California 91608
Tel: 818-889-8246

Archer-Telecine Stock Film Libraries
PO Box 8426
Universal City, California 91608
Tel: 818-889-8246

Archive Films
530 West 25 Street
New York, New York 10001
Tel: 212-620-3955
Fax: 212-645-2137

Aris Multimedia Entertainment
310 Washington Boulevard, Suite 100
Marina Del Rey, California 90292
Tel: 310-821-0234

Beat Club Archive
1151 South Crescent Heights Boulevard
Los Angeles, California 90035
Tel: 213-939-3449

Best Shot Stock Film & Video
4726 North Lois Avenue, Suite A
Tampa, Florida 33614
Tel: 813-877-2118
Fax: 813-874-3655

Blue Sky Stock Footage
PO Box 16741
Beverly Hills, California 90210
Tel: 310-859-4709

Budget Films Stock Footage
4509 Santa Monica Boulevard
Los Angeles, California 90029
Tel: 213-660-0187

Buena Vista Imaging Resources
500 South Buena Vista Street
Burbank, California 91521
Tel: 818-560-12704

Caidin Films
707 Wilshire Boulevard, Suite W7-23
Los Angeles, California 90017
Tel: 213-614-5622

Cameo Film Library
10620 Burbank Boulevard
North Hollywood, California 91601
Tel: 818-980-8700

Cascom International
806 Fourth Avenue South
Nashville, Tennessee 37210
Tel: 615-242-8900

Cinenet
2235 First Street, Suite 111
Simi Valley, California 93065
Tel: 805-527-0093
Fax: 805-527-0305

Classic Images
1041 North Formosa Avenue
West Hollywood, California 90046
Tel: 213-850-2980

Larry Dorn Associates/World Backgrounds
5820 Wilshire Boulevard, Suite 306
Los Angeles, California 90036
Tel: 213-935-6266

Energy Productions
12700 Ventura Boulevard, 4th Floor
Studio City, California 91604
Tel: 800-462-4379/818-508-1444
Fax: 818-508-1293
In New York
Tel: 212-686-4900
Fax: 212-686-4998

Fabulous Footage, Inc.
19 Mercer Street
Toronto, Ontario
Canada M5V 1H2
Tel: 800-361-3456
In Los Angeles
Tel: 213-463-1153
In New York
Tel: 212-571-1227

Film Bank
425 South Victory Boulevard
Burbank, California 91502
Tel: 818-841-9176
Fax: 818-567-4235

Film & Video Stock Shots
10422 Burbank Boulevard, Suite E
North Hollywood, California 91601
Tel: 818-760-2098

Firstlight
15353 Northeast 90 Street
Redmond, Washington 98052
Tel: 800-368-1488/206-869-6600

Fish Films, Inc.
4548 Van Noord Avenue
Studio City, California 91604
Tel: 818-905-1071
Fax: 818-905-0301

Footage
56 Stony Point Road
Rochester, New York 14624
Tel: 716-594-4130

Footage Factory
500-B Santa Rosa Road, Suite 380
Camarillo, California 93012
Tel: 805-987-8191

Footage 91: North American
430 West 14 Street, Room 403
New York, New York 10014
Tel: 800-633-2033

Frontline Video & Film
243 12 Street
Del Mar, California 92014
Tel: 619-481-5566

Great American Stock
Mirage Center, 39-935 Vista del Sol
Rancho Mirage, California 92270
Tel: 619-325-5151

Sherman Grinberg Film Libraries
1040 North McCadden Place
Hollywood, California 90038
Tel: 213-464-7491

Hollywood Film Archive
8344 Melrose Avenue
West Hollywood, California 90069
Tel: 213-933-3345

Hot Shots & Cool Cuts
1926 Broadway
New York, New York 10023
Tel: 212-799-9100
Fax: 212-799-9258

The Image Bank
111 Fifth Avenue
New York, New York 10003
Tel: 212-529-6700/800-TIB-IMAGES

Images Unlimited
75 Bridger Hollow Road
Pray, Montana 59065
Tel: 406-333-4300
Fax: 406-333-4308

Imageways
412 West 48 Street
New York, New York 10036
Tel: 800-862-1118/212-265-1287
Fax: 212-586-0339

International Film & Video
1314 Northwest Irving Street, Suite 503
Portland, Oregon 97209
Tel: 503-223-8689

International Video Network
2242 Camino Ramon
San Ramon, California 94853
Tel: 510-866-1344
Fax: 510-866-9262

Jasmine Multimedia Publishing
6746 Valjean Avenue, Suite 100
Van Nuys, California 91406
Tel: 818-780-3344

Norman Kent Productions
PO Box 1749
Flagler Beach, Florida 32136
Tel: 904-446-0505

Kesser Stock Library
21 Southwest 15 Road
Miami, Florida 33129
Tel: 305-358-7900

L.A. News Service
1341 Ocean Avenue, Suite 262
Santa Monica, California 90401
Tel: 310-399-6460

Harold Lloyd Films
707 Wilshire Boulevard, Suite W7-23
Los Angeles, California 90017
Tel: 213-614-4195

MacGillivray Freeman Films
PO Box 205
Laguna Beach, California 92562
Tel: 714-494-1055
Fax: 714-494-2079

Merkel Films
PO Box 2247
Santa Barbara, California 93120
Tel: 805-882-1904
Fax: 805-882-9104

Miramar Productions
200 Second Avenue West
Seattle, Washington 98119
Tel: 206-284-4700

National Geographic Film Library
1600 M Street, N.W.
Washington, DC 20036
Tel: 202-857-7659

NBC News Archives
30 Rockefeller Plaza, Room 902
New York, New York 10112
Tel: 212-664-3797

Palo/Haklar & Associates
650 North Bronson Avenue, Suite 144
Los Angeles, California 90004
Tel: 213-461-0982

Paradise Stock Footage
1833 Kalakaua Avenue, Suite 404
Honolulu, Hawaii 96815
Tel: 808-955-1000
Fax: 808-949-6948

Paramount Pictures Film Library
5555 Melrose Avenue
Los Angeles, California 90038
Tel: 213-956-5510

Petrified Films/The Image Bank
430 West 14 Street, Room 204
New York, New York 10114
Tel: 212-242-5461

Preview Media
747 Front Street
San Francisco, California 94111
Tel: 415-397-2494

Producers Library Service
1051 North Cole Avenue
Hollywood, California 90038
Tel: 213-465-0572
Fax: 213-465-1671

Pyramid Film & Video
PO Box 1048
Santa Monica, California 90406
Tel: 310-828-7577

Re:Search
28-28 35 Street, Suite 5L
Astoria, New York 11103
Tel: 718-777-1523

Rysher Entertainment
3400 Riverside Drive, 6th Floor
Burbank, California 91351
Tel: 818-846-0030

Ron Sawade Cinematography
PO Box 1310
Pismo Beach, California 93448
Tel: 805-481-0586
Fax: 805-481-9752

Sea Photo, Film & Tape Library
9520 El Granito Avenue
La Mesa, California 91941
Tel: 619-466-2002

Second Line Search
1926 Broadway
New York, New York 10023
Tel: 212-787-7500

SFV International
11219 Bloomington Drive
Tampa, Florida 33635
Tel: 813-884-5963

Sharkbait Pictures
PO Box 3263
Kailua-Kona, Hawaii 96745
The Source Stock Footage Library
738 North Constitution Drive
Tucson, Arizona 85748
Tel: 602-298-4810

Southwest Film/Video Archives
Southern Methodist University
PO Box 4194
Dallas, Texas 75275
Tel: 214-768-1682

Spectra
Time-lapse stock footage
Tel: 503-683-7181
Fax: 503-687-2883

The Stock House
6922 Hollywood Boulevard, Suite 621
Hollywood, California 90028
Tel: 213-461-0061

Stock Shots
North Hollywood, California
Tel: 818-760-2098
Fax: 818-760-3294

Stock Video
1029 Chestnut Street
Newton, Massachusetts 02164
Tel: 617-332-9975

Streamline Archives/Images
432 Park Avenue South, Suite 1314
New York, New York 10016
Tel: 212-696-2616
Fax: 212-696-0021

Tatum Communications
2920 West Olive Avenue, Suite 102
Burbank, California 91505
Tel: 818-841-1155

Travelview International
10370 Richmond Avenue, Suite 550
Houston, Texas 77042
Tel: 713-975-7077

Twentieth Century Fox
10201 Pico Boulevard
Los Angeles, California 90035
Tel: 310-203-2763

21st Century Video Productions
PO Box 7102
Orange, California 92617-7102
Tel: 800-974-4430
Fax: 714-744-4911

Universal Studios Film Library
100 Universal City Plaza, Room 214
Universal City, California 91608
Tel: 818-777-1695

The Video Library
1465 Northside Drive, Suite 110
Atlanta, Georgia 30318
Tel: 404-355-5800
Fax: 404-350-9823

Video Tape Library
1509 North Crescent Heights Blvd.
Suite 2
Los Angeles, California 90046
Tel: 213-656-4330
Fax: 213-656-8746

White Rain Films
111 South Lander, Suite 301
Seattle, Washington 98134
Tel: 206-682-5417

Wish You Were Here Film & Video
1455 Royal Boulevard
Glendale, California 91207
Tel: 818-243-7043
Fax: 818-241-1720

Worldview Entertainment/The Killiam Collection
500 Greenwich Street, Suite 501A
New York, New York 10013
Tel: 212-925-4291

Worldwide Television News (WTN)
1995 Broadway
New York, New York 10023
Tel: 212-362-4440

The WPA Film Library
16101 South 108 Avenue
Orland Park, Illinois 60462
Tel: 708-460-0555
Fax: 708-460-0187

Where to License Music

This list highlights a sampling of suppliers, with phone numbers and opinions.

Associated Production Music
6255 Sunset Boulevard, Suite 820
Hollywood, California 90028
Tel: 800-545-4276/213-461-3211
◇ *All styles; a Hollywood favorite.*

Buyout music and Effects
Tel: 800-468-6874
◇ *Vocals, jingles, synthesizer, large library.*

Capitol/OGM Production Music
6922 Hollywood Boulevard, Suite 718
Hollywood, California 90028
Tel: 800-421-4163/213-421-4163
◇ *Oldest, good sound, 70-minute demos.*

Creative Support Services
Tel: 800-468-6874
◇ *102 CDs of buyout music and effects, free demo.*

Davenport Music Library
Tel: 800-951-6666
◇ *Great preview policy, quality varies.*

Dewolfe Music Library
Tel: 212-892-0220
◇ *Great preview policy, quality varies.*

Dimension Music & Sound Effects, Inc.
PO Box 8495
Jupiter, Florida 33468
Tel: 800-634-0091
Fax: 407-575-3232
✧ *Large library, good sound-effects source.*

Encyclopedia of Sound
Tel: 800-638-5757
✧ *Low cost for educational uses; commercial projects require separate license.*

Energetic Music, Inc.
Tel: 800-323-2972
✧ *Twenty-three volumes of great buyout music, specific themes, one composer.*

Fresh–The Music Library
Tel: 800-545-0688
✧ *45 per disc, orchestral sounds weak, rest better sounding; lifetime buyout; call for free directory CD.*

Gene Michael Productions
Tel: 800-955-0619
✧ *Excellent, will create custom CDs on request.*

Killer Tracks
Tel: 800-877-0078
✧ *Newcomer, some overpriced.*

Magiclips Music Library
Tel: 800-949-7500
✧ *CD–ROM with all formats, many short, linkable synthesized cues.*

Major Music Library
Tel: 800-223-6278
✧ *Soundalikes and traditional sounds.*

Manchester Music Library
Tel: 203-846-3745
Fax: 203-846-0267
✧ *Production music of rare quality. All licensing options available.*

The Music Bakery
Tel: 800-229-0313
✧ *All on approval, 16 low-cost discs, free demo disc.*

Music Madness
Tel: 602-553-8966
✧ *CD–ROMs, synthesized pop, handy edit.*

Omnimusic
6255 Sunset Boulevard, Suite 803
Hollywood, California 90028
Tel: 800-828-6664/213-962-6494
✧ *Excellent production, lots of composers.*

PTBM
Tel: 503-345-0212
✧ *A best buy, wide range of sounds.*

River City Sound Productions
Tel: 800-755-8729/901-274-7277
✧ *Well written, some live, some mono; nature, wedding, country, mellow, sports.*

Sopersound Music Library
Tel: 800-227-9980
✧ *Large buyout selection, free CD demo; for TeleDemo call 415-323-2929.*

Sound Ideas (BO/Blanket)
Tel: 800-387-3030
✧ *Fifty-seven CDs available; you must buy everything.*

Soundquest Music Library
Tel: 914-358-6846
✧ *Short themes, good for special effects.*

TRF Production Music Libraries
Tel: 800-899-6874
Fax: 914-356-0895
✧ *Over 50,000 tracks (4000 discs), free demo.*

Worlds Greatest Music Clips
Tel: 914-426-0400
✧ *Two hundred and fifty short clips on CD–ROM from the Major Music Library, good search utility.*

ZEDZ Music
Tel: 617-324-1989
✧ *A production music botique. High-quality buyout library.*

Packaging Companies

Ace Label Systems
7100 Madison Avenue West
Golden Valley, Minnesota 55427
Tel: 612-933-3105
Fax: 612-545-8771

AET Packaging Films
1313 North Market Street
Wilmington, Delaware 19899-8908
Tel: 302-594-7700
Fax: 302-594-5563

Alpha Enterprises
6370 Wise Avenue N.W.
North Canton, Ohio 44720
Tel: 216-490-2000
Fax: 216-490-2010

Ames Specialty Packaging
21 Properzi Way
PO Box 120
Somerville, Massachusetts 02143
Tel: 617-776-3360
Fax: 617-623-8895

APEX Machine Company
3000 Northeast 12 Terrace
Fort Lauderdale, Florida 33334
Tel: 305-565-2739
Fax: 305-563-2844

AUTODISC, Inc.
1370 Dell Avenue, Suite B
Campbell, California 95008
Tel: 408-376-2700
Fax: 408-376-2712

Bowers Record Sleeve
5331 North Tacoma Avenue
Indianapolis, Indiana 46220
Tel: 317-251-3918
Fax: 317-254-5738

Calumet Carton Co.
16920 State Street
South Holland, Illinois 60473
Tel: 708-333-6521
Fax: 708-333-8540

Edelstein Diversified Co., Ltd.
21 Mount Vernon
Montreal
Canada H8R 1J9
Tel: 514-489-8689
Fax: 514-489-9707

Filam National Plastics
13984 South Orange Avenue
Paramount, California 90723-2083
Tel: 310-630-2500
Fax: 310-408-0712

Gelardi Design
PO Box 2757
Kennebunkport, Maine 04046
Tel: 207-967-0679
Fax: 207-967-2820

Langenpac Kyoto, Inc.
6154 Kestrel Road
Mississauga, Ontario
Canada L5T 1Z2
Tel: 905-670-7200
Fax: 905-670-5291

Multi-Media
9340 Topanga Canyon, Suite 200
Chatsworth, California 91311
Tel: 818-341-7484
Fax: 818-341-2807

PILZ GmbH
Ingrid-Pilz Strasse 1
85402 Kranzberg
Germany
Tel: 011-49-8166-670270
Fax: 011-49-8166-670307

Polyline Corporation
1233 Rand Road
Des Plains, Ilinois 60016
Tel: 708-390-7744
Fax: 708-827-6851

Rose Packaging
17 Cherrymoor Drive
Englewood, Colorado 80110
Tel: 303-761-2815
Fax: 303-761-3519

Shape
PO Box 366
Biddeford Industrial Park
Biddeford, Maine 04005
Tel: 207-282-6155
Fax: 207-283-9130

Vinylweld
2011 West Hastings Street
Chicago, Illinois 60608
Tel: 312-243-0606
Fax: 312-942-0693

Publication Resources

CD–ROM Professional
Pemberton Press
426 Danbury Road
Wilton, Connecticut 06987
Monthly—$55/yr.
❖ *A must get; best magazine in the business; covers only CD–ROM and does it well.*

OEM Magazine
CMP Publications
600 Community Drive
Manhasset, New York 11030
Tel: 516-565-5858
Sent free to qualified system integrators.
❖ *A great source for new hardware announcements in CD–ROM, mass storage, backup systems, and such; often has good features on compression, displays, etc.; highly recommended.*

Video Systems
Intertec Publishing
PO Box 12901
Overland Park, Kansas 66282
Tel: 913-341-1300
Fax: 913-967-1904
Sent free to qualified industry
professionals, otherwise $45/yr.

✧ *Geared toward professional video producers and technicians, but is good to get because it follows the migration of video toward computer discs as a delivery medium.*

Advanced Imaging
PTN Publishing Co.
445 Broad Hollow Road
Melville, New York 11747
Tel: 516-845-2700
Fax: 516-845-2797
Sent free to qualified industry
professionals, otherwise $60/yr.

✧ *For the latest information on graphics formats, image compression, and display technology, this is the best source.*

New Media
Hypermedia Communications
901 Mariner's Island Boulevard, #365
San Mateo, California 94404
Tel: 415-573-5170
Fax: 415-573-5131
Monthly– $38/yr.

✧ *The multimedia market—from Apple Macintosh to PC to CD–ROM and beyond—is growing rapidly. New Media has staked out this considerable turf as its base of coverage in articles ranging from multimedia authoring software to game and cost-reference reviews. A must.*

CD–ROM Multimedia
Universal Multimedia
PO Box 2946
Pittsburgh, New York 12901
Monthly– $19.95/yr.

✧ *A good magazine for following the consumer end of the market.*

Film & Video Monthly
Optic Music
8455 Beverly Boulevard, Suite 508
Los Angeles, California 90048
Tel: 213-653-8053
Fax: 213-653-8190
Monthly– $55/yr.

✧ *Covers high end professional video as well as film. More and more multimedia stuff creeps in every issue.*

Converge
Multi-Facet
PO Box 70758
Sunnyvale, California 94086
Tel: 800-959-5276
Fax: 408-732-1728
Bimonthly– $99/yr.

✧ *If you develop, publish, or sell CD–ROMs then you must get this. It is rich in content and has 32 full pages of information with no ads. Call and ask for a sample issue.*

Wired
544 Second Street
San Francisco, California 94107-1427
Tel: 415-904-0660
Fax: 415-904-0669
Bimonthly– $36/2 yrs.

✧ *A bimonthly explosion of post-information-age news, views, and techno-editorial that is a joy to read and look at. Visually and intellectually alive, the content may not be for all readers, but you owe yourself at least one look. Not technologically specific, it is more a guide to what's fringe, off the edge, or looming on the electronic horizon.*

Business & Legal CD-ROMs in Print

Meckler Corporation
11 Ferry Lane West
Westport, Connecticut 06880
Tel: 203-226-6967
Annual volume–$55.

✧ *An annual review and digest that targets this most vital area of CD–ROM publishing. Any legal or business research professional needs this volume to keep up to date.*

Digital Video
80 Elm Street
Peterborough, New Hampshire 03458
Tel: 603-924-0100
Fax: 603-924-4066

✧ *The definitive source publication for digital media creators; devoted to hands-on evaluation.*

Publish
Integrated Media
501 Second Street
San Francisco, California 94107
Monthly–$39.90/yr.

✧ *Although aimed primarily at the publishing and prepress business, timely articles on Photo CD, multimedia issues, and similar topics make this very worthwhile.*

CDI
Haymarket Publications Ltd.
60 Waldegrave Road
Teddington, Middlesex
TW11 8LG, United Kingdom
Tel: 011-44-81-943-5896
Fax: 011-44-81-943-5993
Bimonthly–rates unavailable.

✧ *A glossy magazine aimed squarely at consumers who favor high-tech applications.*

Computer Graphics World
Penn Well Publishing
10 Tara Boulevard, 5th Floor
Nashua, New Hampshire 03062
Tel: 603-891-0123
Fax: 603-891-0539
Monthly–$39/yr.

✧ *Covers cutting-edge developments and technology in keeping with its title. A good source for animation, modeling, and similar software tools.*

AV Video
Montage Publishing
701 Westchester Avenue
White Plains, New York 10604
Tel: 603-891-0123
Fax: 603-891-0539
Monthly–$53/yr.

✧ *Comes at the computer video market from a broadcasting industry view; good source of video technology tools based in the PC environment.*

PC Graphics & Video
Advanstar Communications
201 East Sandpointe Avenue, Suite 600
Santa Ana, California 92707
Tel: 714-513-8400
Fax: 714-513-8612
Monthly–$24.95/yr.

✧ *Featuring timely articles true to its name, this magazine documents the merging of video into the PC environment. Very good.*

Title Development Software Tools Sources

Advanced Media
695 Town Center Drive, Suite 250
Costa Mesa, California 92626
Tel: 800-292-4AMI

Aimtech Corporation
20 Trafalgar Square
Nashua, New Hampshire 03063-1973
Tel: 603-883-0220
Fax: 603-883-5582

Asymetrix Corporation
110 110 Avenue N.E., Suite 700
Bellevue, Washington 98004
Tel: 206-637-1500
Fax: 206-455-3071

Autodesk Inc.
2320 Marinship Way
Sausalito, California 94965
Tel: 415-332-2344
Fax: 415-491-8308

Caligari Corporation
1955 Landings Drive
Mountain View, California 94043
Tel: 415-390-9600
Fax: 415-390-9755

CMC Research, Inc.
7150 Southwest Hampton, Suite 120
Portland, Oregon 97223
Tel: 503-639-3395
Fax: 503-639-1796

Creative Digital Research
7291 Coronado Drive
San Jose, California 95129
Tel: 408-255-0999
Fax: 408-255-1011

Dataware Technologies, Inc.
222 Third Street, Suite 3300
Cambridge, Massachusetts 02142
Tel: 617-621-0820
Fax: 617-494-0740

Enigma Information Retrieval Systems Inc.
420 Lexingtion Avenue, Suite 608
New York, New York 10170
Tel: 212-599-1400
Fax: 212-338-9242

Executive Technologies, Inc.
2120 16 Avenue South
Birmingham, Alabama 35205
Tel: 205-933-5495

Exoterica Corporation
1545 Carling Avenue
Ottawa, Ontario
Canada K1Z 8P9
Tel: 613-722-1700/800-565-9465
Fax: 613-722-5706

Folio Corporation
2155 North Freedom Boulevard
Suite 150
Provo, Utah 84604
Tel: 801-344-3700
Fax: 801-375-3700

Fulcrum Technologies, Inc.
560 Rochester Street
Ottawa, Ontario
Canada K1S 5K2
Tel: 613-238-1761
Fax: 613-238-7695

I-Mode Retrieval Systems, Inc.
7 Odell Plaza
Yonkers, New York 10701
Tel: 914-968-7008
Fax: 914-968-9187

Innovative Communication Systems
112 Roberts Street, Suite 14
Fargo, North Dakota 58102
Tel: 701-293-1004

Interactive Image Technologies, Ltd.
700 King Street West, Suite 815
Toronto, Ontario
Canada M5V 2Y6
Tel: 416-361-0333

Knowledge Access, Inc.
2685 Marine Way, Suite 1305
Mountain View, California 94043
Tel: 800-252-9273/415-969-0606
Fax: 415-964-2027

Knowledgeset Corporation
888 Villa Street, Suite 500
Mountain View, California 94043
Tel: 415-968-9888
Fax: 415-968-9962

Lenel Systems
290 Woodcliff Office Park
Fairport, New York 14450
Tel: 716-248-9720
Fax: 716-248-9185

Logical Data Expression
5537 33 Street N.W.
Washington, DC 20015
Tel: 206-966-3393

Macromedia
600 Townsend Street
San Francisco, California 94103
Tel: 415-442-0200
Fax: 415-442-0190

Micro Retrieval Corp.
One Broadway
Cambridge, Massachusetts 02142
Tel: 617-577-1574
Fax: 617-577-9517

Microkey, Inc.
15415 Redhill Avenue, Suite B
Tustin, California 92680
Tel: 800-521-3575
Fax: 714-258-3215

Motionworks
524 Second Street
San Francisco, California 94107
Tel: 415-541-9333
Fax: 415-541-0555

Nimbus Information Systems
Guilford Farm SR 629
Ruckersville, Virginia 22968
Tel: 804-985-1100
Fax: 804-985-4625

NTERGAID
60 Commerce Park
Milford, Connecticut 06460
Tel: 203-783-1280
Fax: 203-882-0850

Online Computer Systems, Inc.
20251 Century Boulevard
Germantown, Maryland 20874
Tel: 800-922-9204/301-428-3700
Fax: 301-428-2903

Oracle Corporation
500 Oracle Parkway
Redwood Shores, California 94065
Tel: 415-506-7000
Fax: 415-506-7200

Owl International, Inc.
2800 156th Avenue SE
Bellevue, Washington 98007
Tel: 206-747-3203
Fax: 206-641-9367

Personal Library Software, Inc.
2400 Research Boulevard, Suite 350
Rockville, Maryland 20850
Tel: 301-990-1155
Fax: 301-963-9738

Q-Media Software Corporation
312 East Fifth Avenue
Vancouver, British Columbia
Canada V5T 1H4
Tel: 604-879-1190
Fax: 604-879-0214

RAD Technologies, Inc.
745 Emerson Street
Palo Alto, California 94301
Tel: 415-617-9340
Fax: 415-473-6826

SPINNAKER Software
One Kendall Square
Cambridge, Massachusetts 02139
Tel: 617-494-1200

Textware Corporation
347 Main Street
PO Box 3267
Park City, Utah 84060
Tel: 801-645-9600
Fax: 801-645-9610

Visual Software
21731 Ventura Boulevard, #301
Woodland Hills, California 91364
Tel: 818-883-7900
Fax: 818-593-3737

Glossary

A

A: Hexadecimal representation of the decimal number 10.

absolute sector address: The address of the sector, as counted from the absolute beginning sector of the disc, expressed in minutes:seconds:sectors, or as a logical block number or logical sector number.

access: The retrieval of information from memory or mass storage, such as CD–ROM.

access software: See *search and retrieval software.*

access time: The time span from search command to display of data on the screen. Access time is measured for movement of the read mechanism from the start of the disc until the end.

accessory: Any peripheral of a computer system such as a CD–ROM drive or a modem.

a-characters: Under the ISO 9660 standard, a set of characters (A to Z, 0 to 9, and the symbols [space] ! " % & ' = * + – . / ; : < > ? _) that may be used in certain volume descriptors and other fields. See *volume descriptors.*

accuracy: The absence of error. The extent to which results are error-free.

active lines: The number of horizontal scan lines used to produce a picture on the cathode ray tube of a television. The U.S. standard is 525 lines.

active program: The program that is currently running in a given computer.

adaptive compression: Data compression software that continually analyzes and compensates its algorithm, depending on the type and content of the data and the storage medium.

add-on: Hardware that is added to a computer system to improve overall performance. A common add-on is extended memory.

address: A digital code that specifies where items are located on a CD–ROM and in memory systems.

addressable: Having the capability of being directly addressed within a specific instruction.

addressable space: The smallest addressable space on a disc is the smallest piece of information that can be individually located or addressed. On a compact disc the smallest addressable space is the size of the logical block.

algorithm: A method for solving a problem in which a pattern of set procedures can be iterated until an optimal solution is obtained.

alphanumeric: Characters that include letters of the alphabet, numbers, and other symbols such as an exclamation point or hyphen.

analog: An infinitely variable or continuous characteristic or signal such as time, temperature, or movie video, as opposed to a discretely variable digital characteristic or signal such as a pulse, digitized image, or animated video.

analog-to-digital converter (ADC): An electronic circuit that converts an analog signal into discrete digital data representing the signal.

analog video: A video signal that represents an infinite number of smooth gradations between given video levels. By contrast, a digital video signal assigns a finite set of levels.

AND operation: A Boolean operation that combines two terms. For example, if the search request is traffic AND accidents, all records or documents must contain both terms to be returned as a true match.

ANSI (American National Standards Institute): A standards-setting, nongovernment organization that develops and publishes standards for voluntary use in the United States.

ANSI-labeled tape: A tape that uses a multifile/multivolume label. Each volume has a header whose specification may be found in the American National Standards Institute's *Draft Information Systems File Structure and Labeling Magnetic Tapes for Information Interchange.* A 17-character file name is embedded in the header.

ANSI.SYS: A device that makes a monitor on DOS- and OS/2–based systems conform to ANSI standards.

antialiasing: A form of interpolation used when combining images. Pixels along the transitions between images are averaged to provide a smooth transition.

antialiasing filter: An electronic circuit that deletes extraneous, high-frequency tones from an input signal. If these tones were not removed, they would interact with lower frequencies to create false audio tones called *alias signals.*

append: To add something at the end of a file or database.

API (application programming interface): Collection of routines used to access functions of software modules or layers, that is, a software tool that enables programmers to interface one program or subprogram with another program, operating system, or operating environment.

Appleshare: The software layer of networking capability for Macintosh computers. Appleshare can operate with low-cost Appletalk hardware, but also with Ethernet or FDDI.

Appletalk: The physical and data protocol built into Macintosh computers. At 230 Kbps, it is the slowest—and the least expensive—of networks for the Mac. Appletalk uses a bus topology and collision detection.

application programs: A computer program designed to implement a specific task such as organizing a CD–ROM database. See *application software*.

application software: Software programs designed to perform specific tasks such as search and retrieval of optical text, database management, or word processing. See *application programs*.

archiving: The storage of information over extended periods of time.

ARCnet (attached computer research network): A widely used network operating at 2.5 Mbps over coaxial or twisted-pair cable. Though normally configured in a bus or star topology, ARCnet uses a token-passing protocol to arbitrate communications.

artifact: Term for an ugly roughness that appears in sound or images when they are digitized badly.

artificial intelligence: Computer programs that perform functions that are generally not associated with human reasoning or learning.

ASCII (American Standard Code for Information Interchange): A seven-bit code that represents numbers, letters, and control characters. It is mainly used to transmit data between digital devices. The ASCII code was established by the American National Standards Institute (ANSI).

aspect ratio: The relationship of width and height. When an image is displayed on different screens, the aspect ratio must be kept the same to avoid "stretching" in either the vertical or horizontal direction. Computer screens usually have an aspect ratio of 4:3. Aspect ratio is important in the present context because if you are transferring an image between formats having different aspect ratios, you must decide whether to distort the image or frame it to make it fit.

asymmetrical compression: A compression system that requires more processing capability to compress an image than to decompress an image. It is typically used for the mass distribution of programs on media such as CD–ROM, where significant expense can be incurred for the production and compression of the program.

asynchronous: Not occurring at predetermined intervals, not synchronized.

asynchronous communication: A means of transmitting data in which the timing of character placement on connecting transmission lines is not critical.

A-Time: Absolute time. The time elapsed since the beginning of the disc. It can be used in determining the start and stop times of sound segments for programming an application on a mixed–mode disc, measuring from the very beginning of the data area (including the computer data in Track 1). See *mixed mode*, *data area*, and *Track 1*.

audio frequencies: Those frequencies that can be heard by the human ear; the sound for multimedia systems. Audio frequencies range from 15 Hz to 20,000 Hz.

authoring system: Software that helps developers design interactive courseware. Sometimes called a *search and retrieval engine*.

AUTOEXEC.BAT: A batch file executed at the beginning of DOS operations that gives the computer certain basic parameters for operation, including the paths where certain programs or data may be found.

auxiliary data field: A 288-byte field in a CD–ROM sector that precedes the data field. In Mode 1, it contains error-correction codes; in Mode 2 (CD–ROM) and Mode 2 Form 2 (CD–I) it may be used for data.

A-weighting: An adjustment to an audio signal measurement (usually S/N ratio) that compensates for the range of distortion most noticeable to the human ear.

B

bad byte: A byte that is read back differently than it was originally written.

bandwidth: The number of oscillations expressing the difference between the upper and lower limiting frequencies of a band or a set of adjacent frequencies. This term is also used to mean the maximum number of information units (bits, characters, etc.) capable of traversing a communications path each second.

bar code: A code of lines of variable width that is scanned via optical scanner to receive data.

baseband: A signaling method in which a cable carries a single digital signal at a time.

baud: The number of bits per second transmitted over a communications connection. As an example, at 1200 baud data is transmitted at the rate of 150 typed characters per second. See *bit* and *byte*.

beginning of tape (BOT): A reflective strip that is positioned near the physical beginning of a reel of tape. This strip is located near the top edge of the tape. Data is written to and read from the tape, beginning after this strip. Both the LOAD and REWIND commands position the tape to just after this reflective strip.

bibliographic database: A collection of bibliographic material in the form of bibliographic references to original books, articles, or other literature. CD–ROM is the medium of choice for storing large bibliographic databases.

binary: Pertaining to two state conditions or positions. In computer systems, these two states are 1 and 0 or on and off.

binary search: A search method that entails subdividing a file in half until the desired data is "closed in on" or located.

bit (binary digit): The smallest unit of computer data, represented by 1 (on) or 0 (off) in the binary number system. (See *baud* and *byte*.) Data bits are used in combination to form characters; framing bits are used for parity and transmission synchronization.

bit combination: As per the ISO 2022 standard, "an ordered set of bits that represents a character."

bit map: Representation of characters or graphics by individual pixels arranged in row (horizontal) and column (vertical) order. Each pixel can be represented by either one bit (simple black and white) or up to 32 bits (high-definition color).

bit-mapped graphics: Images that are created with matrices of pixels, or dots. Also called *raster graphics*.

bit plane: In digital video, display hardware that has more than one video memory array contributing to the displayed image in real time. Each memory array is called an *image plane*; however, if the arrays have only one bit per pixel they may be called *bit planes*. See *image plane*.

bit specifications: Number of colors or levels of gray that can be displayed at one time. Controlled by the amount of memory in the computer's graphics controller card. An 8-bit controller can display 256 colors or levels of gray; a 16-bit controller, 64,000 colors; a 24-bit controller, 16.8 million colors. The last is known as true color.

bit stream: (1) A binary signal without regard to groupings by character. (2) A serial sequence of bits.

bit string: A group of binary bits with an arbitrary arrangement.

bits per inch (bpi): The density at which data is written on a tape, optical disc, or magnetic disc. See *density*.

bits per second (bps): A measure of data transmission speed in information systems.

blanking interval: A period in which the monitor receives no video signal while the player searches for the next video segment or frame of play.

block: (1) A sequential group of data, such as sequences of data on a magnetic tape or disk. (2) The user portion of a sector on a CD–ROM disc, commonly referred to simply as user data.

block error correction: Data recovery methods are introduced to a physical block of data during CD–ROM premastering to ensure the recovery of all user data. The block size of user data is 2048 bytes, and EDC and 276 bytes of ECC are used to detect and correct block errors in the user data block.

block error rate: A measure of the capacity of a storage medium to store and transmit blocks of data without errors.

blocking factor: The number of logical records blocked in a physical block. When records are of fixed length, the physical block size is usually an even multiple of the logical record size. Sometimes, particularly in backup data tapes or premastering tapes, the block size is unrelated to the logical record size. Instead, a physical block size is chosen using another criterion, such as a multiple of the disc sector size or a power of two.

BNC connector: A bayonet-type cable connector, found on professional video equipment.

board or card: A board with circuitry and chips that is inserted into a computer or peripheral, usually to enhance or add to its capabilities (such as a fax board or an accelerator board).

Boolean operators: These AND, OR, and NOT connectors comprise a class of keyword search commands enabling one to search for combinations or exclusions of certain specified words of phrases. They are used by more experienced searchers to achieve a higher degree of search selectivity.

Boolean search: A database search request that uses Boolean operators AND, OR, and NOT in various combinations. For example, Vermont AND Utah, dog OR cat, etc.

boot record: A portion of a CD–ROM that contains the operating system; allowable for those systems that may load the operating system from the CD–ROM. In ISO 9660, a record on a compact disc that gives the location of a boot file on the disc.

bootable: A bootable disk or disc is one from which a computer can be started up, because all the necessary operating system software is available from the disc.

bpp (bits per pixel): The number of bits used to represent the color value of each pixel in a digitized image.

bps: (1) Either bits per second (usually abbreviated bps) or bytes per second (usually Bps). Bits per second divided by either 8, 10, or 11 (depending on the communication method being used) gives approximate bytes per second. (2) The number of bits transferred in a data communications system. Measures speed.

brightness ratio: An indication, expressed as a ratio, of the difference between the brightest and the darkest object in the scene.

broadband: A signaling method in which a cable's bandwidth is split into several channels, each of which independently carries analog signals.

browsing: Casually "combing" through a database looking for general topics or information. See *searching*.

buffer: A piece of memory that temporarily stores data, usually a small amount. This can help to compensate for differences in the transfer rate of data from one device to another, or it can be used to store small pieces of information that are likely to be used repeatedly (such as a digitized beep or other sound). Most CD–ROM drives have their own 64-KB buffers, so if you ask for, say, 24 KB of data, the drive will go ahead and read those 24 plus the following 40 into the buffer. If you then need the following 40 KB of data, they will be there for instant retrieval. Otherwise, they are simply wiped out of the buffer when the next set of data is loaded.

bugs: Errors in computer programs.

build engine (indexer): The main part of a database retrieval package, through which data structures such as indexes and linked lists are created. It creates a pointer to data that enables the retrieval engine to quickly locate it.

burst error: An error consisting of a group of consecutive data bits, rather than a single bit, which often results from CD–ROM surface scratches, fingerprints, electromagnetic interference, and other physical irritants. Burst errors are detected in C1 and corrected in C2. The possibility of this happening is 10^{-12}, or one bit error in a trillion bits. See *CIRC*.

burst mode: A way of writing or reading data that will not allow interrupts to occur.

burst transmission: Messages are stored for a time period, then released at a much faster speed for transmission. The received signals are recorded and then slowed down for the user to process.

bus: Also *data bus*. A section of a computer that transfers data between different parts of a computer system.

bus topology: A physical LAN layout in which all computers are connected to a single length of cable (or a series of cables connected to form one long daisy chain) with a terminator at each end.

byte: A sequence of bits generally eight bits long. One byte represents one typed character. It is usually used to measure data capacity of a disc, computer CPU, etc. See *baud* and *bit*.

C

C1: A Reed-Solomon code that corrects random bit errors and detects burst errors of two bits or more for correction by C2.

C2: A Reed-Solomon code that corrects burst errors and detects further uncorrectable errors, which can then be corrected or recovered by the additional EDC and ECC.

cable: The most common LAN medium to connect devices together. See *coaxial cable* and *twisted-pair*.

cache: See *disc cache*.

caddy: The plastic and metal carrier into which a CD must be inserted before it is loaded into a CD–ROM drive.

capacity: See *storage capacity*.

CAV (constant angular velocity): In this disc-rotating system, revolutions per minute are maintained regardless of radial read head position. On CAV discs, data is recorded on concentric tracks. This format is used to store analog signals on 12-inch videodiscs.

CCIR 601: A standard resolution for digital television. 720×840 (for NTSC) or 720×576 (for PAL) luminance, with chrominance subsampled $2:1$ horizontally (only).

CCITT (Consultative Committee for International Telephone and Telegraph): An international standards organization dedicated to creating communications protocols, such as Px64, that will enable global compatibility for the transmission of voice, data, and telecommunications equipment.

CD (compact disc): This is the standard 12-cm (4.75") plastic optical disc created by Philips and Sony to store large amounts of digital information in microscopic pits which can be read by a laser beam. See *Red Book* and *electronic publishing*.

CD–Audio: *See Compact Disc Digital Audio (CD–DA).*

CDDI (copper distributed data interface): A variant of FDDI that substitutes coaxial cable for fiber-optic connections. Transfer rate is maintained, but cable run length is reduced.

CD–I (compact disc–interactive): A compact disc format containing prerecorded digital video, audio, and optical text data. Also known as the Green Book standard (see *Green Book*). Standards have been established by Philips and Sony so that CD–I players will also play CD–ROM discs. CD–I was originally intended to operate via home stereo and television rather than as a computer peripheral.

CD–PROM (compact disc as programmable read-only memory): A CD–ROM disc that can be written to once by the user and therefore can be programmed by the user. See *WORM*.

CD–ROM (compact disc read-only memory): This is the same disc as the audio compact disc except that it contains optical information instead of audio information. Also known as the Yellow Book standard. Extremely large volumes of up to 680 megabytes of optical text (250,000 typewritten pages) are compressed onto small compact discs during manufacture. They can be machine searched to instantly locate and retrieve any desired information upon demand. *Read-only memory* means that the recorded data cannot be erased or altered. This format is ideally suited for storage/access of large reference information databases. See *Yellow Book*.

CD–ROM disc player: A standard type of laser disc player used to play CD–ROM discs. It is interfaced with a personal computer by a controller card attached to an expansion slot in the computer.

CD–ROM drive: See *CD–ROM disc player*.

CD–ROM operating system: See *disk operating system*.

CD–ROM XA (compact disc–read only memory extended architecture): An extension of the CD–ROM standard billed as a hybrid of CD–ROM and CD–I, and promoted by Sony and Microsoft Corporations. The extension adds ADPCM audio to permit the interleaving of sound and video data to animation and with wound synchronization.

CD–Video (CD–V): See *video disc*.

CD–WO (compact disc–write once): A type of compact disc that allows for special discs to be recorded or written once by users at their own terminals.

CDTV (commodore dynamic total vision): Consumer multimedia system from Commodore that includes a CD–ROM/CD–Audio player, a Motorola 68000 processor, 1 MB RAM, and a 10-key infrared remote control.

central processing unit (CPU): The part of a computer that controls data transfer, input/output (I/O), and logical operations by executing instructions received from the computer system's memory.

CGA (color graphics adapter): A low-resolution video display standard, invented for the first IBM PC. CGA pixel resolution is 320×200.

CGM (computer graphics metafile): A standard format that allows for the interchanging of graphics images.

changer: A CD player that holds more than a single disc and can automatically change play from one disc to another. See *jukebox*.

channel: One of the two stereo sound signals (left/right).

channel bit: A bit, as it is transferred from the compact disc to the CD–ROM drive.

channel separation: A measure (in decibels) of the extent to which one stereo channel bleeds into the other.

chapter: A specified sequence of adjacent frames on a CD–ROM.

character string: Any group of characters that are treated as a single unit by a computer system.

check bit: A single bit (binary digit) that is used to determine the parity status of a byte of data. This bit is often called the *parity bit*.

check codes: See *error-correction codes*.

checksum: A number used for detecting data-transmission errors. The values of a set of data bytes are added together, and their sum (the checksum) is transmitted along with the original bytes. The redundant data is checked on the receiving end, and if the checksums differ, the computer knows there's been an error.

chip: Or *integrated circuit*. The basic electronic unit that performs operations in a computer. Contains microcircuits printed on a semiconductor.

chroma keying: A special effects technique used in color TV in which the image from one video source is inserted into the picture of another video source.

chrominance: The color portion of the video signal, which includes hue and saturation information. Requires luminance, or light intensity, to make it visible. Without the chrominance signal, the received picture would be black and white. Also called *chroma*.

CIE (commission internationale de l'_clairage): The international commission on illumination. Developer of color matching systems.

CIF (common intermediate format): Px64 specifies that either CIF or QCIF resolutions must be used.

CIRC (cross-interleave Reed-Solomon code): A series of two different block codes (C1 and C2) combined with data delay and rearrangement techniques. As a result of CIRC, data integrity is 10^{-12} or better.

circuit: A network of electronic components (wire, integrated circuits, resistors, diodes, etc.) that is connected between two or more ports. A circuit allows communication between the ports to which it is connected.

circuit board: See *controller card.*

clean: Up-to-date and free of repetition.

clean room: An equipment room in a CD manufacturing plant that is maintained virtually dust-free to reduce particle contamination of discs during mastering and replication.

client-server LAN: A LAN software design that typically requires one or more dedicated servers and has clients (workstations) that rely on them for services.

clock: A timing device that monitors and records the passage of real time and whose contents are accessible to a computer program. This timing device generates the periodic signal that is the reference for all aspects of timing within a computer system.

clock pulses: The periodic wave generated by a clock in a computer system. See *clock.*

clock rate: The rate at which pulses are generated by a computer system's clock. Also refers to the rate at which data is transmitted from one internal computer element to another. The faster the clock speed, the more commands can be processed per second, and the faster the overall performance will be. Clock speed is measured in megahertz (MHz). See *clock* and *clock pulses*.

CLUT (color look-up table): Also known as *LUT*. A table containing a selection of colors that may be used in a given screen image. Each table entry is a binary number expressing an absolute RGB value. The image is encoded by referring each pixel to a corresponding RGB-coded value, then displayed by matching the code associated with each pixel with the corresponding RGB color value stored in the CLUT. Also known as *indexed color*.

CLV (constant linear velocity): Each sector of data, regardless of its radial position, moves over the read head at the same speed. The disc's rotational speed changes as the head seeks in and out; the range is from 200 rpm to 500 rpm. On CLV discs, data is recorded on one long spiral track. This format is used to store digital optical text on CD–ROM discs on a spiral track approximately 3 miles long.

coaxial cable: Also called *coax*. A cable that consists of a central wire surrounded by insulation, which in turn is surrounded by electrically protective metal mesh or foil and another layer of insulation. The mesh or foil layer protects the inner wire from electrical interference. Thin coaxial cable is used for thin Ethernet LANs. Thick coaxial cable, used for thick Ethernet LANs, has greater protective characteristics and transmits signals reliably for longer distances, but has become unpopular because it is more expensive and difficult to use.

code: A method for inserting digital redundancy into a digital data stream for the purpose of detecting and correcting errors.

color balance: In a color video system, the process of matching the amplitudes of red, green, and blue signals so that the mixture of all three makes an accurate white color.

Color YCC: A device-independent color encoding method developed by Kodak for Photo CD. It separates each color pixel into one 8-bit luma (light intensity) component and two 8-bit chroma (color) components (totaling 24 bits). Photo YCC also defines a method of converting RGB to luma and chroma and vice versa that allows efficient image data compression and sufficient dynamic range and color gamut to support present and future video displays and high-quality color printing devices.

COM file: An executable program file with a .COM filename extension that operates in a specific part of the base memory in DOS and OS/2 systems.

command language: A language used to generate queries and to control the output of the data.

compact disc–digital audio (CD–DA): The official designation of the CD audio industry standard that is licensed by Philips and Sony. All CDs and CD players must conform to this standard. Also called the *Red Book standard*. See *Red Book*.

compact disc–read-only memory (CD–ROM): Defined by Philips and Sony in 1985. A CD–ROM disc offers 600 MB of computer data storage. It is a read-only medium, which means that once data are placed on the disc they cannot be altered.

compact disc–read-only memory extended architecture (CD–ROM XA): This format (defined by Philips, Sony, and Microsoft) combines the formats of CD–ROM and CD–I into a single format. CD–ROM XA discs play on both CD–ROM drives and CD–I players.

compact disc drive: A device for reading the information stored on compact discs. It works by shining a laser beam on the disc's surface and retrieving the reflected beam, which transmits digital data.

compiler A program that transforms a human-language computer program into a machine-readable executable program.

complex field: Database information that has a large number of unique words.

composite video: The complete visual wave form of the color video signal composed of chromatic and luminance picture information; blanking pedestal; field, line, and color synchronizing pulses; and field equalizing pulses.

compressed audio: A method of digitally encoding and decoding audio. By using a buffer to store the audio information, audio may be delivered to accompany images or other data.

compressed video: A digital video image or segment that has been processed using a variety of computer algorithms and other techniques to reduce the amount of data required to accurately represent the content, and thus the space required to store that content.

compression: The removal of insignificant or redundant information to conserve memory space. This is becoming increasingly important in CD–ROM publishing because of the enormous amounts of memory required to store digitized images. All compressed information must be expanded by a reverse operation called decompression.

configuration: The composition of hardware, software, and communications facilities selected to implement a computer system or network.

connectivity: A computer's or program's ability to link with other programs and devices.

constant angular velocity: A rotation mode in which a disk spins at a constant speed, with the result that the tracks nearest the center pass under the reading head at a lower speed than the tracks nearer to the outer edge of the disk. This is the approach normally taken in magnetic disks, so the sectors on the disk are physically shorter near the center and longer near the edge of the disk.

constant linear velocity: A rotation mode in which the speed of rotation is variable, so that all data sectors pass under the reading head at exactly the same speed; the rotation rate of the disc is faster when the reading head is near the center of the disc and slower as the reading head moves further from the center of the disc; sector size is constant. Used with compact discs.

context scrolling: A feature of most search and retrieval software packages that allows the user to move directly to the places in a document where a keyword was found.

continuous tone: An image that has all the values (0 to 100%) of gray (black and white) color in it. A photograph is an example.

contrast: The range between the lightest tones and the darkest tones in an image.

controller card (circuit board): An interface device connecting a CD–ROM player to one of the expansion slots in a personal computer. It controls the flow of information between the computer and the disc player. Controller cards are normally provided along with the CD–ROM players.

CRC (cyclic redundancy check): A technique for detecting data transmission errors.

crop: The camera framing of a picture that excludes part of the originally intended scene.

cross-interleaved Reed-Solomon Code (CIRC): This is the first level of error correction used in CD–ROM and the only error correction needed for CD digital audio. It yields an error rate of one uncontrollable error per 10^9 bytes (1 GB). Further error detection and correction in CD–ROM improves this to one error in 10^{13} bytes (10 trillion, or 10 thousand billion).

CSC (computer supported collaboration): The emerging ability of networked personal computers to enhance and expand work group collaboration by eliminating time and distance barriers to all forms of electronic communication and the exchange of natural data types.

CSMA/CD (carrier-sense multiple access with collision detection): A message arbitration scheme in which network stations are configured in a physical or logical ring. When one station finishes sending messages, it transmits a bit pattern, called a *token*, to the next station. If this station has messages to transmit, it does so at this time, then passes the token to the following station.

cycle: A time interval in which some repeated event or characteristic occurs. Microprocessors in computer systems run in what are called *machine cycles* or *T states*.

D

data area: In ISO 9660, the space on a CD–ROM where the user data is written. It begins at the absolute or physical address 00:02:16, immediately following the system area.

data block: Blocks of data that are written to magnetic tape and delimited by interrecord gaps. They may be virtually any length. The smallest block is one byte, and the largest is 64 KB. Typical block sizes are 4096, 8192, and 16,384 bytes. When logical records are small, they are usually lumped together to form a single larger block which results in more efficient tape usage and a faster data transfer rate. See *interrecord gaps*.

data integrity: The ability to detect and correct all kinds of errors caused by imperfections, damage, or dirt in or on the disc so that the user can view the corrected or recovered data on the screen.

data preparation: The procedure by which existing data on other media is transformed from its present form into a form better suited for delivery on CD–ROM. It includes converting the data into machine-readable format, building the files and file directories, and transferring the data to tape or a write-once disc.

data rate: The speed of a data transfer process, normally expressed in bits per second or bytes per second.

database: A relatively large and complete collection of digitally stored, machine-readable information of the same information category.

database management system: A software program designed to create and organize a database, to store information to the database, and to retrieve information from the database. This program allows speed of access and the ability to automatically produce reports on the database contents.

DBMS: Database Management System. General-purpose software that can create, change, search, sort, and generate reports from a database. Examples are dBASE

IV, Paradox, FoxPro, and Q&A. In a LAN environment, many users can simultaneously manipulate the same database on a server's shared disc.

d-characters: Under the ISO 9660 standard, a set of characters (A to Z, 0 to 9, and the underscore symbol), that may be used in certain volume descriptors and other fields.

DCT (Discrete Cosine Transform): A form of coding used in most of the current image compression systems for bit rate reduction.

decimal equivalent: The decimal number that corresponds to a binary or hexadecimal number representation.

decompression: To reverse the procedure conducted by compression software and thereby return compressed data to its original size and condition.

dedicated server: A LAN-connected computer that acts solely as a server and has no workstation capability. Some peer-to-peer LANs (such as LANtastic and NetWare Lite) permit a server to temporarily act as a dedicated server by running a special program. Stopping the program turns the server back into a nondedicated server without interrupting the work being performed by the server.

default: A value or setting applied to a program when it is first started; it will remain in effect until it is specifically changed during program operation, usually by the user.

de-interleaving: Rearranging interleaved data segments into their original order.

demultiplexing: The process through which multiplexed signals are separated, such as the left and right stereo channels of an audio signal, into its original components. See multiplexing.

density: (1) The number of bits per inch at which data are written on a tape, optical disc, or magnetic disk. (2) The degree of darkness of an image. (3) Percentage of screen used in an image.

descriptor: Under the ISO 9660 standard, a structure containing descriptive information about a volume or a file.

device driver: A small software program needed for a computer to communicate with any external device such as a CD–ROM player or printer. This is normally supplied with the CD–ROM player and may also be incorporated into the software supplied along with some types of CD–ROM disc products.

diacritical marks: Marks that indicate the phonetic value of a letter in a foreign language.

digital: A discretely variable signal or characteristic such as a pulse, digitized image, or animated video, as opposed to an infinitely variable analog signal or characteristic such as time, temperature, or movie video. Computer systems operate solely on digital information. See *analog*.

digital audio: Audio tones represented by machine-readable binary numbers rather than analog recording techniques. Analog audio is converted to digital using sampling techniques, whereby a "snapshot" is taken of the audio signal, its amplitude is measured and described numerically, and the resulting number is stored. More frequent sampling results in a more accurate digital representation of the signal.

digital filtering: Filters that remove unwanted high-output frequencies before the signal is converted to analog form. Almost always used in conjunction with oversampling digital-to-analog converters (DACs).

digital-to-analog converter (DAC): An electronic device that converts discrete digital data into a continuous analog waveform. This circuit is usually implemented in a commercially available integrated circuit.

digital video: A video signal represented by computer-readable binary numbers that describe a finite set of colors and luminance levels. See *analog video*.

digitized speech: Speech that has been converted from an analog signal to a digital signal so that it can be processed by a computer system.

digitizer: A device used to transform two-dimensional textual or graphic information into digital format, thus enabling one to enter sketches into a computer. See *scanner*.

digitizing: (1) The process of transforming two-dimensional textual or graphic information into digital format. (2) The process of sampling an analog waveform at various points in time and converting the waveform into digital data. This is done by sampling the analog signal (e.g., an image or sound waves) at fixed intervals and assigning discrete numeric values to those intervals. The smaller the interval (that is, the higher the sampling rate), the more accurate (closer to the original) the digitized version will be. A digitized version of an analog source is always, strictly speaking, an approximation.

DIN (Deutsche Industrie Norm): German standard for electric equipment. DIN plugs can be three-, five-, or six-pin plugs, depending on their use, although they all have the same outer appearance.

direct color: A method of storing color information in which the number of colors in the system palette equals the bit depth at which the image is stored. That is, if your system palette allows 256 colors, your image is stored at an 8-bit depth.

directory hierarchy: The virtual treelike structure of directories, subdirectories, and files used to help in organizing and using data on a disc or disk.

disc: Or optical disc. Throughout this book, disc with a c is used for optical media, since that is the spelling used in the standards defining compact discs. Contrast with *disk*.

disc cache: A software method that uses RAM to store disc information in order to speed up an application's apparent disc access time by reducing physical I/O to a hard disk or CD–ROM. In CD–ROM applications, the cache is typically used to store directory files.

disc drive: Another name for a disc player. An optical storage device. See *CD–ROM disc player*.

disc replication: The process of copying a master disc. Polycarbonate plastic is injected into a mold and then stamped to make the pits that contain the digital data. The plastic is then coated with a thin layer of aluminum and a protective outer coating of lacquer.

disk: Hard disk or floppy disk or diskette. Refers to magnetic storage media, as opposed to *disc*, which refers to an optical storage medium.

disk drive: A computer device used to read from and write to. Floppy diskettes and hard disks are examples of disk drives. Disk drives are usually magnetic storage devices.

disk operating system (DOS): A software program that instructs a computer how to transfer information to and from peripheral input/output devices. The basic software loaded when the computer boots, which controls basic functions such as saving and retrieving files. MS-DOS, the predominant standard personal computer operating system, must be extended or amplified to operate as a CD–ROM operating system. CD–ROM operating systems include TMS's LaserDOS, Microsoft's MS-DOS with CD–ROM extensions, Digital Equipment Corp.'s Uni-File, and Reference Technology's STA/File. The trend is toward CD–ROM operating systems that are compatible with the proposed High Sierra Group CD–ROM standards.

dithering: In working with digital images, a way to make an image appear to contain more levels of gray or different colors than it actually does. Small patterns are built up out of individual pixels (black-and-white or color) to simulate grays or colors that are not actually available. Used to improve the appearance of low-bit-depth images.

document: Small sections into which large blocks of electronically stored text are divided. Thus, a single publication, such as an encyclopedia, becomes many electronic documents. This is done to make indexing and retrieval faster.

DRAM (dynamic RAM): A RAM memory chip that stores memory as electrical charges. It must be continually refreshed or it will lose its contents.

driver: See *device driver*.

DRDW (direct read during write): The ability to read information during the actual recording process.

DVI (digital video interactive): A technology from GE/RCA, announced in mid-1987, that allows CD–ROM drives to be adapted to play audio and video images in addition to data. This adaptation would, of course, require the addition of some computer circuitry. The system is similar to CD–I, but allows much more video to be stored on each disc (approximately 1 hour). See *CD–I*.

Dvorak keyboard: An alternative keyboard designed for speed where, unlike the standard QWERTY keyboard, the letters making up the most frequent words fall in the middle row of keys.

E

EBCDIC (extended binary coded decimal interchange code): A character encoding scheme that defines 256 characters using an 8-bit code in a computer system. It was developed by IBM and used primarily in their equipment.

EGA (enhanced graphics adapter): A display technology for the IBM PC, which has largely been replaced by VGA. EGA pixel resolution is 640×350.

eight-to-fourteen (8-to-14) modulation (EFM): The process of expanding 8-bit bytes of data into 14 channel bits so that the digital data stream can be efficiently stored in the form of pits on a CD audio disc or a CD–ROM disc.

electronic global publishing: A broad term that covers all of the information distribution possibilities of the CD. The CD–ROM is presently the most attractive candidate in this field.

electronic publishing: The storage and distribution of information in a machine-readable electronic format made accessible to users for viewing on screen, printing, or downloading to storage. The major forms of electronic publishing now include CD–ROM discs and on-line information services. Several other electronic publishing media, such as video text (transmission via television programming to TV sets), have not yet become commercially successful. Future electronic publishing media may include new developments such as transmission via satellite to mass-storage devices.

emulation: Imitation of a computing function by a system that was not originally designed to implement that particular function.

encoding: The process of creating a compressed file.

encryption: Encoding additional digital data on discs for security or commercial protection so that special decoding hardware or software is required for data access.

end of data (EOD): Two consecutive tape marks are usually used to indicate the logical end of tape or the end of data. See tape marks.

end of file (EOF): Indicated by a tape mark that is written on a tape immediately following the data that is in a file.

end of tape (EOI): A reflective strip that is located near the physical end of a reel of tape. This strip is placed near the bottom edge of the tape. Data is not written beyond this point.

EPS (encapsulated PostScript): A graphic file format.

error correction: During CD–ROM premastering, an error correction code is added to each physical block of data (2048 bytes) to ensure detection of any erroneous data.

error-correction code (ECC): (1) Codes added to the digital information of CDs during encoding are used to restore missing data or to correct erroneous data. Also called check codes. (2) A code that is computed from user data on CD–ROMs to achieve the goal mentioned above.

error-correction coding: The process of encoding extra data bits on a CD–ROM disc to detect the presence of erroneously stored data and to return them to their correct value.

error-detection code (EDC): A code that is computed from user data and stored on CD–ROM so that errors in reading user data can be corrected.

error protection: The process of rearranging and expanding data to prevent possible errors in the storage medium.

error rate: The ratio of the amount of data that is written incorrectly to the total amount of data sent or transmitted.

Ethernet: A popular standard for business networks using CSMA/CD collision detect arbitration. Data rate is 10 to 200 Mbps, although 100 Mbps Ethernet rates are currently being discussed.

exabyte tape: An 8-mm magnetic tape widely used in the transportation of CD–ROM data.

EXE file: An executable file with an .EXE extension in a DOS-based system. It is similar to a COM file but is usually larger (not limited to 64 KB) and takes longer to load. Most large programs are stored as EXE files.

expansion slots: Slotlike openings in a personal computer into which controller cards (circuit boards), such as CD–ROM disc player controller cards, can be plugged to add functions to the original equipment. For example, the IBM PC/XT/AT and compatibles contain both long slots for $13^1/_8$-inch-long cards and short slots for $4^1/_8$-inch-long cards.

export: To output data from a software program in some format other than the program's "native" format. See *translate*.

extensions: Programs added to an operating system to give it additional capabilities. For example, extensions must be added to MS-DOS to allow it to recognize files of more than 32 MB such as may be on a CD–ROM.

field: A category of information in a database, such as an address. All operating systems use extensions to enable them to read compact discs.

extent: A set of logical blocks, numbered in ascending order, in which a single file section is recorded.

F

FDDI (fiber distributed data interface): The highest performance of the current established standard, with a raw data rate of 100 Mpbs, it is also the most expensive. Though used less extensively to date than Ethernet, ARCnet, etc., application of FDDI and CDDI is increasing steadily.

fiber optic: A newer type of communications cable in which light-beam signals are sent over glass threads rather than electronic impulses being sent over metal wire.

field: Half the video picture made up of the electronic signal corresponding to the odd or even scanning lines resulting from one passage over the raster area of the TV picture tube by the electron beam. Two interlaced fields compose one frame of a complete video picture.

file: A single logical set of data.

file allocation table (FAT): A table used by the operating system to locate files on a disc.

file mark: See *tape marks*.

file server: A server that provides a shared disc on which users can store, retrieve, and manipulate files of information.

file system: A logical way to organize data on a CD–ROM disc such that an application program need not be concerned with the physical location or structure of the data.

filtering: A process used in both analog and digital image processing to reduce bandwidth. Filters can be designed to remove information content (e.g., high or low frequencies) or to average adjacent pixels creating a new value from two or more pixels. See *antialiasing filter*.

firmware: Software in some type of read-only-memory device; often, cards or boards containing programs.

fixed length: Refers to records or fields that always occupy a set number of bytes. Under the ISO 9660 standard, one can choose to structure data files as sets of records, but all the records within one file must be either fixed length or variable length.

flag: A hardware or software indicator that is used to mark or identify a byte, file, particular location within a program, or a component of a graphics system. A bit may be set to 0 or 1 (off or on) to represent a particular piece of information.

focus: A CD player's ability to maintain precisely the correct distance between the laser pickup and the spiral track of pits that contain the digital information.

form: The CD–ROM XA specification defines two modes for recording physical sectors. Mode 2XA is further divided into two forms. Form 1 is similar to regular CD–ROM Mode 1, as it adds 280 bytes of error detection and correction code, leaving only 2048 bytes per sector free for user data. It is used for computer data that must be accurate. Form 2 is used for recording compressed audio and video or graphics, which do not require extreme precision. Since less error correction is needed, more bytes (2324 bytes per sector) can be used for information storage.

formatter: An optional part of a database retrieval package. Its function is to take raw data and place it into a format that can be used by the indexing portion of the retrieval package.

fractals: Along with raster and vector graphics, a way of defining graphics in a computer. Fractal graphics translate the natural curves of an object into mathematical formulas, from which the image can be later constructed.

frame: (1) The smallest accessible unit of audio on a CD. A single frame contains 1/7 second of stereo sound, and it is made up of 588 channel bits containing twenty-four 8-bit bytes of user data, 8 parity bytes, and 1 control-and-display byte. Ninety-eight frames make up a sector. (2) A single, complete picture in a video or film recording. A video frame consists of two interlaced fields of either 525 lines (NTSC) or 625 lines (PAL/SECAM), running at 30 frames per second (NTSC) or 25 frames per second (PAL/SECAM). Film runs at 24 frames per second.

frame-accurate cueing: An option of CDs that allows extremely precise cueing operations, typically incorporating a dial to enable positioning of the laser pickup to an accuracy of 1/7 second.

frame grabbing: Capturing a single frame from video into a digital format.

frame rate: The speed at which video images are displayed.

frequency: The rate at which a signal vibrates or oscillates, usually measured in hertz (Hz) or kilohertz (kHz). The higher the frequency of a sound, the higher its pitch. Higher frequencies are usually called *treble frequencies*, and lower frequencies are usually called *bass frequencies*.

frequency response: The measurement of an audio system's ability to reproduce each audible frequency without diminishing volume.

full inversion: A means of making an index that includes all meaningful words in a document (that is, excluding articles, pronouns, and prepositions).

full-motion video: Video reproduction at 30 frames per second (NTSC-original signals) or 25 frames per second (PAL-original signals).

full text: Data that consists of words or numbers that are contained in a document (not broken into fields).

full-text database: A database containing the full original text of the subject information.

G

gain: The increase in signaling power as an audio signal is boosted by an electronic device, measured in decibels.

gateway: An opening by means of a physical hardware connection or software interface that permits access between networks and communication systems.

genlocking: The process of synchronization to another video signal. It is required in computer capture of video to synchronize the digitizing process with the scanning parameters of the video signal.

gigabyte (GB): 220 bytes, or 1024 megabytes, often roughly calculated as 1,000 megabytes, or one billion bytes. See *megabyte*.

glass master: The original mechanical master disc from which the dies are made to stamp compact discs. It is a positive image of the disc data (as opposed to the negative image that is the disc).

gold disc: The recordable disc used in CD–WO systems. The blank disc is made, like all other compact discs, of a bottom layer of polycarbonate, but instead of having a series of pits and lands stamped into it, it contains a preformed track spiral, which the recording laser beam will follow when inscribing information onto the disc. This type of disc is therefore called *pre-grooved*. A translucent green layer of recordable material is laid on top of the polycarbonate, then a reflective layer of gold. Then the usual layers of lacquer and label are applied.

gradient: In graphics, having an area smoothly blend from one color to another, or from black to white or vice versa.

granularity: The smallness of the chunks into which information can be divided. Defined by the smallest blocks of information that can be accessed from a disc or disk.

graphical user interface (GUI): Pronounced "gooey"— another example of jargon. A GUI is a layer of software running on top of the computer's operating environment that allows the user to interact with the computer by choosing items from menus or selecting icons on the screen. A GUI may impose or promote some degree of similarity between different software applications, which makes it easier for the user to learn new software under the same GUI. GUIs are considered more user friendly than command-driven operating systems.

graphics: Information that is not character related, such as maps, charts, graphs, and all photographs and pictorial representations. In order to be storable in a database, graphics must be digitized using a scanner. This produces a series of dots that can be handled by a computer but requires large amounts of storage space unless compressed. See *compression*.

grayscale: A method of representing images on screen or paper using tones of gray rather than color or plain black-and-white photographs, which are themselves actually analog images made up of shades of gray.

Green Book: The Philips/Sony specification standard for CD–I.

H

half-height: Used in describing a "thin" floppy disk drive or a CD–ROM drive about 4.5 cm ($1^3/4"$) in height. In many PCs, two half-high drives fit one above the other.

hard read error: A real error; the user cannot read the data, which is scrambled or unrecoverable (i.e., garbage). The possibility of this happening is 10^{-12} or one in a trillion bits. See *CIRC*.

head: The assembly in the CD–ROM drive that contains all components necessary to send a laser beam to the disc, receive the reflected beam, and produce electrical signals from these reflections. The parts of the head include the laser, lenses, prisms, a focusing mechanism, and a photo detector.

header field: Four bytes recorded at the beginning of each sector that tell the address of the sector (expressed as a logical block number) and the mode in which this sector is recorded.

hertz (Hz): A unit of measurement of frequency equal to one vibration or cycle per second. It was named after German physicist, Heinrich R. Hertz (1857–1894). See *kilohertz.*

hidden file: In DOS, a file with a "hidden" attribute doesn't appear on the disc directory, cannot be displayed, erased, or copied, but can be viewed with most file management utilities.

hierarchical file system (HFS): Pyramidlike file system in which each object is linked to those beneath it. Typical format for computer files with directories and subdirectories.

high-resolution: An adjective describing improvement in image quality as a result of increasing the number of pixels per square inch. Called hi-res for short.

High Sierra Group (HSG): A working group of CD–ROM service companies, vendors, and manufacturers that has played the major role in the setting of industry standards. The group is named after its first meeting place.

High Sierra Group standard: This is the informal name of the draft NISO standard ANS Z39.60-198X, *Proposed American National Standard for Information Sciences—Volume and File Structure of CD–ROM for Information Interchange* (see *NISO*). It is the standard format for placing files and directories on CD–ROM discs. The trend is definitely toward CD–ROM products that are compatible with this standard.

horizontal resolution: The specification of resolution in the horizontal direction, meaning the ability of the system to reproduce closely spaced vertical lines.

HSB (hue saturation brightness): With the HSB model, all colors can be defined by expressing their levels of hue (the pigment), saturation (the amount of pigment), and brightness (the amount of white included) in percentages.

hub: A central device to which other devices are connected. Sometimes referred to interchangeably as a *con-*

centrator, although some manufacturers define a concentrator to have additional capabilities.

I

IBM variable-record-length tape: The D-format (variable record length) differs from ANSI-labeled and IBM-labeled in the following manner:

The maximum block length field in header 2 (HDR2) gives the size of the largest block in the data set, and no record may exceed the maximum block size. The first 4 bytes of each record indicate the record length. Records do not overlap block boundaries. Multiple records may be contained in a single block. The S-format (variable record lengths transcending physical block boundaries) is also a part of the variable-record-length tape.

IBM-labeled tape: An IBM-labeled tape that is recorded in F-format (fixed format) and coincides exactly with an ANSI-labeled tape except that the IBM label, the header (HDR), and trailer (TRLR) are written in EBCDIC code rather than ASCII code. See *EBCDIC, ASCII,* and *ANSI-labeled tape.*

illegal character: A character that cannot be used in certain command-driven programs because it is reserved for other functions (e.g., a DOS file name cannot contain an asterisk or comma).

IMA (Interactive Multimedia Association): Formed in 1991 (rooted in IVIA [Interactive Video Industry Association]), it is the industry association chartered with creating and maintaining standard specifications for multimedia systems.

image: See *ISO image*.

image plane: In digital video, display hardware that has more than one video memory array contributing to the displayed image in real time. Each memory array is called an *image plane*. See *bit plane*.

image resolution: The fineness or coarseness of an image as it was digitized, measured in dots per inch (dpi), typically from 200 to 400 dpi.

impedance: A speaker's measure of resistance to the passage of alternating current (AC). It is measured in ohms.

implementation levels: As some operating systems do not support all the proposed features of any level of interchange, the ISO 9660 standard defines two levels of implementation. At Implementation Level 1, the system manufacturer may choose not to implement certain features. At Implementation Level 2, all features must be supported. No operating system currently works at Implementation Level 2.

index: The indexing of a CD–ROM disc is similar to that of a printed book except in degree. The subject index at the rear of many printed reference texts includes the primary locations of the more important book subjects. A CD–ROM disc, by comparison, contains indexes that locate records or words within a file.

injection molding: The process of injecting molten plastic (polycarbonate) into a mold to create the substrate of a CD. See *substrate*.

interactive: Involving the active participation of the user in directing the flow of the computer or video program; a system that exchanges information with the viewer, processing the viewer's input in order to generate the appropriate response within the context of the program, as opposed to linear.

interactive media: An information storage/access format, such as the CD–ROM format, capable of delivering user-requested information in a sequence specified by the user. This represents a significant advancement over the linear format, which delivers information in only one sequence starting at the beginning and continuing to the end.

interactive video: The integration of video and computer technologies in which a video program (moving pictures and voice tracks) and computer programs run together so that the user's choices or actions affect the program outcome.

interchange levels: The three nested levels at which files may be recorded and named under ISO 9660. Level 1 files may consist of a single file section recorded in one extent (i.e., each file must be recorded as a continuous stream of bytes, so interleaving is not possible); with files and directories named according to the strictest set of rules. The only restriction applied to Level 2 is that each file must consist of only one file section recorded in one extent (again, no interleaving). At Level 3 no restrictions apply. Most operating systems and their extensions work only with Interchange Level 1. The exception to date is CDTV, which works at Interchange Level 2.

interface: (1) A circuit, cable, or piece of hardware linking two pieces of computer hardware, such as the controller card connecting a CD–ROM player to a personal computer. See *controller card*. (2) The "connection" between computer software and the person operating it—in a sense, the working environment. See *graphical user interface*.

interframe coding: Compression techniques that track the differences between frames of video and result in more compression over a range of frames than intraframe coding.

interlacing: Scheme to display a video image by displaying alternate scan lines in two discrete fields.

interleaving: (1) The process of subdividing the digital audio data stream into segments that are then recorded so that segments originally adjacent to one another will be spread out on the disc. This process is used in CD–Audio and CD–ROM recording to isolate errors for detection and correction. A sequence of data is read into a grid vertically and read out again horizontally, so that wrong lines are rearranged into individual wrong bits, and can be more easily isolated and corrected. (2) Although a file is one unit of data, it is not necessarily stored in one contiguous block on a disc or disk. On a floppy or hard magnetic disk, where files may be changed or erased many times, files are usually chopped up into many little pieces to make the most efficient possible use of the available storage space. On a compact disc, files may also be deliberately chopped up into pieces so as to get two files as close to each other as possible, putting on the disk, say, 2 Kbytes of a text file, then 2 Kbytes of an image, and then repeating these two operations as many times as necessary. This is useful when you have two or more different kinds of files that must flow together, such as images with a musical background, or images with a voice-over. With interleaving the laser reading head can pick up a small amount of text and then a small amount of sound, play them back together, then move on smoothly to the next small amounts, rather than jumping the head back and forth between two widely separate file locations. Without interleaving, gathering information alternately from the two files would require many seeks. All this frantic head movement would make the application slow at best, if it ran at all.

interpolation: (1) The process of filling in missing data between neighboring audio samples by calculating their average value. (2) The process of averaging pixel information when scaling an image. When reducing the size of an image, pixels are averaged to create a single new pixel; when an image is scaled up in size, additional pixels are created by averaging pixels of the smaller image.

interrecord gap: An erased space on a tape with a nominal length of 0.6 inch. This gap is inserted between consecutive data blocks, as well as between a data block and a file mark. An interrecord gap is recognized by the hardware as the tape is read.

intraframe coding: Compression within each individual frame. Results in less compression over a range of frames than interframe coding.

inverted index: A list of each of the words within a file (except stopwords like *a*, *the*, etc.).

ISO (International Standards Organization): Worldwide group responsible for establishing and managing various standards committees and expert groups, including several image-compression standards.

ISO 646: An international character set standard specifying the 7-bit coded character set for information interchange. The ASCII character set is a subset of ISO 646.

ISO 2022: An international standard specifying the method to extend the 7- or 8-bit coded character set for information interchange to a wider set of Roman characters or completely different character sets (kanji, for instance).

ISO 2375: An international standard specifying the registration procedure of escape sequences used for code extension of a character set.

ISO 8859/1: An international standard specifying the coded character set for the Roman alphabet number 1.

ISO 9660: An international standard specifying the logical file format for files and directories on a CD–ROM.

ISO image: Also *CD–ROM image*, *image*, or *disc* image. An exact representation of the entire set of data and programs, as it will appear on a CD, in terms of content and logical format, simulated on some other medium. This is sent to the disc manufacturer (or a CD–WO recorder) for premastering and mastering.

J

jewel box: The hinged plastic box, the most common way to package CDs.

JPEG (Joint Photographic Experts Group): A working committee under the auspices of the International Standards Organization (ISO) that has defined a universal standard for the digital compression and decompression of still images for use in computer systems. This standard is now an ISO standard.

jukebox: A disc-playing system, similar to the well-known record-playing jukebox, that can hold more than one disc for access one at a time. Prototype models now exist, and commercial models are expected to appear soon. This is one of the two most likely types of multiple disc CD–ROM player systems expected to predominate in university and public libraries. The other is the multiplayer system. See *multiplayer*.

K

K: Short for kilobyte.

kanji: One of four alphabets in written Japanese. It contains about 5000 characters.

key: A group of characters (usually a single field or a set of fields) that uniquely identify a record.

key assignments: Functions that a computer program assigns to specific keys.

key record index: An index that contains field keys as well as the location of the corresponding record in the file.

keying: (1) In a video system, the process of inserting one picture into another picture under spatial control of another signal, called the *keying signal*. (2) The process of mixing the video signal generated by the display processor with the VGA output to combine the PM windows of the VGA with the video. See *VGA*.

keyword: Any word in an electronic database that is indexed to allow its location(s) in the database to be identified on-screen at the user's command. On CD–ROM discs, more than 99% of all words are keywords.

keyword combination: A selective combination of keywords located by advanced keyword search techniques. See *Boolean operators* and *proximity connectors*.

keyword searching: The process of electronically searching a database on a CD–ROM or other optical disc or on-line information service for all locations of any specified keywords or keyword combinations within the database.

kilohertz (kHz): A unit of measurement of frequency that is equivalent to 1000 vibrations or cycles per second. See also *hertz*.

L

LAN (local area network): A network covering a limited area, such as a single office or building.

land: The reflective area between two adjacent nonreflective pits on the spiral track of a CD audio disc or a CD–ROM disc. The translation from pit to land and land to pit represents a binary 1, while the distance between transitions represents binary 0s.

laser (light amplification by stimulated emission of radiation): A device that processes a beam of light through a special crystal so as to produce an extremely narrow coherent beam of vastly increased power. Laser beams are used to record information onto CD–ROM discs by burning microscopic pits into the surfaces of the discs. Weaker laser beams are then used to read the discs.

laser beam: The very narrow and intense beam of light produced by a laser. This beam, unlike most light, has only a single wavelength, thus making it ideal for use as a means for reading the digital data contained on CD–ROM and CD–audio discs. See *laser*.

laser pickup: The mechanism in a CD player that holds the laser and positions it at various points along the spiral track of pits on a CD.

laserdisc: Reflective, optical storage discs. Sizes include the 4$TQ-inch, CD–ROM, 5$OQ-inch, 12-inch, etc.

LaserVision: The former trade name for the laser-read videodisc system that was popularized by Philip, MCA, and Pioneer. In the United States, LaserVision discs come in 5-inch, 8-inch, and 12-inch sizes.

latency: Delay in accessing CD–ROM data as the disc rotates to the desired position. In a CD–ROM reader, for example, the latency is the lag time between the moment the head arrives at a desired track and the moment that the desired sector spins over the head. The average latency for a CD–ROM drive is usually half the rotational period.

LAUD (layered access user diversification): A system in which a single database can have several access layers. Users must present "keys" to move from one access layer to another. This is meant as a control on sensitive restricted data, such as defense maps.

layered EDC/ECC: See *error correction code* and *error detection code*.

lead-in area: On a recordable compact disc (CD–R or gold disc), a data area at the beginning of the disc that is left blank for the disc's table of contents. The table of contents will be recorded when the disc is full and/or it is declared closed.

lead-out area: On a recordable compact disc (gold disc), a data area at the end of the disc that indicates the end of the data has been reached.

linear: A motion sequence designed to be played from beginning to end without stops or branching, like a film; as opposed to *interactive*.

local area network (LAN): A collection of computers and other devices connected in a relatively small geographic area (usually one building) for high-speed sharing of computer files and peripheral devices.

local disc: A hard disc physically connected to a computer. Contrast with *shared disc*.

locking: A method of temporarily gaining exclusive control of a shared file or portion of the file to prevent others users from changing or accessing the data at the same time.

logical block: A subdivision of a logical sector, 2^{n+9} bytes in size. Since a logical block must be smaller than a logical sector, logical blocks can be 512, 1024 or 2048 bytes (that is, 2^9, 2^{10}, or 2^{11} bytes). Logical blocks are needed to allow for finer granularity, that is, for files smaller than 2048 bytes. Otherwise, if you had a 1000-byte file and it had to be stored in a sector all to itself, the leftover 1048 bytes in that sector would be wasted. The logical block is the smallest addressable space on the disc, and each logical block is identified by its unique logical block number (LBN), assigned in ascending order starting from 0. Under the ISO 9660 standard, addressing of all data on a CD is done in terms of logical block numbers.

logical block number (LBN): The most basic address by which information on a compact disc is located.

logical file format: Translates the sector-and-mode view of a compact disc into a virtual "tree" of directories and files, which makes it easier for both people and computers to use the information on the disc.

logical sector: A division of information on a compact disc, under the ISO 9660 standard $2n + 11$ bytes in size; n is set to 0, giving 2048 bytes per sector.

logical topology: The combination of LAN card, physical topology, cable, and access method that establishes a standard method by which nodes communicate on a LAN. The three major types are Ethernet, token-ring, and ARCnet.

lossless compression: Ensures that the original data is exactly recoverable with no loss in image quality.

lossy compression: The original data is not completely recoverable. Although image quality may suffer, many experts believe that up to 95% of the data in a typical image may be discarded without a noticeable loss in apparent resolution.

luminance: Brightness; one of the three image characteristics coded in composite television (represented by the letter Y). May be measured in lux or foot-candles.

M

machine code: The series of bits (1s and 0s), arranged in sets of eight (bytes), that comprise the instructions (program) or data directly acted upon by the computer's microprocessor.

machine-readable information: Digital information electronically stored in a computer or mass storage device that can be keyword searched and manipulated by means of appropriate software programs.

magnetic media: A means for storing information which uses the magnetic polarity of hard disks or floppy diskettes or tapes.

magneto-optical drive: Also called a *rewritable optical drive*. A storage medium using a combination of magnetic and optical (laser) technology for writing information, and a laser for reading it. They are somewhat slower than magnetic hard disks, but are more durable and have a much larger capacity. Several different formats are available.

MAN (metropolitan area network): A network able to link systems across an entire city.

mass storage: A device such as CD–ROM that can hold vast amounts of digital information for later retrieval.

mass-storage device: A device that can hold vast amounts of machine readable information for electronic access upon demand, such as a CD–ROM disc.

master: (1) An original recording of a finished program in audio tape, videotape, or film format. Used for broadcast or to make copies. (2) The process of producing master, mother, and stamper videodiscs that are used for replicating videodiscs.

master disc: A glass disc on which the data for a CD are recorded during the mastering stage of production. Often incorrectly used in reference to a write-once CD.

mastering: The process of producing an original recording "mold" on a glass disc by using a laser to etch pits into the surface of the disc, which is coated with photoresist. This can be compared to a cookie cutter, as it is then used to stamp out future optical discs. It is at this time that error-correction codes are introduced. The stages in producing CD–ROM discs consist of data preparation, premastering to master tape, mastering to CD–ROM disc, and disc replication.

Mbps: Million bits per second, or megabits per second.

MCA (media control architecture): System-level specification developed by Apple Computer, Inc., for addressing various media devices (videodisc and videotape players, CD players, etc.) to its Macintosh computers.

MCI (media control interface): Platform-independent multimedia specification (published by Microsoft Corporation and others in 1990) that provides a consistent way to control devices such as CD–ROMs and video playback units.

megabyte (MB): A data-storage measurement that is equivalent to 1,048,576 characters of information, or approximately one million bytes. The storage capacity of a CD–ROM disc is over 650 megabytes.

menu: An access method that establishes a list of choices in some area of interest. In a computer system, a menu may be displayed on a computer screen. In a voice processing system, a menu is presented as a list of spoken choices.

merge: To combine files.

merging bits: Three extra bits added between bytes on a compact disc to ensure proper separation of transitions.

micron: A unit of length equivalent to one millionth of a meter (about 1/25,000 inch). Also called a *micrometer* (μm).

MIDI (musical instrument digital interface): An industry-standard connection for computer control of musical instruments and devices. It is used to transmit and record performance information from electronic musical instruments to computers for editing, manipulation, and recording.

MIDI sequencer: Software that allows one to edit performance data collected via MIDI from electronic musical instruments.

MIPS (millions of instructions per second): A measure of how fast a computer's CPU can work. Applies to powerful platforms such as workstations.

mixed-mode disc: A compact disc including both computer data and CD–DA tracks. Usually, the computer data is all contained in Track 1 and the audio in one or more following tracks.

mode: There are two recording modes for compact discs. In Mode 1, used with CD–ROM applications, 288 bytes of each sector are used for storing error correction code and the remaining 2048 bytes per sector are available for user data.

Mode 2, used in CD–I and CD–ROM XA, has two forms: Form 1 is similar to Mode 1, as it is also used to record data that requires error correction; Form 2 is used for recording information such as sound or images that does not require such extreme precision. Since less error correction is needed, more bytes in the sector can be freed for information storage, resulting in a data area of 2336 bytes per sector.

modeling: An educational process whereby a computer-based learning system is used to represent another system or process. The learner can change values and observe the effects of the change on the operation of the system.

modem (modulator/demodulator): A unit used to send (modulate) and receive (demodulate) information over bidirectional carriers or digital bit streams. Digital data transfer between two systems over an analog circuit requires a modem at each end of the analog circuit.

modulation: A means of encoding information for transmission or storage. Examples are pulse code modulation (PCM), used for storing audio on CDs, and frequency modulation (PM), used for radio transmissions.

monophonic (mono): Not stereo. Audio information that is processed in a single audio channel.

motion video: Video that displays real motion by displaying a sequence of images (frames) rapidly enough that the viewer sees the image as a continuously moving picture.

mouse: A pointing device for moving the cursor on the screen of a computer. Moving the mouse on a flat surface produces corresponding movements of the cursor. The mouse partitions the screen into horizontal and vertical components, which it uses to adjust the cursor with respect to its position. Clicking buttons on the mouse duplicates many keyboard functions such as Escape and Return.

MPC (multimedia PC): A specification developed by Tandy and Microsoft for the minimum platform capable of running multimedia software. PCs carrying the MPC logo will be able to run any software that also displays the MPC logo.

MPEG (Motion Picture Experts Group): A working committee under the auspices of the International Standards Organization (ISO) that has defined standards for digital compression and decompression of motion video/audio for use in computer systems. The first phase of the committee's activity was addressing methods for encoding video within the 1.5 MB/s CD–ROM data rate. Their standards have recently been adopted by the ISO and are called MPEG-1.

MPEG-2: (1) Evolving standard intended to extend MPEG compression and decompression capabilities encompassing support for digital, flexible, scalable video transport. (2) Developing standard for digital video coding covering multiple resolutions, bit rates, and delivery systems.

MS-DOS (Microsoft Disk Operating System): A disk operating system distributed by Microsoft. See *disk operating system*.

multifile volume: A single reel of tape containing at least two files.

multifile/multivolume: Multiple files that occupy multiple volumes of tape.

multimedia: Refers to the delivery of information that combines different content formats (motion video, audio, still images, graphics, animation, text, etc.).

multiplexing: The process of combining multiple streams of data, such as the left and right channels of a stereo audio signal, into a single, continuous stream of data.

muting: The act of silencing the audio output for a fraction of a second when the CD player encounters uncorrectable data errors. Although the listener may notice a dead spot during playback, the possibility of hearing a very unpleasant frequency is eliminated.

N

natural frequency: The highest pitch occurring in a sound (e.g., a piece of music); usually the highest pitch audible to the human ear (22 kHz) is taken as a default.

network: A series of devices or locations connected by communications lines. SCSI and SASI are types of networks. See SCSI and SASI.

network operating system (NOS): The system software that runs on each workstation or server in conjunction with the computer's regular operating system (such as MS-DOS) to allow computers to communicate and share server resources.

NIC (network interface card): A plug-in board to connect a computer or workstation to a network.

NISO (National Information Standards Organization): Establishes U.S. national standards for libraries, information sciences, and publishing, including CD–ROM. See *High Sierra Group Standard*. National Information Standards Organization, National Bureau of Standards, Gaithersburg, Maryland, (301) 590-0097.

node: A LAN-connected computer, whether a server or a client/workstation. In some cases, a node can also be a LAN-connected peripheral, such as a printer or terminal.

nondedicated server: A server that can also act as a workstation at the same time it acts as a server.

NOT operator: Boolean operator that gives a TRUE reading if its operand is FALSE, and a FALSE reading if its operand is TRUE.

notepad: This is an electronic work and storage space with word processing capabilities incorporated into certain published CD–ROM discs. This enables one to type in ideas or comments in combination with information extracted from the database to produce letters, reports, or memos for printing or storage.

NTSC: National Television Systems Committee of the Electronics Industries Association (EIA), which prepared the standard of specifications approved by the Federal Communications Commission, in December 1953, for commercial color broadcasting. NTSC is still the TV standard for the United States, Japan, etc.

NTSC format: A color television format having 525 scan lines, a field frequency of 60 Hz, line frequency of 15.75 kHz, frame frequency of 1/30 second, and a color subcarrier frequency of 3.58 MHz. See *PAL* and *SECAM*.

object code: The computer programming machine-readable instructions produced by a compiler.

object oriented programming: When programmers define the types of functions that can be applied to a data structure, as well as the data structure itself.

OCR (optical character recognition): A method of digitizing printed information without actually typing the information into a computer. Similar to bar-code readers in stores.

offset factor: When using A time to create a mixed-mode disc, the offset factor is the length of Track 1 (the data track) plus its pre- and postgaps.

on-line: A system in which database information may be accessed via modem. This can be a time-consuming and thus expensive data retrieval mechanism.

operating system: See *disk operating system*.

operating system extensions: See *extensions*.

optical disc: A high-density storage device whose data are both encoded and played back using low-powered lasers. This includes both analog video/audio information discs (movies and interactive video) and digital audio/graphics/textual information discs.

optical publishing: See *electronic publishing*.

optical scanner: See *scanner*.

optical storage technology: The use of lasers to read data by reflecting light off irregular surfaces such as those caused by the pits in a CD–ROM. The on or off pulses are read as bits of information by a photodetector.

Orange Book: The Philips/Sony specification for compact disc–magneto-optical (CD–MO) and compact disc–write-once (CD–WO) systems. Includes the specification for the Hybrid disc technology on which Kodak's Photo CD is based.

orders of magnitude: An order of magnitude is a power of 10: 1000 (10^3) is an order of magnitude less than 10,000 (10^4). This phrase is much used in the computer industry, especially when talking about prices or speeds.

OSI (Open Systems Interconnect): A document, released in 1978, covering the structure of standards for computer networks. OSI is not a standard in itself but describes the parts, or layers, of a network, such as physical cabling, data rates, protocols, etc.

overhead: The amount of storage space required by the index of a full text database, sometimes 40 to 50 percent of the storage space required for the information contained in the database.

oversampling: A technique in the digital-to-analog conversion process that reads the digital data at two or four times the standard sampling rate of 44.1 kHz. It is done so that digital filters may be used to delete unwanted high-frequency signals from the digital audio.

P

PAL format: Phase alternation line. The European video standard, except for France. It uses interlaced scans with 25 frames per second and 625 lines per screen. See *NTSC* format and *SECAM* format.

parity: A method of error detection that uses a percentage of redundant information to check the user's data.

parity bits: Extra data bits that are encoded on the disc during the error-protection stage of encoding. These bits are later used to correct erroneous or missing data.

parity check: A check that helps determine the validity of data. This test determines if the number of 0s and 1s of a byte of data is even or odd, adds up the number of bits, and compares it to the number of bits in the original data.

parse: To separate transferred data into separate columns to fit correctly in a spreadsheet.

path: The location of a file in terms of the route used to reach it through directories and subdirectories.

path length: The total length of the character string needed to give the path to a particular file or directory.

path table: A set of records describing the exact location of every file and directory on a disc, in terms of its logical block number, using one record for each. The path table enables an application program to learn the location of a file in only one seek.

PCM (pulse code modification): The most common method of encoding an analog signal into a digital bit stream. A digitization technique, not a universally accepted standard.

Photo CD: A recently introduced digital imaging system from Eastman Kodak that stores up to 100 photographic color images on one CD. With correct software, such as Adobe Photoshop, the digital images can be transferred from a CD–ROM XA drive to a computer hard drive and manipulated. Photo CDs can be produced from traditional 35-mm negatives or color slides.

photoconductive cell: See *photoresist.*

photodetector: A light-sensitive electrical device that senses the pulses of laser light that are reflected from the disc's metallic film during the playback process. These light pulses are transformed into electrical signals by the photodetector. The photodetector is located on the head of the CD–ROM drive.

photoresist: A coating on the surface of the master disc into which a low-powered laser burns the microscopic pits during the mastering process.

physical block size: The size (in bytes) of the blocks of data written on a tape or optical disc.

physical format: For a compact disc, the standard laid down by the Philips/Sony Yellow Book for how information is physically recorded on the disc, the size of physical sectors, and so on.

physical sector: As mandated by the Yellow Book standard, each compact disc is divided into 270,000 physical sectors of 2336 bytes each.

PIH (paper in hand): The opposite of POD. See *POD*.

pits: Oblong microscopic indentations in the plastic substrate of CDs that represent the digital data recorded. These pits on a CD are approximately the size of bacteria, 0.11 microns deep and 0.5 micron wide, and their length varies from 0.8 to 3 microns. See *land*.

pixel: An abbreviation for *picture element*. It represents a single bit of information that is displayed on a computer screen. It is the minimum raster display element, represented as a point with a specified color or intensity level. One way to measure picture resolution is by the number of pixels used to create images.

platform: A specific set of hardware and operating system, for instance, DOS platform, Macintosh platform.

PLV (production-level video): Highest-quality motion video compression algorithm today. Compression is achieved off-line (non-real-time), while playback (decompression) is real-time (asymmetrical compression). Independent of the technology in use, off-line compression will always produce a better image quality than real-time or symmetrical compression because more time and processing power are used per frame.

POD (paper on demand): A present-day technology in which important information such as technical reference manuals and so on are stored in a database and are easily retrievable multiple times. This allows referenced items to be stored on CD–ROM with the following advantages:

1. User searches are simpler and faster.
2. Cross referencing is faster and organizational guide-lines can be present.
3. Entire databases can be carried in one shirt pocket and backed up on another.
4. Sections can be printed on demand, then discarded if desirable.

point: In typography, a unit of measure equal to 1/72 inch.

polycarbonate: The plastic material from which CDs are constructed.

port: A connection point on a CPU through which a computer workstation or another device can communicate directly with the CPU.

pre-emphasis: A signal processing technique that prevents signal loss or attenuation during playback. This method is not used for CD–ROM data.

prefix operator: This is a useful keyword searching feature incorporated into certain published CD–ROM discs to locate all words with common beginnings but different endings.

pregrooved: A recordable compact disc with a spiral track preformed in the polycarbonate substrate for the recording laser beam to follow when inscribing information onto the disc.

premastered tape: A magnetic master tape ready for recording on an optical master disc.

premastering: The process by which information is prepared for mastering and pressing into optical discs. This includes formatting the data, some error-correction encoding, and other technical tasks. The stages in producing CD–ROM discs consist of data preparation, premastering to master tape, mastering to master CD–ROM disc, and disc replication. Premastering requires both knowledgeable computer professionals and computer processing power. During this stage, 288 bytes of EDC and ECC are added to each block of user data (2048) to ensure the full recovery of user block data. The result of premastering may be a tape ready to go for mastering, or, in the case of CD–WO systems, premastering and mastering may be done in one operation, resulting in a ready-to-read compact disc.

program: The software that carries out a task on the computer such as word processing, database retrieval, spreadsheets, and so on.

program calibration area (PCA): On a recordable compact disc (gold disc), an area in which a brief initial test run is made to calibrate the recording laser for that particular disc.

program memory area (PMA): On a gold disc, an area containing track numbers and their starting and stopping points.

PROM (programmable read-only memory): A storage device that can be programmed only once. After the initial program is stored data can be retrieved from the device but not written to it. CD–ROM is a form of PROM.

proximity connectors: These connectors comprise a class of keyword search commands that enable one to search for certain specified words or phrases occurring in sequence or in close proximity. They are used by more experienced searchers to achieve a higher degree of search selectivity.

proximity determination: A method of text searching that looks for keywords based on how close they are (separated by how many words in a sentence) to other keywords.

proximity word search: A information search and retrieval strategy that allows the user to perform adjacent word searches in the same document, page, paragraph, and sentence via proximity connectors. See *proximity connectors.*

Px64: Also known as CCITT Recommendation H.261. A draft standard for motion video compression in videophone and teleconferencing, designed around 64 Kb/second transmission channels.

QR

quantization: The scheme of representing amplitude measurements as discrete subdivisions.

quantizing: One step in the process of converting an analog signal into a digital signal. The three steps are sampling, quantizing, and encoding.

QWERTY keyboard: The layout of keys on a standard typewriter-style keyboard; the first six letters on the top alphabetic line.

RAM (random access memory): A method of data storage found in computer systems that allows access of data on a random basis. In other words, a set of chips in the computer in which information can be held for very fast access by the microprocessor. The operating system and application programs are loaded into RAM, where the computer can use them to perform operations as requested. This is as opposed to an orderly, sequential basis. This memory device may be read from and written to.

random bit error: A bit error that has no correlation with other bit errors. May occur as a result of transmission noise in the circuitry, imperfections of production materials, damage during production, and so on; random bit errors are detected and corrected in C1.

raster graphics: Images defined as a set of pixels or dots in a column-and-row format. Also called *bit-mapped graphics*.

raw bit error: Physical data errors on a CD–ROM disc that, without the use of a CD–ROM drive's decoding and correction system, would be transferred to the computer as data errors.

RDBMS (relational database management system): A relational database management program to create, install and maintain customized database applications.

read: To acquire or retrieve data from one storage medium to another; the opposite of *write*.

real-time: In computing, refers to an operating mode under which data is received, processed, and the results returned instantaneously.

Red Book: The Philips/Sony standard for audio (CD–DA) compact discs.

redirected disk: A workstation's disk drive name that refers to a server's shared disk. Also sometimes called a *mapped* disk. A workstation accesses a server's hard disk by redirecting an unused disk drive name, such as L:, to the server's hard disk. From that point on, any time the workstation user issues a command to the L: disk, the network operating system redirects the command to the server's disk.

relevance: The ratio of the number of relevant records retrieved in a database search to the number of relevant records actually present in the database.

replication: The process of mass-producing copies of compact discs.

resolution: A measure of the density of dots per unit area of a digitized image. More dots per unit area means higher resolution and better picture (i.e., fineness of detail). In computer monitors it is measured in pixels (usually horizontal × vertical) or in pixels per inch. Resolution in laser printers is measured in dots per inch (dpi); the most common laser printer resolution at the moment is 300 dpi. Resolution in digital sound refers to the number of bits used to describe each sound sample; the higher the resolution, the more dynamic range can be represented.

retrieval engine: Software that provides access to the data stored in CD–ROM or other mass-storage media.

RGB (Red-Green-Blue): A type of computer color display output signal comprised of separately controllable red, green, and blue signals, as opposed to composite video, in which signals are combined prior to output. RGB monitors offer higher resolution than composite.

RISC (reduced instruction set computer): A CPU where processing capabilities have been reduced to increase speed.

ROM (read-only memory): The type of memory or storage device for prerecorded permanent information that cannot be erased or altered. That is, a memory device that once written to cannot be rewritten to. Intended for the storage of data that will be useful for extended periods of time. The CD–ROM is of this type. Personal computers have ROM chips whose circuits contain the most basic commands needed to start up and operate the computer. The term *ROM* was also adopted for compact discs because they could be reproduced only by the mastering and replication process, and as far as the personal computer was concerned they were read-only.

root directory: The highest-level directory in DOS, ISO 9660, and other logical formats. All files and subdirectories branch off from the root.

rotational delay: The delay in the access of data due to the disc's positioning time. See *latency*.

RRIP (Rock Ridge Interchange Protocol): A standard for recording UNIX/POSIX file system information (longer file names, deeper levels of hierarchy) while remaining compliant with ISO 9660.

RS232: The Electronic Industry Association (EIA) standard that defines a computer interface.

RTV (real-time video): On-line, symmetrical, 30-fps video compression algorithm.

S

sample: The measured value of the amplitude of an analog signal at some point in time.

sample-and-hold circuit: An electronic circuit that momentarily holds, or stores in memory, the digital value of a sample so that the sample can be processed for conversion to digital or analog.

sampling: The first step in the process of converting an analog signal into a digital representation. This is accomplished by measuring the amplitude of analog signals at consistent time intervals, called *samples*. These values are then encoded to provide a digital representation of the analog signal.

sampling rate: The rate at which an analog waveform is sampled. The sampling rate of CD audio is 44.1 kHz, or 44,100 samples per second. See *sampling*.

SASI (Shugart Associates systems interface): A simple interface with less intelligence than SCSI, though much more powerful than "dumb" controllers in connecting peripherals to microcomputers.

saturated colors: Strong, bright colors (particularly reds and oranges) that do not reproduce well on video. They tend to saturate the screen with color or bleed around the edges, producing a garish, unclear image.

scalability: The ability to vary the information content of a program by changing the amount of data that is stored, transmitted or displayed. In a video image, this translates into creating larger or smaller windows of video on screen (shrinking effect). Also refers to the ability of video to be played over systems with varying performance capabilities.

scaling: Process of uniformly changing the size of characters or graphics.

scanner: A device that scans and digitizes two-dimensional information consisting of pictures, graphics or text into a stream of bits. Also called *optical scanner.* Scanners are incorporated into several different types of devices such as WORM drives. See *WORM.*

SCSI (small computer system interface): Pronounced "scuzzy." An 8-bit parallel bus interface for connecting peripherals to microcomputers. Any device on the bus can initiate activities. A terminator is required with the last device on the network. Up to eight systems and peripherals may be connected on the same SCSI bus.

search and retrieval software: This is a software program enabling one to use the CD–ROM discs supplied by a particular publisher. Most publishers claim their software to be superior, and it does not appear likely that one universal standard search and retrieval software program will evolve. This is not a serious problem, however, inasmuch as all CD–ROM discs produced in accordance with the proposed High Sierra Standard can be played on the same standard disc players controlled by the same computers.

search engine: See *search and retrieval software.*

search hit: The product of a successful keyword search; that is, each location of the keyword or keyword combination retrieved and displayed on the screen.

searching: Locating specific information by systematically examining the indexes of databases for all data available. See also *browsing.*

SECAM (séquentiel couleur à mémoire [sequential color with memory]) format: The French color TV system also adopted in Russia. The basis of operation is the sequential recording of primary colors in alternate lines. See *NTSC* and *PAL*.

sector: The smallest addressable unit of a disc's track, it consists of 2352 consecutive bytes. Every sector contains its own error-detection-and-correction coding and has its own unique address on the disc.

seek: To read back data from a CD–ROM disc in an attempt to find a particular piece of information. Because seeking is so time-consuming on a CD–ROM, it is desirable to have few seeks that access large blocks of data.

seek error: Occurs when the CD–ROM drive's laser is unable to locate the data desired. This error can be the result of physical and/or mechanical problems, such as vibration, disc surface irregularities, and poor laser focusing. The possibility of a seek error happening is 10^{-6} or one in a million tries.

seek time: The time required to position the read head of the CD–ROM drive in the correct location for reading the desired information. On a CD–ROM this requires altering the rotational speed of the disc if the information desired is at a different radial position from where the read head is presently located.

serial port: A port for serial communication that also makes sure that transmissions and receptions occur without loss of data. Also called a *serial interface*.

serialization: Serialization of compact discs means a serial number printed on the disc's surface. This number cannot be encoded in the disc data, so serial numbers on compact discs cannot be used in software protection schemes.

server: A LAN-connected computer that makes available its shared resources (hard discs, printers, mail modems, or CD–ROM drives) to other LAN-connected computers. Contrast with *workstation*.

servo: See *servomechanism*.

servomechanism: An electrical device that makes small mechanical movements in response to electrical signals. It continually follows some variable quantity, using feedback to maintain a constant rotation. Its movement is bidirectional with respect to some center. Servos are used to keep the laser on track and in focus in a CD player.

settling time: The time that it takes the CD player's read head to settle into position at the desired location. This includes time to find a synchronization pattern and then read the sector header, which verifies that the current address is the one desired.

SHARE: A DOS program that must be run on an MS-DOS-based peer-to-peer LAN server to coordinate multiple users accessing the same files at the same time.

shared disc: A disc on a server, available for use by workstations via redirection over a LAN.

sideways search: This is a useful keyword searching feature incorporated into certain published CD–ROM discs. The user can initiate a secondary or "sideways" search from within the text of the database and return to the same point when sideways searching has been completed.

signal-to-noise (S/N) ratio: A measure of the difference in level (in decibels) between system noise and the loudest signal that can be produced without distortion. This is a common specification given by manufacturers of stereo audio components.

site license: Licensing whereby a software publisher allows an organization to make copies of a program for internal use at a cost that's less than buying that number of programs. Also called a *software license*.

SMPTE code: Created by the Society of Motion Picture and Television Engineers, this is a method of numbering each individual frame of a video to allow synchronization with sound, indexing, and so on.

soft read error: An error that comes and goes; this kind of error is not a result of an error on the disc but rather occurs during the reading process because the laser is out of focus, there is noise in the circuitry, and so on. This error is related to the mechanics of the reading process and can be corrected by rereading. The odds of this occurring are 10^{-3} or once in every 1000 tries with a 10^{-9} (one in a billion) possibility of the data being in error or nonrecoverable after rereading and error correction.

software: Any stored data that requires hardware for playback and/or observance. Examples of software are CDs, CD–ROMs, LPs, and cassettes. See *hardware*.

spatial resolution: Horizontal and vertical resolutions as a result of subdividing and quantizing a screen into individual parts.

specification: A set of "rules" that hardware or software must follow, usually to ensure compatibility with specific platforms, software, or hardware.

speech synthesis: Artificially generated speech that is produced by a computer with specific software programs that synthesize human speech from ASCII text information.

SRAM (static random access memory): Pronounced "ess-ram." A RAM memory chip that is faster, more dependable, and needs to be refreshed less often than DRAM.

standard: A set of specifications for a product or process or combination thereof, which the standard-makers hope will become accepted as the "correct" way to do things. Some standards, such as the Yellow Book standard for the physical format of CDs, can be enforced because they are owned by the companies who invented the technology. User companies, in order to work with the product, must agree not to make changes which do not meet the specifications.

Standards are advantageous to consumers because they eliminate market confusion. People tend to be leery of spending money on a new technology if it's being offered in several different flavors because they don't know which will be the eventual winner. Widely accepted standards mean the consumer is not faced with making a choice that may prove to be painfully wrong.

Hardware and software manufacturers, on the other hand, are not necessarily fond of standards, because if they are all competing to make machines that do exactly the same thing, they have little room to add on goodies that make their machines more competitive than Brand X. This is especially painful when Brand X is made very cheaply by someone else, so some manufacturers argue that standards are bad for competition.

stereophonic (stereo): Recorded and replicated in two audio channels, right and left.

stopwords: Words that are deliberately excluded from an index because they have no use in locating information within a database. These are words such as *a, the, it,* and so on.

storage capacity: The measure of how much a memory system can hold. The storage capacity of a CD–ROM is 625 MB, which, by today's standards, is an incredibly large amount for such a dimensionally small device.

subcode: Extra data stored on CDs that includes track and timing information. Additional subcode storage space is available for other data, such as graphics and text, that CD–ROM utilizes.

substrate: The base material from which a CD–ROM is fabricated, a strong and transparent polycarbonate plastic. It comprises the bottom layer of a compact disc, into which the data spiral is pressed.

SUSP (system use sharing protocol): Proposed by the Rock Ridge Group as a standard for utilizing the ISO 9660's system use areas to record information useful to various operating system extensions.

S-video: Type of video signal used in the Hi8 and S-VHS videotape formats. It transmits luminance and color portions separately, using multiple wires, thus avoiding the NTSC encoding process and its inevitable loss of picture quality. Also known as *Y-C Video.*

symmetrical compression: A compression system that requires equal processing capability for compression and decompression of an image. This form of compression is used in applications where both compression and decompression will be utilized frequently.

synchronization information: Information contained in the header field of a compact disc sector to tell the CD drive how fast it should spin to correctly read the information in that sector.

system area: The space on a CD–ROM between the physical or absolute addresses 00:00:00 to 00:02:16. Under the ISO 9660 standard this space is available for expansion.

system data: The 288 bytes of EDC and ECC per block (2048 bytes) of user data that can be added during premastering to ensure full recovery of that block of user data.

system noise: Audible hum and/or hiss produced by an audio component when no signal is input to the device.

T

table of contents (disc): Shows the number of tracks, their starting locations, and the total length of the data area of the disc.

tape marks: Lengths of tape written with a reserved magnetic pattern that is not used for recording user data. Tape marks are usually used to separate data sets or to mark the end of a file.

terabyte: A unit of memory equal to approximately 1 trillion bytes.

terminal: Any input/output device for a computer. It allows the user to communicate with the system, and it also allows the computer to communicate with the user.

text: Legible character strings usually stored or transmitted in ASCII format. See *ASCII code.*

text file: A file consisting solely of ASCII characters, containing no other codes or control characters.

text-to-speech: Converting ASCII text to voice information. See *speech synthesis*.

three-beam pickup: A laser pickup mechanism that actually splits the laser beam, creating two secondary beams on either side of the primary beam. The secondary beams are used for tracking control; the primary beam is used for focus and to reflect the data to the photo detector.

TIFF (tagged image file format): A bit-mapped file format for describing and storing color and gray scale images.

time code: A frame-by-frame address code time reference recorded on the spare track of a videotape or inserted in the vertical blanking interval. It is an 8-digit number encoding time in hours, minutes, seconds, and video frames (e.g., 03:45:30:18).

total harmonic distortion (THD): A measure of the system noise in a CD system.

tpi (tracks per inch): A measurement of the density of tracks on a disc.

track: A continuous audio segment on a CD that is identified by a track number (an audio CD may have as many as 99 tracks), or the continuous spiral of pits on a CD–ROM (it is three miles long).

track postgap: The 4-second gap of silence after a track on a compact disc.

track pregap: The 2-second gap of silence before a track on a compact disc.

track relative time: A method of determining the start and stop times of sound segments for programming an application on a mixed-mode disc, measuring each segment's offset from the beginning of its track.

tracking: The ability of a CD player's laser to stay in alignment with the spiral of pits on the CD as the disc rotates.

transfer rate: (1) The speed at which information is transferred from the CD–ROM drive or CD player. For the CD–ROM, about 150,000 bytes per second. (2) The speed at which data can move from one device to another. Within a computer, such as between a hard disk and a processor, a transfer rate is normally specified in bytes per second. Communications devices such as LANs and telephone lines usually specify transfer rates in bits per second.

trichromatic: The technical name for RGB representation of color to create all the colors in the spectrum.

truncation: In video compression, the techniques of reducing the number of bits per pixel by throwing away some of the least significant bits from each pixel.

turnkey system: A communications system with all software, hardware, and facilities components, assembled and installed by a single vendor, and sold as a package.

UV

undelete: To restore all or part of a file or document that has been deleted.

underflow error: What happens when a computer tries to represent a number that is smaller than its predefined range of values.

undo: Returning to a previous condition by retracting the most recent command. Some programs support an unlimited number of undos. Some have a special undo key.

uninterruptable power supply (UPS): A device with battery storage that continues to provide electrical power to connected devices for a limited length of time if regular commercial power fails. Often a desirable device for a LAN server because of its importance in a work group.

UPS (uninterruptable power supply): A backup battery charged by line current that turns on when the main power supply fails.

VDRV (variable-data-rate video): In digital systems, the ability to vary the amount of data processed per frame to match image quality and transmission bandwidth requirements.

vector graphics: Images defined by sets of straight lines, defined by the locations of the end points.

vertical blanking interval: Lines 1–21 of video field one and lines 263–284 of video field two, in which frame numbers, picture stops, chapter stops, white flags, closed captions, and so on may be encoded. These lines do not appear on the display screen but maintain image stability and enhance image access.

vertical resolution: The number of scan lines.

VESA: Video Electronics Standards Association.

VGA (video graphics array): Standard IBM video display standard. Provides medium-resolution text and graphics. VGA pixel resolution is 640 × 480.

video disc: This is a 12-inch-diameter laser disc used for years for recording analog video and audio, mostly movies. This disc is used successfully for interactive video, primarily for training and educational purposes.

video display: Television-type CRT (raster format) that decodes and displays information from a video source signal.

video stream: Three component streams: Y, U, and V. The AVK software extracts the compressed video from blocks. The sequence of compressed video frames from the AVK software creates the video stream.

volume descriptors: In ISO 9660, fixed-length records containing vital information about the CD and how to read it.

volume space: In ISO 9660, the set of all logical sectors containing CD–ROM data.

VTOC (volume table of contents): The portion of the CD–ROM disc containing basic information about the disc. This might include copyright information, the name of the disc, dates, and so on.

W

wait state: A period of time when nothing happens. Programmed into many computer systems to allow slower components, such as RAM, to catch up with faster CPUs.

watt (W): A unit of power used to measure the audio output capacity of amplifiers and the input audio capacity of speakers and headphones. The watt is named after Scottish engineer James Watt (1736–1819).

wide area network (WAN): A series of local area networks in different geographic areas that are connected together using telephone lines or other telecommunications links.

wildcard: A symbol used in keywords and computer commands to indicate positions where any value is acceptable. The asterisk (*), at sign (@), and question mark (?) are often used as wildcards. In database searches, they can be used for variations of a keyword to aid in hit rate. For example, a search using CD would retrieve documents with CD and all words beginning with CD, like CD–ROM, CD–audio, CDV, and so on.

windows: Microsoft Windows, a graphical user interface (GUI), which runs "on top of" the MS-DOS operating system.

wireless LAN: A LAN that makes connections between nodes without cables, such as by using radio signals or infrared signals. Some wireless LANs are hybrids that connect clusters of wired nodes using wireless methods.

workstation: A microcomputer-based terminal connected to the various peripherals needed for specific applications. This may include a CD–ROM drive, printer, modem, monitor, and so forth.

WORM (write once read many): This is a laser disc system for custom database creation. The user begins with a blank disc and scans or writes any information desired, such as employee medical records, etc. This system uses a 5¼-inch-diameter disc and a different disc player, and so is not compatible with CD–ROM WORM systems that are now commercially available. Usually the discs can be written during many sessions, but once an information block is filled, it cannot be changed or overwritten.

write protected: A disk or disc is "locked" so that information can neither be added nor altered. A CD–ROM is by definition locked.

WYSIWYG (What you see is what you get.): Pronounced "wizzy-wig." Where what you see on the display screen looks like what you'll get when the display is printed.

XYZ

XAR (extended attribute record): In the ISO 9660 standard, a record which contains extra attributes of a file (beyond attributes listed in the file's directory record), such as permissions, dates, escape sequences, etc. Use of XARs is optional.

XGA (extended graphics adapter): New IBM graphics standard that includes VGA and supports higher resolutions, up to 1024 pixels by 768 lines interlaced at 256 colors.

X Windows: A graphical user interface for the UNIX operating system, which is the system used in powerful workstations such as those made by Sun and NeXT.

Y-C: Super VHS component video format. See *S-video*.

Yellow Book: The CD–ROM standard for the physical format of compact discs to be used for information storage as defined by Sony and Philips.

YUV color system: A color encoding scheme for natural pictures in which the luminance and chrominance are separate. The human eye is less sensitive to color variations than to intensity variations, so YUV allows the encoding of luminance (Y) information. It transmits the color information by using one channel for brightness, one for color hue, and one for color saturation.

zero-slot LAN: A LAN that connects computers together without the use of a LAN card, and therefore does not take up an expansion slot in a PC. Connection is made instead using serial ports, parallels ports, or modems and telephone lines.

zero-wait-state computer: Refers to computers that don't have to wait for slower components to catch up with faster ones. See *wait state*.

Index